FUNDAMENTALS OF PSYCHOLOGY
PROCESSES OF HUMAN EMPOWERMENT

As per CBCS Syllabus for +3 Pass, Hons., Elective, PG & Competitive Examinations

STERLING≡ BOOKS ON PSYCHOLOGY

General Psychology
S. K. MANGAL

2019
978 93 86245 76 2
6.5"x9.5
432 pp
Paperback
₹ 350
520 gms

Abnormal Psychology
S. K. MANGAL

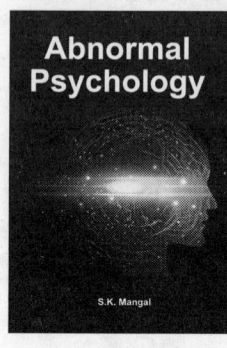

2019
978 93 86245 65 6
6.5"x9.5"
388 pp
Paperback
₹ 325
570 gms

Child Psychology & Development
S K MANGAL AND SHUBHRA MANGAL

2019
978 93 86245 54 0
6.75×9.5"
536pp
Paperback
₹ 350
756 gms

Exceptional Children
Their Psychology and Education

CHINTAMANI KAR

2016
978 81 207 9533 4
6.75"x9.5"
288pp
Paperback
₹ 270
180 gms

An Introduction to Psychology
S. K. MANGAL

2017
978 81 207 1840 1
5.5"x8.5"
232pp
Paperback
₹ 160
210 gms

FUNDAMENTALS OF PSYCHOLOGY
PROCESSES OF HUMAN EMPOWERMENT

As per CBCS Syllabus for +3 Pass, Hons., Elective, PG & Competitive Examinations

Chintamani Kar
Former Head, Department of Psychology
F.M. (Autonomous) College,
Balasore, Odisha

STERLING PUBLISHERS (P) LTD.
Regd. Office: A1/256, Safdarjung Enclave,
New Delhi-110029. CIN: U22110DL1964PTC211907
Tel: 26387070, 26386209
E-mail: mail@sterlingpublishers.in
www.sterlingpublishers.in

Fundamentals of Psychology: Processes of Human Empowerment
© 2020, Chintamani Kar
ISBN 978 81 944007 2 1

All rights are reserved. No part of this publication may be reproduced, stored in a retrieval system or transmitted, in any form or by any means, mechanical, photocopying, recording or otherwise, without prior written permission of the original publisher.

Printed and Published in India by

Sterling Publishers Pvt. Ltd.,
Plot No. 13, Ecotech-III, Greater Noida -201306, U.P. India

Dedicated to My Teachers

Late Muralidhar Samanta
and
Buli Nanee

Contents

UNIT - I : BASICS OF EMPOWERMENT

1 : INTELLIGENCE   2
- Introduction
- Meaning and Definition of Intelligence
- Early Studies of Intelligence
- Intelligence Quotient (I.Q.)
  - Evaluation of Binet's Test of Intelligence
  - Distribution of I.Q.s in the Population
  - Constancy of I.Q.
  - How Reliable and Dependable Are Intelligence Tests?
  - Limitations of I.Q. Tests
  - Uses, Misuses and Abuses of Intelligence Tests
  - Culture-Free and Culture-Fair tests
  - Intelligence Testing in India
- Contemporary Approaches to Understanding Intelligence
  - Psychometric Approach
  - Information Processing Approach
  - PASS Model of Intelligence
  - Cognitive–Development Approach
- Factors Affecting Intelligence
- Creativity and Intelligence
- Intelligence: Unified or Multifaceted?
- Fluid and Crystallised Intelligence
- Is Intelligence Innate or Acquired?
- New Directions in Intelligence
- Key Terms
- Chapter Summary and Review
- Questions

2 : SELF AND PERSONALITY — 39

- Introduction
- Allport's Definition of Personality
- Characteristics of Personality
- Classification of Personality
  - Pre-Scientific Classification
  - Kretschmer's Classification
  - Sheldon's Classification
  - Jung's Typology
- Trait Theory of Personality
  - Source Traits and Surface Traits
  - Allport's Trait Theory
  - Single-Trait Research
- Assessment of Personality
  - Psychometric Tests
  - Projective Techniques
  - Self-Report Tests of Personality
  - Assessment of the Big Five Factors
  - How Useful Is Personality Assessment?
- Self and Personality
  - What is Self?
  - Self as Subject and Object
  - Different Aspects of Self
  - Self-Regulation
  - Techniques for Self-Regulation or Self-Control
  - Self in the Indian Tradition
- Key Terms
- Chapter Summary and Review
- Questions

UNIT - II : SOURCES OF POWER

3 : THEORIES OF PERSONALITY — 66

- Introduction
- Perspectives in Personality Theory
- Sigmund Freud and Psychoanalysis
  - The Structure of Personality: Id, Ego and Superego
  - Self Protection by Ego: Defence Mechanisms
  - Psychosexual Stages of Development
- Theories of Personality by Neo-Freudians: Other Psychoanalytic Views
  - Similarities between Freud and Erikson
  - Distinction between Freud and Erikson

- Current Thoughts on Freud and Psychoanalysis
- Humanistic Psychology
  - Rogers's Self Theory: Becoming a Fully-Functioning Individual
  - Maslow's Self-Actualisation Theory
  - Characteristics of Self-Actualised People (Maslow)
  - Criticism of Humanistic Psychology
  - Can Humanistic Concepts be Studied or Experimented?
  - Humanistic Theories: An Evaluation
- Social Cognitive View of Personality
- Albert Bandura's Social Learning Theory
  - Role of Self-Efficacy
  - Sources of Self-Efficacy
  - Principles of Observational Learning
  - Vicarious Learning
  - Summary of Bandura's Social Cognitive Theory
  - Evaluation of Bandura's Theory
- Trait Theories of Personality: Seeking the Key Dimensions of Personality
- Allport's Definition of Personality
  - Concept of Trait and Personal Disposition
  - Characteristics of Traits
  - Types of Traits
  - Common Traits versus Individual Traits
  - The Proprium: Development of Selfhood
  - Functional Autonomy
  - Types of Functional Autonomy
    - The Mature Personality
  - Application: The Study of Values
- Raymond Cattell's Trait Theory of Personality
  - Formula for Personality
  - Categories of Traits
- Hans Eysenck's Trait-Type Theory of Personality
  - Hierarchical Taxonomy
  - Three Dimensions of Personality
  - Causal Aspects
  - Neurophysiological Basis of Traits and Types
  - Psychoticism and Gonadal Hormones
  - Basic Personality Types
  - Measurement of Personality
  - Differences between Extroverts and Introverts
- The Big Five Factors: The Basic Dimensions of Personality
  - The Big-Five Factors: An Evaluation
  - The Big-Five Theory

- Advantages of Big-Five Structure
- Measurement of Big-Five Inventory
- Trait Theories: An Evaluation
- Best Ways to Describe Personality
- Current Thoughts on Trait Perspective
- The Biology of Personality: Behavioural Genetics
- Key Terms
- Chapter Summary and Review
- Questions

4 : MOTIVATION   143

- Introduction
- Needs, Drives and Incentives
- Intrinsic and Extrinsic Motivation
- Motivational Cycle
- Homeostasis
- Types of Motives
  - Biological Motives
  - Social Motives
  - Psychological and Personal Motives
- Theories of Motivation
- Unconscious Motivation
- Measurement of Human Motives
  - Direct and Indirect Measurement of Motives
- Key Terms
- Chapter Summary and Review
- Questions

5 : EMOTION   172

- Introduction
- What is Emotion ?
  - Understanding Emotion
  - Development of Emotion
  - Definition of Emotion
  - Feeling and Emotion
  - Differences between Feeling and Emotion
  - Basic Human Emotions
  - Functions of Emotions
  - Organic (Physiological) Changes During Emotion
- Theories of Emotion
  - James–Lange Theory of Bodily Reactions
  - Cannon–Bard Theory of Central Neural Processes

- Activation Theory of Emotion
- Lazarus–Schachter Theory of Cognitive Arousal
- Role of Cerebral Cortex in Emotion
- Role of Hypothalamus in Emotion
- Role of Limbic System in Emotion
- Key Terms
- Chapter Summary and Review
- Questions

UNIT - III : EMPOWERED PRACTICES

6 : SOCIAL THOUGHT AND SOCIAL BEHAVIOUR 192
- Introduction
- Attribution
  - Biases in Attribution: To Err Is Human
- Social Cognition: Understanding Others
  - Impression Formation
  - Attitudes and Social Cognition
    - Attitude Change
    - Information-Processing Routes to Persuasion
    - The Link between Attitudes and Behaviour
- Key Terms
- Chapter Summary and Review
- Questions

7 : POSITIVE PSYCHOLOGY 206
- Introduction
- Traditional Psychology and Negative Focus
- Negatives Are More Important in Human Life
- Disease Model
- Emergence of Positive Psychology
- Relation of Positive Psychology with Other Branches of Psychology
  - Relationship of Positive Psychology with Health Psychology
  - Relationship of Positive Psychology with Clinical Psychology
  - Relationship of Positive Psychology with Developmental Psychology
  - Relationship of Positive Psychology with "Survey Research" and "Subjective Well-Being"
  - Relation of Positive Psychology with Social/Personality Psychology and Psychology of Religion
  - Positive Psychology: Assumptions, Goals and Definitions

- Life above Zero
- Culture and Meaning of a Good life
- Why Are We Interested to Know about Positive Psychology?
- Positive Psychology Is Not Opposed to Psychology
- Positive Psychology and the Status-Quo
- Key Terms
- Chapter Summary and Review
- Questions

8 : THE PSYCHOLOGY OF HAPPINESS — 224

- Introduction
- Two Traditions
  - Hedonic Happiness
  - Eudaimonic Happiness
- Positive Affects and Meaningful Life
- Subjective Well-Being: The Hedonic Basis of Happiness
- Measuring Subjective Well-Being (SWB) or Happiness
- Life Satisfaction
- Positive Affect, Negative Affect and Happiness
- Self-Realisation: The Eudaimonic Basis of Happiness
  - Psychological Well-Being and Positive Functioning
  - Need Fulfilment and Self-Determination Theory
- What Makes a "Good" Day?
- Comparing Hedonic and Eudaimonic Views of Happiness
  - Definition and Causes of Happiness and Well-Being
  - Complementarity and Interrelationship
- Subjective Well-Being, Age and Personal Growth
- Key Terms
- Chapter Summary and Review
- Questions

Key Terms in Psychology — 247

Abbreviations — 258

Preface

The behavioural science, psychology, speaks with many voices to diverse students, offering a personal message to each one of them. No doubt, this discipline can provide a better understanding of people's behaviour. But for some people, it is also a path to self-understanding. To some individuals, psychology offers the potential of a future career, and some are drawn to psychology because it gives them an opportunity for intellectual discovery.

This book, *Processes of Human Empowerment*, presents the discipline of psychology in a way that engages and excite students about human empowerment, no matter what led them to take an introductory course or what level of motivation they initially brought to the course. The book is particularly designed to draw them into its way of looking at the world and to increase their understanding of psychological issues. It provides a wide, comprehensive introduction to the field of psychology, covering basic theories and research, as well as highlighting current applications outside the laboratory.

This book includes extensive coverage of both traditional areas of human empowerment and applied topics, including motivation, emotion and personality. Some topics of positive psychology were also included. It also features many application-oriented chapters such as intelligence, pro-social behaviour and happiness. Ultimately, this book presents a combination of traditional core topics and contemporary applied subjects, providing an extensive and current view of the field of psychology. The flexibility of the book's organisation and structure, a hallmark of this text, is considerable. Each chapter is divided into three or four manageable, self-contained units – such as text, key terms, chapter summary and model questions.

Building on the strong tradition of facilitating student learning, this edition of *Processes of Human Empowerment* contains several new and improved features. Advances in such areas as evolutionary perspectives, intelligence, emotion, motivation, cognition, social behaviour and cultural approaches to psychological phenomena receive expanded and new coverage. In addition, the content is updated and covers a broad range of topics.

I am grateful to all those who have helped me, directly or indirectly, in the preparation of this manuscript. I also express my sincere thanks to those teachers of psychology in different colleges and my own colleagues to whom I read out a few chapters in the early stages of preparation of my manuscript, for their appreciation of its value and their encouragement. I am also grateful to a number of experts for their helpful suggestions and constructive criticisms.

My thanks also go to my daughter Leny and son Amitanshu who helped in bringing this book to fruition. In completing this book, I had to adopt and borrow a few examples from several sources. Unfortunately, it is not now possible to locate the actual source of some of the illustrations. I take this opportunity to acknowledge my indebtedness to the sources both anonymous and known.

It is my sincere hope that this book will receive appreciations from the students, teachers and experts. Any suggestion for the improvement of this book will be highly appreciated.

I am especially indebted to Mr. M.R. Mishra, Balasore and Mr. M.C. Nayak, Dr. J. Mishra, Mrs. S. Das and some of my students who have inspired me to accept this challenge. Finally, I am most thankful to Mr. S.K. Ghai, Managing Director Sterling Publishers Pvt. Ltd., for showing keen interest in publishing my books.

Chintamani Kar

"HITAISEE", Charampa, Bhadrak
Mobile : 9861106206

UNIT I
BASICS OF EMPOWERMENT

CHAPTER - 1

INTELLIGENCE

❑ *Intelligence is the complex mental capacity to profit from experience – to go beyond what is perceived and to imagine symbolic possibilities and use them to act effectively.*
❑ *Intelligence is the aggregate or global capacity of the individual to act purposefully, to think rationally and to deal effectively with the environment.*

❑ This chapter covers:
- Meaning and definition of intelligence
- Early studies on intelligence
- Intelligence Quotient (I.Q.)
- Evaluation of Binet's test of intelligence
- Constancy of I.Q.
- Distribution of I.Q.s in the population
- Different approaches for understanding the nature of intelligence
- Factors affecting intelligence
- Limitations of I.Q. Tests
- Creativity and intelligence
- How reliable and dependable are intelligence tests?
- Is intelligence innate or acquired?
- New directions in intelligence: emotional and artificial intelligence (AI)
- Key Terms, Summary and Questions

Intelligence 3

❑ *By the end of this chapter, you will be able to:*
- Define intelligence
- Describe the nature of intelligence
- Explain the multiple facets of intelligence
- Discuss the cultural differences in conceptualising intelligence
- Acquaint yourself with different methods of assessing intelligence
- Describe different approaches of intelligence
- Know about the factors which influence intelligence
- Find out the relationship between creativity and intelligence
- Understand about artificial and emotional intelligence

Introduction

In our day-to-day conversations, we often comment that a particular individual is intelligent or is not intelligent. All such comments are based on our observation of performance or behaviour of that individual in comparison to others in the group. Further, humans differ from the other species in their ability to control the environment. The intellectual skills place humans as the most superior species in the animal kingdom. Underlying all human abilities lies the essential attributes of intelligence.

Though intelligence is a commonly-used popular term, it is so complex that it is difficult to give a comprehensive and precise definition of intelligence. As a term, it refers to the ability to understand, act, interpret and predict the future. Thus, it is a commonly used word to express universal capacity required for survival and progress beyond the present.

No doubt, it is a process of cognition. Cognition refers to how we acquire, store, retrieve and use knowledge. All the basic psychological processes such as learning, perception, memory, concept formation, thinking, reasoning, problem solving, decision making and creativity are related to intelligence. However, intelligence cannot be observed directly, but it can only be estimated through the individual's performance on tests and real-life situations. The concept of intelligence has now been broadened to include terms such as emotional intelligence, spiritual intelligence, artificial intelligence, practical intelligence, social intelligence, musical intelligence, and so on.

Meaning and Definition of Intelligence

Each person is unique in this universe. Individuals differ from one another in both physical and psychological characteristics. They also differ from one another in their colour, height, weight, size, strength and life style. Some people react quickly and are very sensitive. Others are dull, shy and withdrawn. They are passive individuals. Some people are gregarious and sociable, whereas others are introverts, who try to live in seclusion. In a classroom situation, a teacher comes across different type of students. Some are very bright, intelligent and creative and others are just average or dull.

Then, very often, people are confused about what intelligence is. In one survey conducted by Robert J. Sternberg (1981), people were asked to define what they meant by intelligence. Their answers indicated three major components of intelligence: (a) Problem-solving abilities, (b) Verbal abilities and (c) Social competence.

Firstly, people who reason logically and identify more solutions to problems were seen as intelligent. Secondly, verbal abilities were thought to exemplify intelligence. Finally, social competence, which means the ability to show interest in others and interact effectively with them, was regarded as an indication of intelligence.

The intelligence of an individual can be expressed through his or her intellectual activities which can be measured both formally as well as informally. Informal assessment of one's intellectual activities can be made through observing some actions, explaining a concept or observing the process of adapting to a novel situation.

Intelligence has been defined in several ways. For your reference, a few definitions are given below. The following important characteristics are prominent in all the definitions:

(a) Intelligence is a cognitive process involving *rational* and *abstract thinking*.
(b) Secondly, it is *goal-directed* and *purposeful*. Intelligent activities are planned to reach a self-determined goal.
(c) Finally, it involves *social competence* to help individuals adjust to their environment and surroundings.

Definitions

1. Intelligence is the ability to think abstractly. (Lewis Terman, 1921)
2. Intelligence is what the intelligence tests test. (E.G. Boring, 1923)
3. Intelligence is a particular instance of biological adaptation. (Jean Piaget, 1952)
4. Intelligence is a person's capacity for goal-directed adaptive behaviour. (Robert Stenberg & Salter, 1982)
5. Intelligence is the innate general cognitive capacity. (Francis Galton, 1984).
6. Intelligence is the global and aggregate capacity of the individual to think rationally, to act purposefully and to deal effectively with the environment. (David Wechsler, 1972)

David Wechsler (1972) has given a commonly accepted definition of intelligence. He says that intelligence characterises the individual's behaviour as a whole. But some critics expressed the view that intelligent behaviour does not include "acting purposefully", since it is the conative aspect of one's behaviour, whereas intelligence is related to the cognitive process.

The terminology and language used in defining intelligence apart, there seems to be some agreement among the psychologists. They agree on the following points:

(a) Intelligence must be understood as the mental capacity or mental energy available with an individual at a particular time in a particular situation.
(b) This mental capacity helps him in the task of both theoretical and practical manipulation of things, objects or events present in his environment in order to adapt to or face new challenges and problems of life as successfully as possible.
(c) His capacity or the fund of mental energy available with him can be judged only in terms of the quality of his behaviour or performance.

Taking all the above factors into consideration, we may attempt a viable definition of intelligence. Intelligence is a sort of mental energy, in the form of mental or cognitive abilities available with an individual, which enables him to handle his or her environmental situations as effectively as possible.

Early Studies of Intelligence

The formal tests of intelligence were developed in the early 1900s. Sir Francis Galton (1885) was one of the early proponent of mental tests. In an international health exhibition at London's South Kenisington Museum, he tested more than 9,000 men and women visitors without their knowledge. The term "test" became popular after his study in 1884. Galton measured characteristics such as head size, visual acuity, reaction time and memory for visual form. Since he was a naturalist and mathematician, he tried to discover individual differences. He was very interested to know how and why people differed in their abilities.

Galton was sure that intelligence could be measured by objective tests. He raised many important issues concerning intelligence – the degree of its inheritance, its ways and procedures of measurement and its components.

Another American, psychologist, J. McKeen Cattell was also interested to study about individual differences during the last part of nineteenth century. He believed that sensory, perpetual and motor processes constituted the core of intelligence.

In 1904, Alfred Binet was requested by the French ministry of education to identify mentally disabled children from the normal school children. He tried to know why children at that time were not able to benefit from the standard school curriculum. Being requested by the ministry of education, Binet and his student Simon developed an intelligent test. This test had 30 different parameters. The range of the parameters was from the simple ability of touching one's nose or ear to more complex abilities of defining abstract concepts.

Alfred Binet (1857–1911)

The concept of mental age (M.A.) was first developed by Binet. According to him, mental age is the average age at which normal individuals achieve a particular score on a measure of intelligence. It is different from chronological age (C.A.). C.A. is the number of years or months since the child is born. Binet and his associates tried to devise age-appropriate test parameters so that a large number of children's responses could be compared.

The parameters in Binet's test were chosen objectively without being influenced by environment, impulsive judgement or rote memory. The parameters were based on rational judgment and reasoning.

For his test, Binet has taken normal children of different ages. Then the average score for each age was determined. Then each child's performance was compared to the average of all other children of the same age.

The results were interpreted in terms of the average age at which normal children achieved a particular score. This measure is called mental age (M.A.). For example, when the obtained scores of a child on different parameters of a test add to the average score of a group of 6-year-olds, the child is said to have a mental age of 6, irrespective of his or her actual age, i.e., chronological age. Alfred Binet defined mental retardation as being two mental age years below the chronological age. When a child's mental age is more than the chronological age, the child is called a bright child. On the contrary, a dull child's mental age will fall below the chronological age.

Intelligence Quotient (I.Q.)

William Stern (1871–1938), a German psychologist first developed the idea of intelligence quotient (I.Q.) in 1912. According to him, intelligence quotient is just a number. It is an age-related measure of intelligence level. I.Q. is determined by the child's mental age divided by chronological age multiplied by 100.

$$I.Q. = [M.A. / C.A.] \times 100$$

Here, the number 100 is used as a multiplier to avoid a decimal point. When M.A. equals the C.A., then the I.Q. is equal to 100. On the other hand, when M.A. is less than C.A., the I.Q., is less than 100. If the M.A. is above the C.A., the I.Q. becomes more than 100.

Evaluation of Binet's Test of Intelligence

Four characteristics are pertinent in Binet's intelligence test. These are:
(a) The score on Binet's newly developed test was an assessment of the current performance. But it was actually a measure of inherited attributes, as pointed out by some critics.
(b) The test scores obtained by Binet were to be used to identify weak children who needed special help and there should be no stigma attached to them for their weakness.
(c) Binet strongly believed that intelligence can be influenced by training and opportunity. He tried to identify the areas in which special education can benefit the performance of these children.
(d) Binet did not try to develop a theory of intelligence. But he developed his test empirically on the basis of how the performances of children were observed.

The original test of Binet has been revised several times in his country and in England. In 1916, Terman, a professor of Stanford University, revised Binet's test. This popular test became popularly known as Stanford–Binet test of intelligence. Revisions of this test were made in 1937, 1960 and 1972. The present Stanford–Binet test has a wide variety of verbal and non-verbal items. The latest test of Stanford–Binet for adults released in 2003 has five components, that is, knowledge, quantitative reasoning, visual-spatial processing, working memory and fluid reasoning.

The Stanford–Binet test is a popular and most widely used test of intelligence. The test captures complex mental processes such as memory, imagery, comprehension and judgement. The following table shows the classification of people on the basis of their I.Q.s:

Interpretation of I.Q. on Stanford–Binet Test

I.Q.	Description of I.Q. Level	Percentage in each group
Above 139	Very Superior	01
120–139	Superior	11
110–119	High Average	18
90–109	Average	46
80–89	Low Average	15
70–79	Borderline	06
Below 70	Mentally Retarded	03

It can be assumed that the higher the economic standing of an occupational group, the higher would be the average I.Q. keeping other factors constant. This is a comparative rather than absolute measure of intelligence.

Distribution of I.Q.s in the Population

When a suitable population of individuals of some age is taken for intelligence measurement, the I.Q. can be represented graphically in the following manner:

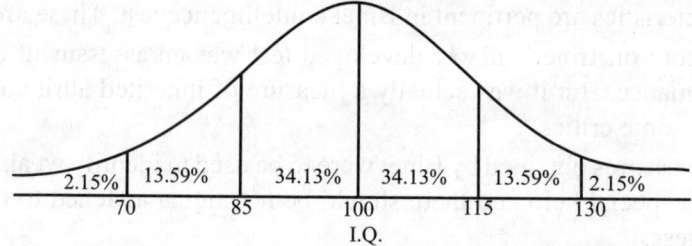

Fig. 1.1: *Graph showing distribution of I.Q. in the population*

Here, on the horizontal axis, the measured score of I.Q. is presented. On the vertical axis, the percentage of children for each score of I.Q. is presented. From the curve, it is obvious that 2.15 per cent children have an I.Q. score between 0 and 70, 13.59 per cent between 70 and 85, 34.14 per cent between 85 and 100 and another 34.13 per cent between 100 and 115. In summary, the maximum number of children have I.Q. between 85 to 115 in a population.

Constancy of I.Q.

Different studies reveal that a child will remain in the same relative position in the group as he or she grows up. Of course, I.Q.s are not static in pre-school years. But studies indicate that, on the whole, I.Q. remains essentially constant throughout childhood and adolescence, when other conditions like health, type of education, home situation and other environmental facilities do not have a significant change.

Some empirical studies indicated that adverse physical conditions like deficiency of thyroxin, insufficient food and nutrition may affect I.Q. level to some extent. Likewise, unusual environmental conditions and lack of normal educational opportunities may affect the I.Q. level.

How Reliable and Dependable Are Intelligence Tests?

Any test used for measuring human traits or characteristics should satisfy the criteria of reliability, validity, objectivity, comprehensiveness and practicability. It should also have suitable standardised items relevant to local situations and should be essentially administered in conditions most favourable to the subject(s).

However, the assessment of intelligence has following drawbacks:

(a) No intelligence test can ever measure the true psyche potential or mental functioning of an individual. These tests can assess the I.Q. rather than the real cognitive ability of an individual.

(b) It is very difficult to obtain the same scores of I.Q. of the same person when he or she is administered different types of I.Q. tests. It is quite surprising and rather confusing when an individual scores very high in one test and very low on another.

(c) No intelligence tests, including the most refined performance tests, can be claimed as culture-free or culture-fair tests.

(d) In fact, intelligence tests can not assess an individual's overall potentiality because they do not go beyond the subject's cognitive abilities. As a result, it becomes impossible to draw conclusions from these tests about one's aspiration, motives, aptitudes, attitudes, interests, etc.

(e) The scores of the tests may be highly influenced by the conditions prevailing at the time of testing. Physical conditions such as mental as well as physical fatigue and ailments seem to interfere with performance. *Test anxiety* also plays a key role in testing situations. Emotional and other psychological factors must be taken into account during test administration.

Therefore, it may be concluded that too much reliance cannot be placed on the results of intelligence tests. These tests cannot be accepted as the sole measure of school achievements, profession and future life. The results of achievement tests, aptitude tests, attitude scale, interest inventory, measurement of motives and personality tests should also be considered along with I.Q. scores while making decision about the future education and profession of children.

Limitations of I.Q. Tests

Psychological tests can either be used or misused. Ability tests help both parents and teachers divide the children into different groups or can be used to label some children as dull and incompetent. Poor performance on an intelligence test may result in a stigma for the child, inviting teacher and parental discrimination. Experts view that discriminatory practices on the basis of performance on intelligence tests are unethical and should be abandoned.

One important limitation of I.Q. tests is that these tests tap only a part of human's overall competence. There are many more skills to be assessed, such as creativity, competence in social situations, etc.

It is impossible to separate intelligence from scholastic achievement. Robert Sternberg propounded the triarchic theory of intelligence. He did very poorly in intelligence tests. But he became the professor of psychology at the Yale university. He held that intelligence is more than what I.Q. tests measure (Sternberg, 1985, 1987).

According to him, intelligence tests have three major limitations:

(a) The I.Q. tests fail to measure creative insight.
(b) They ignore the practical side of intelligence.
(c) Since I.Q. tests limit the time taken to complete the test, they wrongly equate intelligence with speed.

A criticism labelled against intelligence tests is that these tests are biased in favour of the middle-class and higher class populations. They underestimate the intellectual potentialities of children belonging to minority groups and other cultures. In many studies, it was seen that the Blacks scored 15 points lower on I.Q. tests than the White Americans (Brody & Brody, 1976). In these cases, language and the nature of the test items create problems in estimating intelligence.

Another drawback of I.Q. tests pointed out by Miller-Jones (1989) is that answers to some intelligence test items seem to have been arbitrarily decided. When scores obtained in I.Q. tests are thought to give a fixed and unchanging indicator of an individual's intelligence, it brings misjudgment.

An example is the 1973 edition of the Stanford–Binet intelligence test. There is a question in the test: "What a house is made of?" A child may answer: "A house is built of walls." According to the test developer, the correct answer should be: "A house is made of wood, bricks and stone." Here the answer of the child is not wrong, but he or she will fail to earn a score.

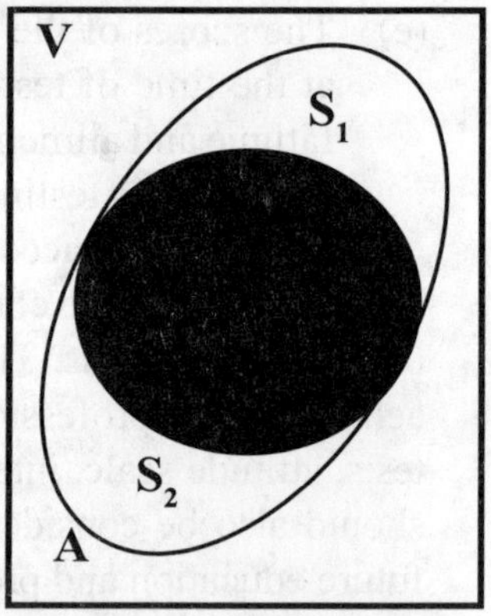

In their theories, many psychologists pointed out that intelligence tests are less predictive of creative abilities that lead to scientific discoveries and inventions. These tests provides less meaningful information for the actual planning of educational instruction. I.Q. tests provide an A.Q. or Academic Quotient predictive of academic achievement (Kagan & Ernest, 1976).

Fig. 1.2: A diagram representing Spearman's 'g' and 's' factors of intellectual activities

In spite of all the limitations discussed above, I.Q. tests provide important information about the individuals and students, when used judiciously by trained and expert investigators.

Uses, Misuses and Abuses of Intelligence Tests

Intelligence tests became popular because they were based on basic principles or capacities which we use not only in schools and colleges, but in understanding and solving our day-to-day problems. It is true that if an individual shines in one activity, he or she may be mediocre in another and dull in some other. Everyone cannot be good at everything all the time. This fact led to extensive application of intelligence tests in all walks of life to identify how intelligent an individual was, so that what was best in him could be exploited.

In the Western world, intelligence testing has acquired the status of a policy instrument in the educational system. Entry into the institutions is possible only after being subjected to some kind of intelligence testing. I.Q. reports are maintained along with the progress reports of students. The students who score very low are rejected because they are supposed to belong to the special schools (i.e., schools for mentally retarded children).

In the army, mental tests are used for selection and placement of officers. Today, testing intelligence along with aptitudes begins at the kindergarten level in order to decide the child's future education, training and profession. In some Oriental countries like Japan and Korea, children of 4 to 5 years who are identified as having potentials to play games like table tennis or badminton are sent to special schools. They are also reared under special conditions with rigorous training so as to make them perfect in playing that particular game.

On the whole, I.Q. is not a "birth mark". An evaluator testing intelligence often tags the subject with a value called I.Q., which determines the subject's education, profession and eventually his or her entire life. Numerous longitudinal studies reveal that intelligence can grow or diminish in terms of I.Q. points. Evidence indicated that I.Q. level depends upon education, income, social status, nutrition, etc.

Rampant use of these tests in educational institutions and workplaces has made more and more people realise that intelligence tests are nothing but a big fuss over a few monkey tricks. An individual exposed to these tricks a couple of times is able to do very well in subsequent tests and earn a score of superior intelligence, though he or she may not really be very intelligent. Thus the I.Q. is what the given test can measure rather than the real cognitive capacity of the person.

Though the theoretical concepts and tests of intelligence have reached every corner of the world, still they suffer from many drawbacks. Educationists and psychologists have recognised some of these loopholes and were interested for the construction of better tests.

Culture-Free and Culture-Fair Tests

Many intelligence tests are biased towards a particular culture in which they are developed. A test is culture-biased, when it has language elements. But some tests are language-free tests. When a test is culture-biased, the norms for this test are almost entirely based upon these cultural groups. To overcome these problems, non-verbal and performance tests were developed. These tests are considered as culture-fair tests because people of any culture could take them. But it has been noticed that these tests also show cultural bias.

It is almost impossible to design a culture-free test which is devoid of all culture-related content. Therefore, psychologists have tried to develop tests that can be considered culture-fair or culture-reduced, where the cultural elements are minimum.

In brief, culture-fair tests were developed to reduce culture-bias. There are two types of culture-fair tests. The first category contains the items that are assumed to be known to individuals from all socio-economic and ethnic backgrounds. For example, one individual can be asked "How are the birds different from animals?" Every individual in the world is acquainted with birds and animals, and there is no culture bias in the question.

The second category of culture-fair tests do not have any verbal items. An example is Raven's Progressive Matrices test (RPM). It is called a culture-fair test of intelligence. But one criticism against this test is that educated people score higher in RPM than the less educated people.

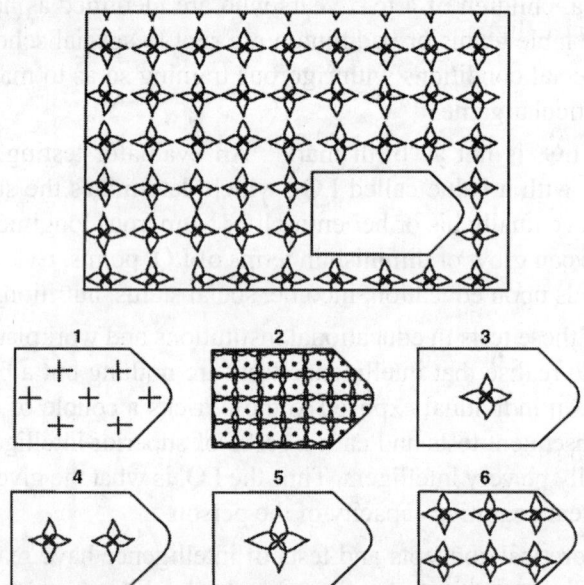

Fig. 1.3: A sample item from Raven's Progressive Matrices test

Another culture-fair test was developed by Mercer and Lewis (1978). The test is popularly known as System of Multi-cultural Pluralistic Assessment (SOMPA). The test is made for 5 to 11-year-old children belonging to low-income families.

The Kaufman Assessment Battery for Children (K-ABC) developed by Kaufman (1983) is another culture-fair test of intelligence. This test is meant for children from 2 to 12-and-a-half years of age. This test has taken into account representative samples of minority and handicapped children. But it has certain limitations.

It can be concluded that a culture-fair test is difficult to construct taking into account all possible cultural and ethnic variations across the world.

Intelligence Testing in India

In his book *Working Mind*, J.P. Das (1998) reviewed the short history of intelligence testing in India. The first systematic test of intelligence (Binet's test) was made by Dr. Rice in Urdu and Punjabi in 1930s. Prof. S.M. Mohsin is one of the pioneers of intelligence testing in India. He constructed an intelligence test in Hindi in the year 1930. In the year 1966, Long and Mehta prepared a mental measurement handbook listing out 103 tests of intelligence developed in many Indian languages. The Bhatia test of intelligence is very popular in India. Some tests developed in India are given below:

Verbal Tests	Performance Tests
1. Group Test of Mental ability by S. Jalota	1. CIE Non-verbal Test
2. Indian Adaptation of Binet Simon Scale by S.K. Kulshrestha	2. Performance Test of Intelligence by C.M. Bhatia
3. Group Test of Intelligence by Prayaga Mehta	3. Draw-A-Man Test by Pramila Pathak
4. Test of General Mental Ability by M.C. Joshi.	4. Adaptation of Wechsler
5. The Bihar Test of Intelligence by S.M. Mohsin.	5. Adult Performance Intelligence Scale by R. Ramalingaswami

Contemporary Approaches to Understanding Intelligence

Different approaches adopted by psychologists from time to time have tried to uncover the components or elements of intelligence. The psychologists attempted to answer the questions: Is intelligence a single ability or does it consist of multiple abilities? Is it fully inherited or is it shaped by environmental factors? Should intelligence be conceptualised as abilities or processes? Are there qualitatively different stages of intellectual development? Is there one type of intelligence or several types of intelligences?

These questions inspired the experts to develop different theories of intelligence. Mainly there are three groups of theories or three major approaches to study intelligence. These are: (a) Psychometric approach (b) Information processing approach and (c) Cognitive development approach.

(a) The psychometric approach depicts intelligence as the ability or as aggregate of multiple abilities. It assesses intelligence in quantitative terms and expresses the performance of an individual of a test in the form of scores. The theories developed by Charles Spearman, Louis Thurstone, Raymond Cattell, J.P. Guilford, Arthur Jensen and Howard Gardner are some of the examples of the psychometric approach to the study of intelligence.

(b) The information processing approach encompasses the underlying processes of intelligent behaviour. It describes the processes people use in intellectual reasoning and problem solving. The theories developed by Robert Sternberg and J.P. Das are of this kind of approach.

(c) The cognitive development approach emphasises the functional significance and development of intelligence. It reveals that intellectual development proceeds in the form of qualitatively distinct developmental stages. The theory of intelligence developed by Jean Piaget is the most prominent cognitive development approach to the study of intelligence.

Psychometric Approach

Charles Spearman (1923) advanced a theory of intelligence popularly known as Two-Factor Theory. It was an approach of trait organisation based on the statistical analysis of test scores. According to him, all intellectual activities have a single common factor called the general factor or "g" factor. There are also a number of specific or "s" factors. Each of the s-factors refers to a specific, single activity.

Spearman explored statistically the interrelations among scores obtained by many persons on different tests. He said that positive correlation between any two mental functions was attributed to the g-factor. But the s-factors have low correlations among them.

In addition to the general factor, there are specific capabilities which give an individual the ability to deal with specific problems. For example, an individual's performance in English is partly due to his or her general intelligence and partly due to some specific aptitude for language which they might possess, i.e., $g + s_1$; in mathematics the performance may be the result of $g + s_2$; in drawing it may be due to $g + s_3$ and so on. The factor "g" is thus present in all specific activities. The total ability or intelligence "A" of an individual, thus, will be expressed by the following equation:

R.B. Cattell

$$g + s_1 + s_2 + s_3 + \ldots = A$$

However, the opinions of Spearman are not free from criticisms.

(a) Spearman held that intelligence may be expressed in terms of two factors. But as we have seen, there are not only two, but several factors (such as g, s_1, s_2, s_3, etc.).

(b) According to Spearman, each job requires some specific ability. This view was criticised because it implied that there is nothing common to different jobs except a general factor. But we have found that in some jobs like nursing and medical professions, there are some common and overlapping factors.

Raymond B. Cattell (1965) developed a theory of intelligence with Horn (1978). They have suggested that general intelligence can be broken down into two relatively independent components: fluid intelligence and crystallised intelligence. Fluid intelligence denotes reasoning, memory and information processing capabilities. It is required for learning and problem solving. It is dependent on neurological development and is relatively free from the influences of education and culture. It is derived more from biological and genetic factors and is less influenced by training and experience.

Fluid intelligence is measured by the test of block designs and spectacle visualisation. It grows rapidly in early childhood and reaches full development by the end of an individual's adolescence.

Crystallised intelligence is not a function of one's neurological development and, therefore, it is not innate. It depends on learning, training, education and culture. It is measured by tests of vocabulary, arithmetic and general information. Research works indicate that crystallised intelligence increases across the life-span of an individual. Both the types of intelligence are partly inherited and partly learned.

Howard Gardner (1983) proposed a different theory of intelligence. According to him, intelligence consists of numerous abilities, each of which are equally important. In other words, Gardner believes that we have multiple intelligences, each of which are relatively interdependent of the others.

Gardner's theory was first appeared in his book, *Frames of Mind: the Theory of Multiple Intelligence* in 1983. By introducing this concept, Gardner challenged the notion of general intelligence 'g' and then questioned the very basis of prevailing intelligence tests by asking how an individual's intellectual capacities could be captured in a single measure of intelligence. Gardner tried to give a broad base to the concept of intelligence and its measurement by providing a multiple frame. He asserted that human intelligence or cognitive competence can be described as a set of an individual's multiple abilities, talents and mental skills related to a multiple number of domains of knowledge in a particular cultural setting.

Gardner concluded that we possess seven types of intelligence, each relatively independent of the others. These grow and develop differently in different people, depending on their hereditary characteristics and environmental influences. By calling them independent, Gardner meant that each intelligence is a relatively autonomous intellectual potential which is capable of functioning independently of the others. He identified the following seven intelligences:

(a) *Linguistic Intelligence*: This type of intelligence includes skills involved in the production and use of language. It is responsible for all kinds of linguistic competence, abilities, talents and skills available in human beings. This can be best broken down into components like syntax, semantics and pragmatics as well as more school-oriented skills such as written or oral expression and understanding. This type of intelligence is most visible among professionals like lecturers, lawyers, writers, lyricists, etc.

Examples of individuals strong in this component of intelligence are Rabindranath Tagore, T.S. Eliot and Shakespeare.

(b) *Logical-Mathematical Intelligence*: This type of intelligence is responsible for all types of abilities, talents and skills in areas related to logic and mathematics. This intelligence is concerned with skills in scientific thinking and problem solving. This involves one's ability to think logically and critically, which is essential for scientific inventions and discoveries. This intelligence is, of course, required for academic achievements. Scholars, scientists and Nobel prize winners have this kind of intelligence. Professionals like mathematicians, philosophers and physicists are found to exhibit this type of intelligence in abundance. Some individuals who were strong in this intelligence were Albert Einstein, Archimedes, Madam Curie, C.V. Raman and H.G. Khorana.

(c) *Spatial Intelligence*: This includes the skills in spatial configurations such as those used by artists and architects. This type of intelligence is concerned with the abilities, talents and skills involving the representation and manipulation of spatial configuration and relationship. Many adults make use of this kind of intelligence in their sphere of work. For example, painters and artists may be seen to demonstrate spatial intelligence through their use of space when applying pigments to a canvas.

Besides these, navigation in space and seas without instruments, use of mental images, spatial configuration and piloting aeroplanes are some examples of spatial intelligence. Michaelangelo and Leonard da Vinci were very strong in spatial intelligence. This is also true of professional like land surveyors, architects, engineers, mechanics, sculptors and chess players who are found to rely upon spatial intelligence in their own way.

(d) *Musical Intelligence*: This type of intelligence covers the abilities, talents and skills pertaining to the field of music. This is primarily related to skills in tasks involving music. This may be well demonstrated through one's capacity for pitch discrimination, sensitivity to rhythm, ability to hear themes in music in its most integrated forms, and the production of music through performance or composition. Beethoven, Yehudi Menhuin, Zubin Mehta, M.S Subbulakshmi and Lata Mangeshkar are some examples.

(e) *Bodily-Kinesthetic Intelligence*: This type of intelligence is concerned with the set of abilities, talents and skills involved in using one's body or its various parts to perform skilful and purposeful movements. Sports persons, dancers, actors, athletes and people showing acrobatics demonstrate such abilities. The great football player Pele, Olympic gold medallist Jesse Owen's, footballer Maradona, cricketers like Tendulkar and Bradman, dancers like Birju Maharaj and Sanjukta Panigrahi demonstrated high bodily-kinesthetic intelligence.

(f) *Interpersonal Intelligence*: This intelligence is related to the skills used in interacting with people while being sensitive to their moods, temperaments and motives. This type intelligence consists of the ability to understand other individuals and one's relations with others. It includes the ability to act productively based on the understanding of others. The knowledge and understanding of others are required for social interactions in one's daily life. Individuals having strong interpersonal intelligence can understand the perspectives of others easily, can establish good relationships with people and help others develop insight into their problems. In practical life, this type of intelligence is most visible among psychotherapists, teachers, politicians and religious leaders. Sigmund Freud, Mother Teresa and Vinoba Bhave are some examples.

(g) *Intrapersonal Intelligence*: This kind of intelligence consists of people's abilities to know their own selves. It includes knowledge and understanding of one's own cognitive strengths, styles and mental functioning. In short, intrapersonal intelligence helps individuals to understand their own self by providing an insight into their total behaviour: what they feel, think or do. Therefore, it is one of the private intelligences that a person possesses.

Due to its secret and private nature, this type of intelligence in an individual is available only through self-expression, i.e., through music, language, visual arts and similar creative forms of expression. Religious leaders and philosophers are strong in this kind of intelligence. This type of intelligence is also demonstrated by yogis, saints and masters of Zen. Vivekananda, Aurobindo, Victor Frankel and Ramakrishna Paramhansa are some of the examples.

Gardner's theory of multiple intelligence provides a broad and comprehensive view of human abilities, extending from linguistic and logical mathematical abilities on the one hand, to interpersonal and intrapersonal abilities on the other. Out of these seven categories, whereas the linguistic, logical-mathematical and spatial abilities have been accepted widely as the types and components of intelligence, the last four have been the subjects of great controversy as to whether they should be categorised as separate types of intelligence or as different talents. Anyhow, so far as the broader and global assessment of one's intellectual competencies and abilities is concerned, there is sufficient truth in the assertion of Gardner's theory that all the seven types of intelligence are essential for the true assessment of one's level of intellectual functioning.

In his book, Gardner said that out of these seven intelligence, the first two abilities (linguistic intelligence and logical-mathematical intelligence) were promoted more by the Western society and the other attributes were nurtured more by other societies. He also suggested that these separate intelligences do not operate in isolation. Any activity encompasses several kinds of intelligences, working together. His model has led to a number of advances in our understanding of the nature of intelligence.

Liouis L. Thurstone's Theory of Intelligence

L.L. Thurstone (1938) revealed that intelligence is a composite of seven distinct primary mental abilities (PMA). He tried to analyse the inter-correlations of a set of fifty six mental test and finally identified seven factors, each of which he called as a primary mental ability.

Table: 1.1. lists out the seven primary abilities described by L.L. Thurstone.

Table: 1.1 The Seven Primary Mental Abilities (Thurstone)

	Ability	Brief Description
V.	Verbal comprehension	The ability of reading comprehension; grasping meaning of words, concepts, and ideas; verbal reasoning.
N.	Numerical abilities	The ability to use numbers with speed and accuracy, to compute answers to problems. It is the ability to measure and use computational skills.
S.	Spatial relations	The ability to visualise and manipulate patterns and forms and visualise geometric relations in space.
P.	Perceptual speed	Speed of perceiving details, i.e., the ability to grasp details quickly and accurately, and to determine similarities and differences between stimuli.
W.	Word fluency	Speed of manipulation of single words, i.e., the ability to use words quickly and fluently in performing tasks, such as rhyming, solving anagrams, and doing crossword puzzles and naming words.
M.	Memory	The ability to recall simple material, such as lists of words, mathematical formulas, definitions, etc.
I.	Inductive Reasoning	Logical reasoning ability, i.e., the ability to derive general rules and principles from the presented information.

Liouis Thurstone

Thurstone considered each of the mental abilities to be independent of the other and that each could be assessed separately. He believed that there was no single source of an aggregate intelligence. His Primary Mental Abilities Test (PMAT) was widely used during the second and third decades of 20th century.

Arthur Jensen's Theory

Jensen (1969) proposed a different approach of intelligence. He developed a two level-theory of mental abilities which invited a debate on the association of heredity versus environment with intelligence. In his work, he clearly mentioned that there was a clear-cut difference in the average intelligence of races and social classes. His studies got published in the *Harvard Educational Review* in 1969.

Jensen said that two genetically based levels of intelligence exist. This means that intelligence consists of two levels of abilities. The Level-I ability is associative learning, which includes short-term memory (STM), rote learning, attention and simple associative skills. The Level-II ability is called the Cognitive Learning, which consists of abstract thinking, symbolic thought, conceptual learning and the use of language in problem solving.

He mentioned that Level-I ability, i.e., associative learning is equally distributed across all racial and national groups, but, on the contrary, Level-II, i.e., cognitive learning is concentrated more in the middle class Anglo-American population than in the lower class black populations. He believed that genetic differences in intelligence exist among people coming from different races, nationalities and social classes.

He conducted many studies on identical and fraternal twins. Identical twins have identical genetic dispositions for which their I.Q.s are assumed to be similar. On the other hand, fraternal twins like ordinary siblings are genetically less similar, which results in the assumption that their I.Q.s are also less similar. On the basis of his studies, he believed that genetic factors are more important than environmental factors for one's intelligence.

J.P. Guilford's Approach

J.P. Guilford (1967) advanced a model of intelligence which was based on factors analysis. He attempted to make logical explanations of the factors involved in mental functions. Guilford developed a "Structure of Intellect" model which stated that all mental activities are conceptualised within a three dimensional framework. This simply means that there are three features of intellectual tasks – the content on the type of information, the product or the form in which the information is represented and the operation, or type of mental activity performed.

The Structure of Intellect model shown in Fig: 1.4 shows five types of contents (visual, auditory, symbolic, semantic and behavioural); five kinds of operations (cognitions, memory, divergent production, convergent production and evaluation) and six varieties of products (units, classes, relations, systems, transformation and implications).

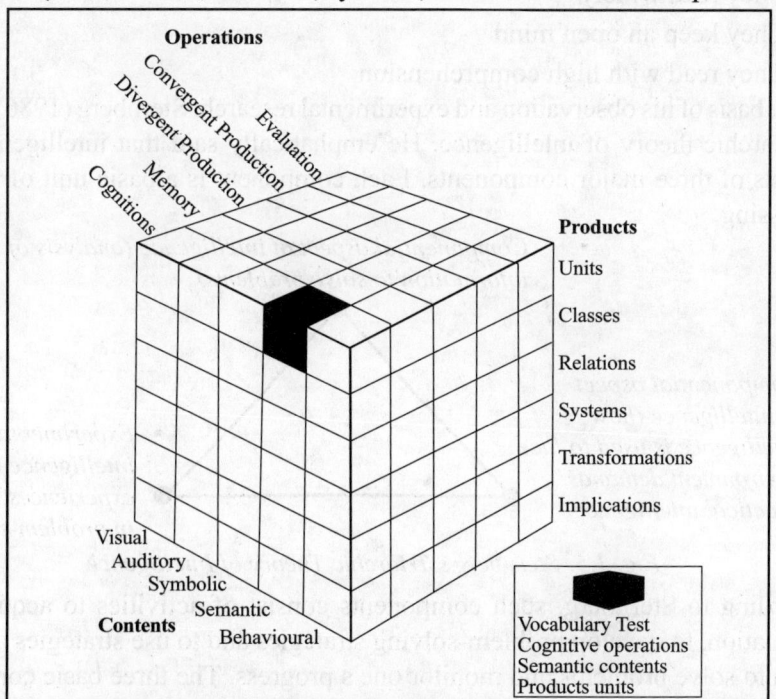

Fig. 1.4: J.P. Guilford's model of the Structure of Intellect

Each task performed by an individual can be identified according to a particular type of content, product and operation involved. By simple calculation, since there are five types of content, five different operations and six different kinds of products, there are, altogether,150 (5×5×6) separate kinds of mental abilities. For example, a test of vocabulary assesses one's ability for cognition of units with semantic content, while learning a form of dance requires memory for behavioural contents.

In Guilford's model, convergent and divergent thinking are considered to be generally involved in creativity and intelligence. In addition to other operations, creative abilities involve divergent operations. On the contrary, the production of single connect response is related to estimate intelligence in convergent thinking.

Information Processing Approach

Some cognitive psychologists have made significant contributions towards understanding the nature of intelligence very recently. An American psychologist, Robert Sternberg (1985) has put forward a theory of intelligence by adopting an information processing approach to cognition or problem solving. The cognitive psychologists do not focus on the structure of intelligence, but on the processes underlying intelligent behaviour.

Robert Sternberg of Yale University, USA, asked people to identify the characteristics of intelligent persons. The most frequently given answers were the following :

(a) They read logically and well
(b) They read widely
(c) They keep an open mind
(d) They read with high comprehension

On the basis of his observation and experimental research, Sternberg (1986) formulated the triarchic theory of intelligence. He emphatically said that intelligent behaviour consists of three major components. Each component is a basic unit of information processing.

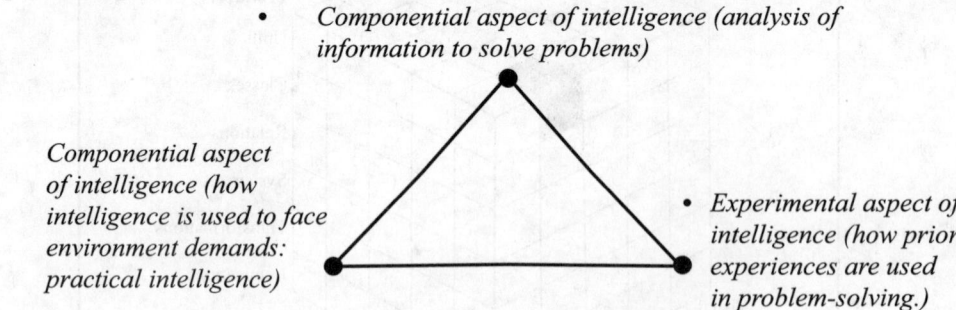

Fig. 1.5: Sternberg's Triarchic Theory of Intelligence

According to Sternberg, such components consist of activities to acquire or store information, to develop problem-solving strategies and to use strategies according to a plan to solve problems and monitor one's progress. The three basic components of intelligence are:

(a) Componential intelligence (analysis of information to solve problems)
(b) Experiential intelligence (using prior knowledge and information in problem solving and creating new ideas)
(c) Contextual intelligence (using intelligence to adapt to environmental demands, i.e., practical intelligence)
(d) *Componential Intelligence*: Componential intelligence is reflected in the I.Q. scores obtained through test administration. It is the knowledge acquisition component of learning new facts. Intelligent behaviour of a person consists of three information-processing components. These are: (1) Learning how to do things (2) Planning what things to do and how to do them and (3) Actually doing things. The individuals having this type of intelligence perform excellently in standard tests and they usually show rational behaviour.
(e) *Experiential Intelligence*: This component is involved in using the past experience creatively to solve novel problems. Thus, experiential intelligence is reflected in creative performance. The scientists develop new theories by using their past experience. This type of intelligence was shown by many scientific genius in the past. The bright examples are Newton, Einstein, C.V. Raman, etc.
(f) *Contextual Intelligence*: This component of intelligence involves *practical intelligence*. People manage practical, day-to-day life problems, get rid of trouble and try to be sociable using this type of intelligence. The contextual aspect is composed of adaptation to the present environment, selection of a relatively favourable environment instead of the existing one and modifying the present environment to fit to one's needs, skills and values.

Contextual intelligence is commonly called "street smartness" or "business sense". Individuals become successful by controlling their environment easily if they have a high component of contextual intelligence. It is difficult to measure contextual and experiential intelligence by standard I.Q. tests.

A Critical Evaluation of Sternberg's Theory

According to Sternberg, this kind of practical intelligence is the "tacit knowledge" and this tacit knowledge is more important than "bookish knowledge" for success in life. His test measures tacit knowledge of the individual. Further, the test also measures sensitivity to the non-verbal cues. Recent research of intelligence has focused more on Sternberg's contextual aspect of intelligence. Later on, Sternberg expanded his theory to the field of personality. He viewed "mental self-government" in describing personality dispositions of individuals. In a nutshell, Sternberg provided a clearly promising perspective in the field of cognition to understand the nature of intelligence.

PASS Model of Intelligence

The PASS model is a model of cognitive processing known as planning, attention, simultaneous and successive processing. This model of intelligence has a strong neurological foundation. It is an extension of the information processing approach. This model was based on Luria's analysis (Luria 1973, 1980) of human brain structures and cognitive psychological research (Broadbent, 1958; Simen, 1981).

An approach was developed by J.P. Das, Naglieri and Kirby in 1994. It is a modern theory of intelligence. J.P. Das said that intelligence is information processing which is dynamic in nature. It is not static or constant like ability.

Human cognitive processes involve three functional systems or units which work in harmony (Luria, 1980). The participation of all the three functional units is essential for any type of mental activity. The three functional units are:

(a) *First Functional Unit*: It is responsible for cortial arousal and attention. This unit is associated with the activities of the brain stem and the lower portion of the cerebral cortex.

(b) *Second Functional Unit*: This unit analyses, codes and information using simultaneous and successive processes. Simultaneous processing is associated with the parietal and occipital lobes of the brain, whereas successive processing is associated with the frontal-temporal lobes of brain.

(c) *Third Functional Unit*: This unit is important for planning, self-monitoring and structuring of cognitive activities. It is located in the frontal lobe of the brain.

Generally we receive informations through our sense organs such as eyes, ears, nose, skin, etc. When information is analysed, the central processing becomes active. The four components of the central processing mechanisms are: (a) Planning (b) Attention (c) Simultaneous processing and (d) Successive processing. All these four constitute the PASS processes.

These four processes work out on the existing knowledge base. This knowledge base is the outcome of learning, emotions and motivations. As J.P. Das said, "It is as if PASS processes are floating on a sea of knowledge". It is just like a boat floating on water – without water, the boat will sink.

The three units mentioned are together responsible for attention, simultaneous and successive processing and planning. These processes are enumerated in detail:

(a) *Attention*: Attention is the first functional system. The human cognitive processing starts from the proper wakefulness condition and it prepares the individual to receive and process information. This functional system involves maintaining an appropriate level of arousal followed by effective performance known as "attention".

When an individual's consciousness is focused on a stimulus, it is simply called attention. Of course, it is a complex cognitive activity. We receive information through our receptors. Attention comes after receiving information. The process of attention is voluntarily controlled.

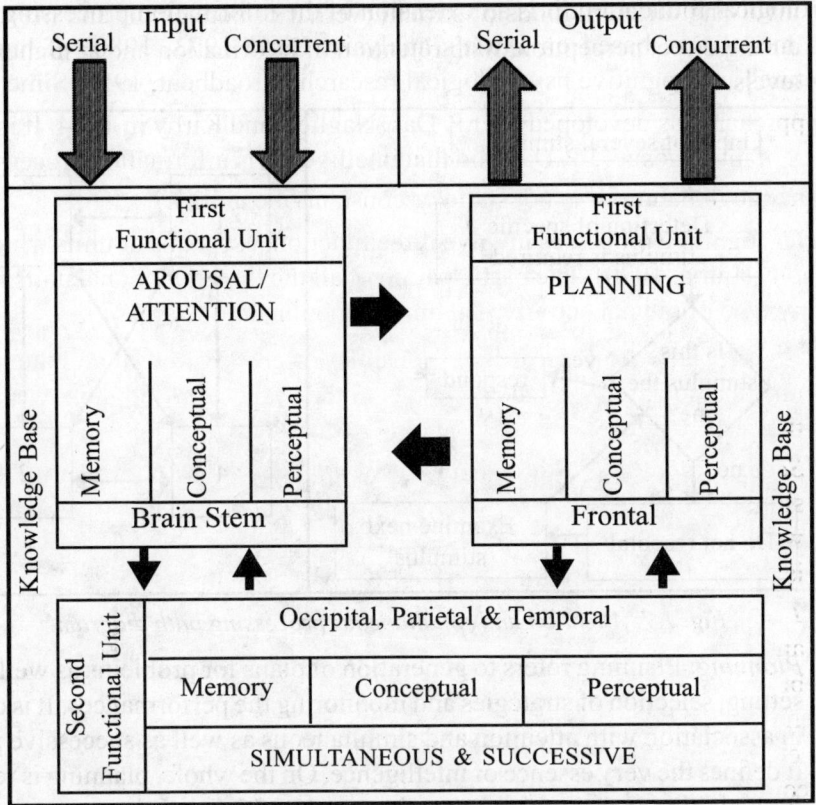

Fig. 1.6: The PASS model of intelligence

After cortical arousal and wakefulness, attention may be selective or divided. In selective attention, the individual focuses or acts on a single relevant stimulus and ignores the irrelevant stimuli. Selective attention is also known as voluntary discrimination of stimuli. Selective attention is an important activity of the first unit of the PASS system of intelligence.

(b) *Simultaneous and Successive Processes*: This is the second functional unit which is related to processing and retaining information received from the external world. Here two types of information processing take place: (i) Simultaneous Processing and (ii) Successive Processing.

Simultaneous processing is holistic in nature and involves integration of stimuli into harmonious groups. It organises information into a meaningful composite pattern. Through this process, an individual recognises that a number of stimuli share a common characteristic. Learning of digits and alphabets comes under successive processing. It refers to the processing of information in a serial order. Successive processing integrates the stimuli into a particular series forming a chain-like progression. Both simultaneous and successive processes can be applied to the tasks of various modalities (auditory, visual, kinesthetic, etc.)

involving different kinds of stimuli (verbal or nonverbal) and may take place during direct perception, with retention of information and at higher cognitive levels.

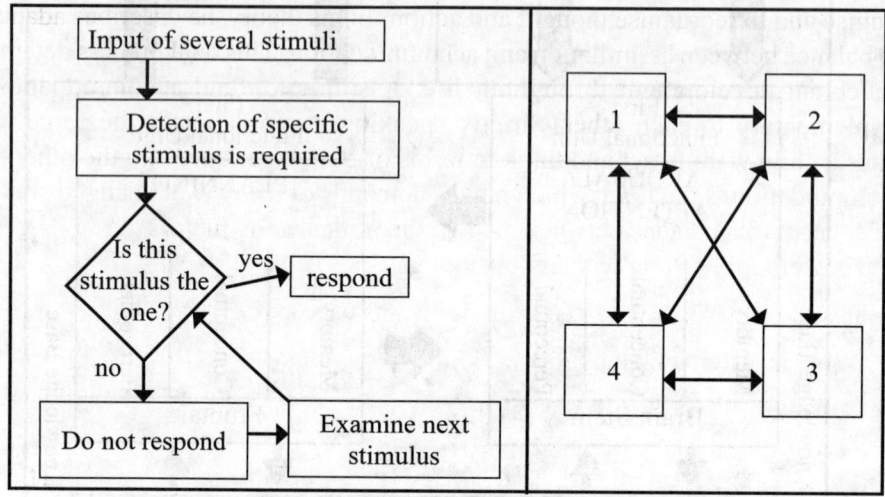

Fig. 1.7: *Attention and simultaneous processing path diagram*

(c) *Planning*: Planning refers to generation of plans for problems as well as to goal setting, selection of strategies and monitoring the performances. It is carried out in association with attention and simultaneous as well as successive processes. It defines the very essence of intelligence. On the whole, planning is responsible for activities such as asking questions and problem solving.

Evaluation of PASS Model

The Das-Naglieri Cognitive Assessment System (CAS) was based on PASS theory. CAS is a battery of tests developed by Das and Naglieri (1994). The system employs verbal and tests presented through visual and auditory sensory channels. All PASS processes are dynamic and interactive in nature. Still each process has its own function. All processes are not equally involved in a task. PASS model has also demonstrated how Luria's conceptualisation of human brain structures and functions can be used to operationalise intelligence. According to Wills (1998), PASS model provides a strong theoretical basis for psycho-educational assessment.

Cognitive–Development Approach

Jean Piaget (1970, 1972), a Swiss psychologist, developed a different theory which differed from the psychometricians to understand human cognition. The psychometricians were interested in studying individual differences in cognition, but Piaget was interested in understanding the nature of intellectual development in normal children. Piaget was a genetic epistemologist who was concerned with nature of knowledge, the structure and processes by which it is acquired. He argued that "much of our knowledge comes not from without but from within the forces of our own logic – a fact often forgotten in education".

Piaget makes constant reference to the interaction between an active organism and the environment. According to him, intellectual activities are adaptive. Intelligence is seen as an aspect of biological adaptation. Intelligence helps the individual to cope, to organise and to reorganise thought and action. In his theory, he describes adaptation as a balance between assimilation and accommodation. This dual process determines intellectual development throughout life. Assimilation and accommodation are complementary to each other. Strictly speaking, assimilation is the force which makes a child want to act and think in terms of past experience. On the other hand, accommodation is the force which makes demands of the new or changed situation. The concept of a balance between the two theoretical constructs is the central theme to Piaget's theory of intellectual development.

Piaget was primarily concerned with three questions:

(a) What is it that which changes with development?
(b) How do cognitive changes take place?
(c) How can cognitive development be ordered?

Piaget believed that specific cognitive structures or schemes change as a function of age. For infants, the schemes are the patterns of motor action. As the child advances in age, the schemes move from an action-based level to a mental level. Gradually, it becomes symbolic. The schemes are continuously modified and adapted to the environmental demands. Cognitive changes take place as a result of this modification and adaptation. What changes with the development are the schemes or the cognitive structures of children.

(e) How do cognitive changes take place?

Piaget identified two intellectual functions: adaptation and organisation to explain how cognitive changes take place. Adaptation is made up of two complementary processes, assimilation and accommodation. He borrowed these terms directly from the field of biological growth. During assimilation, we interpret the external world in terms of our existing cognitive structures. In accommodation, we modify the existing mental structures to take account of new information.

(f) How can cognitive development can be ordered?

Piaget opined that the cognitive changes take place in a systematic and orderly manner. Children pass through four qualitatively distinct stages of development. These are: (i) Sensorimotor stage (ii) Preoperational stage (iii) Concrete operational stage and (iv) Formal operational stage.

These stages are universal. This means that every child in this world goes through these stages. The first one, i.e., sensorimotor stage, lasts from birth to two years. During this time, understanding of the world is limited to sensory and motor organs. Through his or her motor actions, the child gradually learns that actions produce effects on the environment. This is the most important period of development in which accommodation is required to meet the environmental needs. The child masters three important capacities during this span: cause-and-effect relationship, object permanence and deferred imitation.

First, the child develops an understanding that he or she can manipulate the environment to produce interesting effects. Second, the child develops the concept of object permanence i.e., understanding that objects exist even when they are not visible. Also the child develops the ability to remember and copy behaviours of others who are not immediately present. This is called "differed imitation".

The preoperational stage lasts from 2 to 7 years. During this stage, the child develops representational ability, i.e., the capacity to think using mental images of people and objects. In other words, the child learns to carry out symbolic thinking. Symbolic thinking is the ability to make one thing represent or act as a symbol for another thing. It is reflected in many activities of children such as acquiring and using language and symbolic or make-believe play and drawings.

The concrete operational period spans from 7 to 11 years. It is a major turning point in cognitive development. This period is characterised by logical thought and loss of egocentric thinking. During this period, the children become more logical, flexible and organised in their cognition.

Formal operational stage begins after 11 years. It is the final stage of cognitive development. Here children's thinking becomes formal, hypothetical and abstract like adults. Another important characteristic of this stage is propositional thinking. Children can evaluate the logic of propositions or verbal statements without referring to real world circumstances.

The theory of cognitive development developed by Piaget provides the most important and powerful perspective on children. It is a grand theory in developmental psychology. But his theory is not free from criticisms. Piaget believed that development proceeds in a stage-like manner. But some developmental psychologists suggest that development is a continuous process and cannot be broken down into different stages as Piaget proposed. They believe that development is more quantitative than qualitative in nature. Another serious criticism levelled against Piaget is that he has seriously underestimated the cognitive capacities of infants and young children. Again, it was found that many older children, adolescents, college students and adults do not show formal operational thinking. This is another drawback in Piaget's theory. Piaget has underestimated the role of society in the development of children's cognitions. On the contrary, Piaget overemphasised the aspects of cognition in developing his theory. Other dimensions of development like social, emotional and moral development have not been given due attention by Piaget.

Factors Affecting Intelligence

There are individual differences in people's intellectual abilities. Some people are more intelligent than others. Why are there individual differences? What are the factors which influence the people's intelligence? The individual differences are the products of two broad factors: hereditary and environmental.

Hereditary factors are based on the genetic makeup of the individual, whereas the environmental factors consist of the influence of family, parents, friends, society, schooling, culture and all other experiences to which the child is exposed. The question of whether heredity or environment is important in determining intellectual growth is known as nature-nurture controversy. Nature refers to hereditary factors and nurture to environmental influences. The nature-nurture controversy has philosophical roots. During the 1960s, John Locke, a British philosopher held that the mind of a newborn is a blank slate or "tabula rasa" on which experiences are written. Locke believed that environment acts as the sole determinant of development. On the contrary, Rousseau suggested that genetic factors mostly influence the developmental process.

The nature-nurture question has been debated for years together. At present, psychologists agree that both nature and nurture interact to produce specific developmental patterns. Now the question is shifted to evaluating how and to what extent heredity and environment shape the developmental process.

Hereditary Factors

The genetically transmitted characteristics from one generation to the next are called heredity. We inherit the genetic code from our parents. A person's genetic heritage is called genotype. The genotype expresses itself in observable appearance and behaviour, which is called phenotype. This phenotype includes height, weight, eye, colour and other psychological characteristics such as intelligence, personality and creativity. The genetic code provides the base on which phenotype grows and manifests.

Very often, the question asked is – how can we know that human intelligence has a genetic basis? To answer this question, we have to infer the underlying genotypes from the observable phenotype behaviour.

Several studies have been conducted on identical twins to know the influence of heredity on intelligence. On the basis of some studies, Francis Galton (1885) opined that intelligence is largely inherited. Correlations between I.Q.s of brothers, sisters, children and their parents indicate that intelligence has a strong hereditary component.

Prof. Arther Jensen (1969) published an article, "How much can we boost I.Q. and Scholastic Achievement" in *Harvard Education Review*. It has brought a revolution in thinking and led to a lot of debate on the role of heredity in the development of intelligence. His findings also indicate that heredity has 80 per cent role in intellectual development, whereas environment has 20 per cent.

Environmental Factors

Heredity alone is not responsible for the individual differences in intelligence. Rather, environment also has a role to play. The child is exposed to a wide range of stimulations in the environment. He or she lives and grows in the environment. Several studies have been conducted to examine the role of environment as a determining factor of intelligence. The most illuminating study was done by Hussen (1960).

From the very moment of conception of the mother, the environment starts showing its actions. Both prenatal environment and postnatal environment influence the intellectual development of children.

(a) *Prenatal Environment*: During prenatal stage, rapid development takes place in major organs and brain cells. If anything goes wrong during this period, the effects are very difficult to rectify. The important prenatal environmental influences are mother's nutrition, emotional state of the mother, illness of the mother, mother's use of drugs and birth complications.

Lack of nutrition has an adverse effect on the mental development of the child. Anxious and tense mothers are likely to deliver infants who would be irritable and would have sleeping and eating problems in future. Maternal diseases like AIDS, diabetes, hypertension, rubella and syphilis produce permanent adverse effects on the child. The brain cells may be damaged and the intellectual development may be arrested. Drugs, alcohol and nicotine are very dangerous for pregnant mothers. They may result in retarded mental growth of the babies. If the neonate suffers from birth complications such as lack of oxygen at the time of birth, he or she may suffer from permanent brain damage.

(b) *Postnatal Environment*: Postnatal environment means the environment a child faces after birth. Enriched environment accelerates cognitive development whereas impoverished environment produces the opposite effect.

The home is the first place of learning for children. So home environment plays a significant role in their intellectual development. The home provides an identity to the children, builds their self-concept and prepares them to face the world. All the mental and behavioural transaction are possible in the home environment. The environment may be supportive or stressful for the child. A supportive home environment encourages curiosity, exploration and self-reliance which are conducive for intellectual growth of children. Where the parents are strict and authoritarian, the child's intellectual competence becomes low. The emotional and motivational aspects of children are also closely attached with intellectual competence.

(c) *Parent-Child Interaction*: Parents are the first teachers of their children. The mental and behavioural transactions between the parents and children have significant influence on intellectual competence. The intellectual development of children becomes faster when the parents provide emotional security, make the family environment more supportive and praise the achievement of their children. On the other hand, the intellectual development suffers where parents encourage dependence and family condition is stressful.

Parental values and expectations also play a vital role in fostering intellectual abilities of children. In a study, Harold Stevenson revealed that parental expectations for boys and girls differ and these then get reflected in their achievements. In another study, it was found that high achievement in boys was associated with high maternal reinforcement and encouragement during the first three years of life.

(d) *Social and Environmental Deprivation*: Poor cognitive performance is evident if environmental opportunities and stimulations are low. This was the result in a study conducted by Skeels (1966). In an Indian study conducted by Dash and Das (1984, 1989), it was found that schooling influences children's cognitive capacities significantly. In a study in rural India, they have shown that schooled children show superior performance on a variety of intellectual tasks compared to their unschooled age-mates. No doubt, a school provides an enriched social environment for children. Similar results were also found in another study conducted by Scribner and Cole (1979) in African countries. On the whole, researchers and experts have shown that early intellectual retardation can be overcome by providing adequate enriched environmental experiences.

(e) *Socio-Economic Status (SES)*: It is seen that children in upper socio-economic strata are exposed to more intellectual stimulation. The index of socio-economic status (SES) is based on parental education, occupation and income. The higher the socio-economic status of the parents, the higher is the I.Q. of children. In another study, Harrell and Harrell (1945) revealed that parental occupation is closely related to the I.Q. level of children.

In an Indian study, Jachuk and Mohanty (1974) found that children of high SES performed significantly better than children from low SES on a variety of intellectual tasks. Rath, Dash and Das (1979) reported the adverse effects of social class on intellectual reasoning.

(f) *Race and Culture*: Culture refers to a system of beliefs, attitudes and values which are passed from one generation to another. Many studies show that racial and cultural differences are prominent in intellectual development. In their study, Jensen (1969) and Kennedy (1966) found that there was a clear difference in cognitive competence between whites and blacks. In India, there are many sub-cultures with their own values. The socialisation practices in these sub-cultures are different. In Odisha, many studies were conducted by Das, Singha, Rath and Jachuck (1974) and they have reported significant differences in the cognitive levels of children.

(g) *Sex differences*: Evidence indicates that sex differences affect performance for particular kinds of cognitive abilities. Females are superior in language skills, verbal fluency and reading, whereas males are superior in mathematical reasoning and spatial abilities. It appears that the two sexes show different patterns of intellectual abilities. But intelligence is also related to personality characteristics. Boys are socialised in a manner so as to promote self-reliance and competence, which are positively correlated with intelligence. But many researchers differ in their convictions regarding sex differences. They believe that differential abilities are the products of some combination of genetic and environmental factors.

(h) *Personality Dispositions*: Some evidence suggests that changes in I.Q. are related to a child's general pattern of adjustment and personality. Personality traits like assertiveness, independence, self-initiation and competitiveness have positive impact on intellectual development. If these personality traits are not socially acceptable, the advantages would be minimised. It was observed that the children who showed temper tantrums had drops in their I.Q.s. (Peskin, 1964; Sontag, Baker and Nelson, 1958).

(i) *Physiological Conditions*: Empirical studies of intellectual development reveal that the physiological conditions such as nutrition, health, drugs, disease and physical injury affect the cognitive competence of children. This supports the adage that a healthy body has a healthy mind. The mental development of a child is associated with biochemical processes and hormones within the body. Poor health retards the growth of brain cells and ultimately the intellectual skills also. Similarly brain injury, intoxicating drugs and alcohol consumption also adversely affect the biological processes and the development of brain cells.

Creativity and Intelligence

Robert Sternberg (1987) talked about three types of intelligence in his theory. These are: analytic, creative and practical.

Creativity is a process which requires the balance and application of the different aspects of intelligence. The creative intelligence is the ability to go beyond the given data to generate novel and interesting ideas. Highly intelligent people may or may not be creative, but highly creative persons are highly intelligent. No doubt, a creative individual is a good synthetic thinker. He or she can visualise the relationships what others cannot see. Creative people have the ability to analyse and evaluate ideas.

The practical intelligence is the most important aspect of creativity. It refers to the ability to translate theory into practice and transfer abstract ideas into practical tasks. On the whole, while an intelligent person is high only on analytical intelligence, a creative person is high on all the three aspects.

Intelligence: Unified or Multifaceted?

Very often, the question arises: Is intelligence a single characteristic or does it consist of several distinct parts?

Some psychologists viewed intelligence as a general, unified capacity. Spearman (1927) believed that performance on any cognitive task depends on a primary general factor (g-factor) and on one or more specific factors relating to that particular task.

According to him, people who score high or low on one kind of test of intelligence tend to score at a similar level on other tests too.

On the contrary, some experts believe that intelligence is composed of many separate mental activities which operate more or less independently. One of the strongest proponents of this position was Therstone (1938). He suggested that intelligence is a composite of seven distinct primary mental abilities. According to him, assessment of one's intelligence requires measurement of all seven abilities. Some related theories (Gardner, 1983 & Guilford, 1985) have divided intelligence into different patterns of components, but the basic underlying idea remains the same – intelligence is multifaceted.

Fluid and Crystallised Intelligence

Cattell (1987) emphatically viewed that intelligence consists of two major components: fluid intelligence and crystallised intelligence.

Fluid intelligence involves the abilities to form concepts, reason and identify similarities. It is more intuitive and active in forming new mental structures rather than in making use of existing ones. On the other hand, crystallised intelligence includes those aspects of intelligence which involve drawing on previously learned information to make decisions or solve problems. For example, classroom tests, vocabulary tests and many social situations involve *crystallised intelligence*.

Is Intelligence Innate or Acquired?

A very pertinent question often comes to our mind: Is intelligence innate or acquired? The scientists who claimed that intelligence is innate regarded that intelligence is genetically determined at conception or is controlled by heredity. According to these theorists, an individual is born with a certain degree of intelligence which is constant and continues to be the same throughout his or her life. In his famous book, *Hereditary Genius*, Sir Francis Galton emphasised biological heredity as the only factor which determines individual differences in intelligence.

On the contrary, the environmentalists viewed that some part of intelligence is inherited, whereas some part is acquired. According to them, intelligence can be increased or diminished due to individual experiences. It can be acquired and modified during one's life-span. Some pioneering studies emphasising the role of environment on intelligence were undertaken at the University of Iowa under the leadership of Martha Wellman. The results indicated that I.Q. can be enhanced by providing proper environment.

Some studies have shown that the effects of early experiences like extreme loneliness due to parental rejection, institutionalisation, isolation of members of the lower class and death of loved ones can be so drastic that not only intelligence, but the whole cognitive abilities of an individual can be irreversibly impaired.

Some experts believe that both heredity and environment have significant roles in the growth of intelligence. They believe that intelligence is an outcome of the interaction between heredity and environment. The environment can help to unfold the capacities that are innate by providing opportunities at the right time and the right place. It may be concluded that heredity can find its outlet only through the environment.

New Directions in Intelligence

(a) *Emotional Intelligence:* Psychologists Peter Salovey and John D. Mayer coined the term "Emotional Intelligence" in 1990 describing it as "a form of social intelligence that involves the ability to monitor one's own and others' feelings and emotions, to discriminate among them, and to use this information to guide one's thinking and action". They emphasised five broad types of abilities as central to emotional intelligence. These are (a) Knowing one's emotions (b) Managing emotions (c) Recognising emotions in others (d) Motivating oneself and (e) Handling social relationships

Danial Goleman developed the concept in 1995. He argued that our view of human intelligence is limited because it has not included a set of abilities which are crucial for the happiness and success of individuals. Scientists recognise that in the practical world, emotional intelligence is more important than academic intelligence measured by I.Q.

Emotional intelligence refers to the set of capacities which are independent of I.Q., but essential for excelling in the workplace, social interaction and intimate relationships. According to Goleman, one's EQ or "Emotional Quotient" consists of seven qualities or abilities. These are self-awareness, self-motivation, persistence when frustrated, impulse control, mood regulation, empathy and hope or optimism.

Goleman held that emotional intelligence helps in building better careers, encourages developing better relationship and better health in later life. He also suggested that a child's emotional intelligence can be better developed in the right direction if parents try to become emotionally healthy from the beginning itself. Little mistakes and carelessness during early childhood may lead to serious repercussions. Goleman rightly said, "You can be a highly effective life-long teacher for your child's emotional intelligence for better or worse by how you model emotions and handle your child every day."

Components of Goleman's E.Q.
❏ *Self-Awareness*
❏ *Self-motivation*
❏ *Persistence*
❏ *Impulse Control*
❏ *Mood Regulation*
❏ *Empathy*
❏ *Optimism*

(b) *Practical Intelligence*: An individual's high I.Q. score does not guarantee success in life, if it is without practical intelligence. Observation indicates that Sternberg's concept of contextual intelligence represents practical knowledge. This type of intelligence can be applied to solving day-to-day life problems. Sternberg calls it as "tacit knowledge". Tacit knowledge includes all the useful and need-based information about getting along in the real world, which is not taught in schools or colleges. The use of practical intelligence is seen in politics, business, social communication and science. Sternberg cites the example of a graduate student named Celia who was also street-smart. She knew well how to manipulate the environment. Her score in traditional tests were not very high, but she could succeed in almost every social context. Sternberg developed some tests of practical intelligence which are different from traditional I.Q. tests.

(c) *Spiritual Intelligence*: This is also known as Spiritual Quotient (S.Q.). Very often, it is considered as the *ultimate intelligence*. The term spiritual intelligence and spiritual quotient is mostly attributed to Danah Zohar and Ian Marshall based on their pioneering book published in 2001, *SQ: Connecting With Our Spiritual Intelligence*.

This concept is related to higher values and meaningful existence in larger holistic context. Meditation helps in achieving spiritual intelligence. Possibly, Swami Vivekananda, Buddha, Shankaracharya and Mother Teresa had high spiritual intelligence. Spiritual intelligence allows human beings to be creative to change the rules and to alter situations by extending the boundaries. It takes us beyond the present moment and ourselves.

As indicated by authors, S.Q. operates out of the brain's centre and integrates all our intelligences. S.Q. makes us fully intellectual, emotional and spiritual creatures that we are. S.Q. does not have connection with religion.

(d) *Artificial Intelligence:* Artificial Intelligence has been defined in many different ways as it covers a vast field. No definition of AI can be so comprehensive that it will cover all the dimensions of AI. Some definitions are mentioned here:

AI refers to an artificial creation of human-like intelligence that can learn, reason, plan, perceive or process natural language to bring immense socio-economic opportunities, while also posing ethical and socio-economic challenges.

AI is any technique that enables computers to mimic human intelligence, using logic, if–then rules, decision trees and machine learning including deep learning.

AI may be defined as a computerised machine that exhibits intelligent-like behaviour.

AI can do many things better than humans – not just routine tasks, but also more complex ones, if there is enough opportunity for the AI system to learn them. For example, AI could be helpful in sentiment analysis of psychiatric patients having suicide tendencies so as to prevent suicides by early detection and follow-up treatment. A project at IBM (Watson) attempts to infer people's personalities, emotions and intentions using social media data and machine learning techniques. Sentiment analysis is used by e-commerce companies and by National Health Scheme (NHS) of UK for gathering feedback from users on the quality of services provided.

❑ Key Terms

1. Accommodation
2. Achievement test
3. Adaptation
4. Aptitude
5. Assimilation
6. Chronological age (C.A.)
7. Crystallised intelligence
8. Emotional intelligence
9. Environment
10. Fluid intelligence
11. g-factor of intelligence
12. Gifted children
13. Heredity
14. Intellectual development
15. Intelligence
16. Intelligence Quotient (I.Q.)
17. Mental age (M.A.)
18. Mental retardation
19. Nature vs nurture
20. Non-verbal tests
21. Norm
22. PASS theory of intelligence
23. Practical intelligence
24. Psychometric tests
25. Reliability
26. s-factor of intelligence
27. Spiritual intelligence
28. Standardisation
29. Validity
30. Verbal tests

❑ Names to Know

1. Alfred Binet
2. Arthur Jensen
3. C.M. Bhatia
4. Charles Murray
5. Charles Spearman
6. Danah Zohar
7. Daniel Goleman
8. David Wechsler
9. Francis Galton Sir
10. Henry Goddard
11. Howard Gardner
12. Ian Marshall
13. J.P. Das
14. Jean Piaget
15. Lewis Terman
16. R. Rath
17. Raymond Cattell
18. Robert Sternberg
19. S.M. Mohsin
20. William Stern

❑ Chapter Summary and Review

1. Intelligence may be understood to be a mental energy available with an individual which enables him to cope with his environment in terms of adaptation and dealing with novel situations as effectively as possible. According to David Wechsler, "Intelligence is the global and aggregate capacity of the individual to think rationally, to act purposefully and to deal effectively with the environment."
2. The formal intelligence tests were developed in the early 1900s. Galton (1885) is considered as the father of mental tests. He believed that intelligence could be measured by objective tests.
3. J. McKeen Cattell tried to study the nature of individual differences. He believed that sensory, perceptual and motor processes constitute the core of intelligence.
4. In 1904, Alfred Binet devised a method to identify mentally disabled children from the normal school children. Binet and Simon developed an intelligence test on being requested by the French Ministry of Education. The concept of Mental Age (M.A.) was first developed by Binet.
5. Intelligence Quotient (I.Q.) is just a number devised by a German psychologist, William Stern. It is an age-related measure of intelligence level.
6. I.Q. is determined by the individual's Mental Age (M.A.) divided by Chronological Age (C.A.) multiplied by 100.

    $$I.Q. = [M.A. / C.A.] \times 100$$

7. Wechsler Scales are most widely used intelligence tests. These scales were developed by David Wechsler of the Bellevue hospital in New York. There are three scales (a) the Wechseler Adult Intelligence Scale -Revised (WAIS-R), the Wechsler Intelligence Scale for Children Revised (WISC-R) and Wechsler Preschool and Primary Scales of Intelligence (WPPSI). These scales have gone through successive revisions.
8. There are three main approaches to the study of intelligence:
    (a) Psychometric approach
    (b) Information- Processing approach
    (c) Cognitive- Developmental approach
9. The psychometric approach studies intelligence as the ability or an aggregate of multiple abilities. But information-processing approach describes the processes people use in intellectual reasoning and problem solving. (Sternberg and J.P. Das). The cognitive-developmental approach places emphasis on functional significance and development of intelligence (Piaget).
10. Charles Spearman advanced a two-factor theory of intelligence in 1927. He revealed that all intellectual activities have a single common factor called the general factor or "g" factor. He also said that there were a number of specific factors or "s" factors. Each s-factor refers to a specific single activity. The g-factor runs through all abilities and forms the basis for prediction of the individual's performance.

11. R.B. Cattell indicated that general intelligence can be broken down into two relatively independent components: fluid intelligence and crystallised intelligence.
12. Fluid intelligence denotes reasoning, memory and information-processing capabilities, whereas Crystallised intelligence is the knowledge that an individual has already acquired and the ability to access that knowledge.
13. L.L. Thurstone (1938) suggested that there are seven distinct primary mental abilities (P.M.A.) which constitute intelligence. These seven primary mental abilities are: (a) Verbal comprehension (b) Numerical abilities (c) Spatial relations (d) Perceptual Speed (e) Word fluency (f) Memory (g) Inductive reasoning.
14. Arthur Jensen (1969) proposed a two-level theory of mental abilities. The *Level* I ability is associative learning, which consists of Short Term Memory (S.T.M.), rote learning, attention and simple association skills. The Level II ability is called Cognitive Learning, which consists of abstract thinking, symbolic thought, conceptual learning and the use of language in problem solving.
15. In 1967, J.P. Guiford advanced a model of intelligence based on factor analysis. According to him, there are three features of intellectual tasks, (a) the content or type of information (b) the product or the form in which the information is represented and (c) the operation or type of mental activity performed.
16. Howard Gardener (1983) believed that we have multiple intelligences, each relatively independent of the others. These are: Linguistic intelligence, Logical–Mathematical intelligence, Spatial intelligence, Musical intelligence, Bodily–Kinesthetic intelligence, Interpersonal intelligence and Intrapersonal intelligence. These are essential for successful adaption and survival.
17. Robert Sternberg of Yale University, USA, formulated the triarchic theory of intelligence. According to him, the three basic and major components of intelligence are: (a) Componential intelligence (b) Experiential intelligence and (c) Contextual intelligence.
18. The PASS model of intelligence was developed by J.P. Das and Naglieri (1994). It is a model of cognitive processing known as Planning, Attention, Simultaneous and Successive processing (PASS). This model has a strong neurological foundation.
19. The Swiss psychologist, Jean Piaget (1970, 1972) developed a theory of intellectual development of children. According to him, intelligence is a particular instance of biological adaptation. Piaget revealed that the four successive stages of cognitive development are: (a) Sensorimotor stage (b) Preoperational stage (c) Concrete Operational stage (d) Formal Operational stage.

20. Generally two factors affect intelligence: (a) Hereditary factors and (b) Environmental factors. An individual's genetic heritage is called genotype. It expresses itself in observable behaviour. This observable appearance or behaviour is called phenotype. The phenotype includes intelligence, personality and creativity.

21. Both the prenatal and postnatal environments play vital roles in the development of cognition and intelligence. The prenatal environment includes mother's nutrition, mother's emotional state, illness of the mother, mother's use of drugs and birth complications. The postnatal environment includes home environment, parent–child interaction, society, socio-economic status, culture, sex differences and personality dispositions.

22. I.Q. tests have many limitations. These tests tap only a part of a human's overall competence. The I.Q. tests fail to measure creative insight, ignore the practical side of intelligence and wrongly equate intelligence with speed.

23. Very often, intelligence tests are biased in favour of the middle class and higher-class populations. Further, the answers to some intelligence test items seem to have been arbitrarily decided. They provide little meaningful information for the actual planning of educational instruction.

24. Intelligence tests having language elements have a cultural component in them. It is almost impossible to design a culture-free test. Instead, the psychologists and experts have tried to develop tests which can be considered culture-fair or culture-reduced, where cultural influence is reduced to some extent.

25. New directions of intelligence include emotional, practical and spiritual intelligence. Denial Goleman (1995) has given new direction to Emotional Intelligence although the idea was first developed by Salovey and Mayer. Components of Goleman's EQ are: (a) Self-awareness (b) Self-motivation (c) Persistence (d) Impulse control (e) Mood regulation (f) Empathy and (g) Optimism.

26. Sternberg's contextual intelligence is otherwise known as practical intelligence. It is the tacit knowledge which includes all the useful and need-based information about getting along in the real world.

27. The concept of spiritual intelligence (SQ) was first developed by Danah Zohar and Marshall (2000). It is considered to be the ultimate intelligence. We address and solve problems of meaning and value with this type of intelligence.

QUESTIONS

1. Define intelligence. Discuss the nature of intelligence.
2. What is the nature of intelligence? How it can be measured?
3. How can you relate intelligence to adaptation, shaping and selection?
4. Discuss briefly the multiple intelligences identified by Gardner.
5. Distinguish between Sternberg's theory and Gardner's theory of intelligence.
6. What are the components of PASS model of intelligence?
7. Define intelligence. Briefly discuss different approaches to the study of intelligence.
8. What is I.Q.? How can you differentiate between verbal and performance tests of intelligence?
9. What are the different types of intelligence tests?
10. Critically examine Sternberg's triarchic theory of intelligence.
11. What is intelligence? Discuss different factors affecting intelligence.
12. Critically examine whether intelligence is determined by hereditary or environmental factors.
13. Elucidate different theoretical positions regarding whether intelligence is unitary or multifaceted.
14. Discuss briefly the Piagetian conception and theory of intellectual development.
15. Discuss the nature-nurture controversy in intelligence.
16. Explain various theories of intelligence.
17. Write short notes on the following:
    (a) WAIS-R
    (b) Creativity and intelligence
    (c) Emotional Intelligence
    (d) PASS model of intelligence
    (e) Artificial Intelligence
    (f) Spiritual Intelligence
    (g) 'g' factor and 's' factor in intelligence
    (h) Fluid intelligence

CHAPTER - 2
SELF AND PERSONALITY

❑ *Personality refers to a person's unique and relatively stable qualities which characterise behaviour patterns across different situations and over a period of time.*
❑ *The study of self and personality tries to understand human beings in totality.*

❑ **This chapter covers:**
- What is personality?
- Allport's definition of personality
- Classification of personality
- Type Theory of personality
  - (a) Hippocrate's typology
  - (b) Kretschmer's typology
  - (c) Sheldon's typology
  - (d) Jung's typology
- Trait theory of personality
- Surface traits and source traits
- Assessment of personality
  - (a) Psychometric tests
  - (b) Projective tests (TAT, RIT, WAT)
- Self and personality
- Key Terms, Summary and Questions

❑ **By the end of this chapter, you will be able to:**
- Define personality
- Classify personality into different types
- Know about the traits of personality
- Assess personality administering different tests
- Describe the concept of self
- Understand the meaning and some of the methods of regulating self
- Explain the Indian notion of self

Introduction

Personality is perhaps the most controversial concept in psychology. People as well as philosophers have different ideas of what the term "personality" stands for.

The word "personality" is derived from the Latin word "persona" which was a theatrical mask used by actors in those days to indicate their role in a theatrical play. Today, people take personality to mean reputation or physical attractiveness.

Often, people are heard saying, "that person has got a wonderful personality" or "that person does not possess any personality". But such conceptions are erroneous. Every person has a personality. Personality does not simply mean the outward appearance of a person. Personality is the totality of an individual's inner as well as outer qualities, interacting with each other.

Several attempts have been made to define personality in different ways. It is true that personality has no standard meaning. Probably fifty definitions of personality are available. All these definitions mostly seek to include the total person, i.e., his or her external appearance, abilities, tendencies and innate and acquired characteristics.

According to G.W. Allport, all these different definitions could be divided into two groups:

(a) Mask Approach,   (b) Substance Approach

In the Mask approach, the emphasis was placed on superficial aspect of behaviour. It is concerned with outward appearance. But in the Substance approach, emphasis is placed on the underlying nature of the individual.

Allport's Definition of Personality

One of the most adequate definitions of personality has been given by G.W. Allport. He defined personality as "the dynamic organisation within the individual of those psychophysical systems that determine his or her unique adjustment to his or her environment". An analysis of Allport's definition points out the following characteristics of personality:

(a) *Dynamic Organisation:* Personality is not static. It is not a simple addition of traits and qualities. Rather, it is an active organisation which constantly changes and develops. These changes in organisation are due to motivation. In an abnormal personality, there is a disorganisation of various physical and psychological traits.

The term "organisation" refers to physical and mental traits combined into one. Physical traits refer to intelligence, general physique, colour of the eyes, hair, shape of the nose, body structure, complexion, etc. The psychological traits refer to attitude, interest, motives, sociability, honesty, etc.

(b) *Psychophysical System*: Personality is neither exclusively mental nor exclusively physical. It is a combination of the two. Traits denote distinct mode of behaviour. They are more or less permanent. According to Kimble and Germazy (1980), a trait is a stable and enduring attribute of a person that is revealed consistently in a variety of situations. They are dynamically interrelated and each trait is influenced by the other.

(c) *Determine*: The traits which constitute personality have determining tendencies and when aroused by suitable stimuli provide these adjectives and expressive acts by which personality comes to be known.

(d) *Unique*: Every person has a unique personality. It is different from every other person. No two personalities in this world are exactly the same. The adjustment of each individual with the environment and with the society is unique in every respect. Because of this uniqueness, every person is completely different from the others.

(e) *Adjustment to the Environment*: The personality of a person adapts to changing situations and circumstances. Moreover, adjustment and adaptation becomes a mode of survival. Here adjustment includes maladjustment and environment includes both behavioural and geographical environment.

In a nutshell, personality is the sum-total of the physical and mental traits of an individual, which are dynamic and liable to change. The traits of personality help an individual to adjust to his or her environment. In other words, personality refers to a person's unique and relatively stable qualities that characterise behaviour patterns across different situations and over a period of time. We often show consistency in behaviour, thought and emotion across situations and across time periods. Understanding uniqueness and commonality within and across individuals is a great challenge for psychologists.

Common observation reveals that different people respond to the same situation in different ways. Underlying the behaviour of each individual, there seems to be some coherence, order and consistency. Briefly speaking, "personality" is used to characterise these aspects of an individual.

Table 2.1 gives some personality related terms and how to distinguish them.

Table 2.1: Distinguishing Personality Related Terms

Temperament	Biologically based characteristic way of reacting.
Disposition	Tendency in the individual to react to a given situation in a characteristic way.
Character	Total pattern of regularly occurring behaviour.
Trait	Constant, persistent and specific way of behaving.
Type	Distinct category to which people with a pattern of traits are assigned.
Habit	Learned mode of behaving.
Values	Goals that are considered worthwhile.

Characteristics of Personality

(a) Personality is unique. Every individual has his or her own set of personality characteristics.

(b) There are certain characteristics of personality which remain relatively persistent and permanent.

(c) An individual's personality represents a dynamic orientation of an organism to the environment.

(d) Personality is also influenced by social interaction. As a child grows up, he or she develops interaction through socialisation and ultimately this influences personality development.

(e) Personality represents an unique organisation of persistent, dynamic and social predisposition.

Now the question arises: How is personality expressed? Personality is expressed in three ways:

(i) Firstly, personality is expressed by the overt action which involves the gross bodily muscles and habits.

(ii) Secondly, personality is expressed through verbal and communicative activities. But these activities are only possible for human beings.

(iii) Lastly, personality is also expressed through our thoughts and some internal processes like emotions, impulses and language. When the same words are uttered differently, personality is revealed in a different manner.

Classification of Personality

Pre-Scientific Classification

Pre-scientific classification of personality was based on body humours. It was made by Hippocrates. He believed that the peculiarities in one's temperament and character were caused by body humours (fluids). According to him, there were four types of personality: the sanguine, phlegmatic, choleric and melancholic (Table 2.2).

He also revealed that the type which an individual belongs depends on whether the predominant fluid in his or her body is blood, phlegm, yellow bile or black bile.

Sanguines have surplus of blood and being warm-blooded, they are quick, gay, cheerful and active. The phlegmatic people have surplus of phlegm and they are slow, dull, calm and unexcitable.

Hippocrates also believed that the choleric people have surplus of yellow bile, whereas the melancholics have black bile to the maximum extent. Cholerics are irritable, quick tempered and angry, whereas the melancholic people are sad, depressed and pessimists. But this classification by Hippocrates invited many criticisms and one of the major criticism is that it is not classified on a scientific basis.

Table 2.2: Prescientific Classification of Personality

Type	Fluid	Temperament
1. SANGUINE	Surplus of Blood	Quick, gay cheerful and active
2. PHLEGMATIC	Surplus of Phlegm	Slow, dull, calm and unexcitable
3. CHOLERIC	Surplus of Yellow bile	Irritable, Quick tempered, angry
4. MELANCHOLIC	Surplus of Black bile	Sad, depressed and pessimist

Kretschmer's Classification

In 1925, Kretschmer classified individuals in terms of their physical form and structure. He was a German psychiatrist who noticed during his treatment that certain body types were associated with particular types of mental disorders. The schizophrenic patients have tall and slim physique, while the manic depressive psychotics have plump and short body structure. Later on, he observed the body structure of the normal people and classified human personality into three types. These are: Pyknic, Athletic and Asthenic.

- *Pyknic*: The pyknic persons are short, stout, fatty, thick and round-faced. They are sociable, easy going, informal, tolerant, good humoured people.
- *Athletic*: These persons are tall, well-built and muscular. They are active, practical, tolerant, jovial and adjustable.
- *Asthenic*: These people are tall, long-limbed, having sickly physique. By temperament, they are shy, sensitive, gentle, intolerant, idealistic, formal and romantic. Asthenic people are generally introverts.

Table 2.3: Kretschmer's Classification of Personality

Type	Physical Structure	Temperament
PYKNIC	Short, fatty, thickened and round-faced	Sociable, easy going, jovial, internal, tolerant
ATHLETIC	Tall, well-built and muscular	Active, practical, tolerant, jovial and adjustable
ASTHENIC	Tall, long limbed, sickly physique	Shy, sensitive, gentle, intolerant and idealistic

Sheldon's Classification

Sheldon (1942) divided personality into three types. His typology has much in common with that of Kretschmer. In fact, it is an outgrowth of Kretschmer's classification. Very often, it is called Sheldon's Somatotype Theory (Table 2.4).

Sheldon studied 200 college students for five years. Finally, he classified his observations. These are: (a) Endomorphy, (b) Mesomorphy and (c) Ectomorphy.

According to him, the viscerotonic people are characterised by physical comforts. They enjoy eating and relaxation. They always feel insecure.

The somatotonic persons are characterised by bodily activities like energetic movement, aggressiveness, competition, etc.

The cerebrotonic personality is characterised by an influence of cerebral processes resulting in being restrained, thoughtful, shy, etc. These people are non-adventurous and do not withstand pain easily.

Sheldon's classification invited many criticisms. No doubt, his observation was based on the study of 200 college students over a long span of time. Experts viewed that Sheldon's table of correlations had serious computational errors. Some of these correlations are mathematically impossible. Subsequent studies on body type and temperament indicated no practical relationship (Hood, 1963 and Lubin, 1950).

Table 2.4: Sheldon's Typology of Personality

Body Type	Physical Structure	Temperament
PYKNIC	Short, fatty, thickened and round-faced	Sociable, easy going, jovial, internal, tolerant
ATHLETIC	Tall, well-built and muscular	Active, practical, tolerant, jovial and adjustable
ASTHENIC	Tall, long limbed, sickly physique	Shy, sensitive, gentle, intolerant and idealistic

Typical Traits

Endomorphy	Viscerotonia	Fond of food, apprehensive, insecure, amiable, sleeps well.
Mesomorphy	Somatotonia	Adventurous, likes strenuous exercise, dresses informally, withstands pain easily and willingly.
Ectomorphy	Cerebrotonia	Asocial, unnameable, lacks desire for exercise, non-adventurous, does not withstand pain easily.

Jung's Typology

C.G. Jung's classification of personality has occupied a prominent place in the personality domain. He divided personality into two types: (a) Extroverts and (b) Introverts.

(a) *Extroverts*: Extroverts share a tendency to be outgoing, friendly and talkative. They are mobile, exuberant, liv*ely and i*nclined towards direct action. They are also sociable, gregarious and take interest on other people. These people are insensitive to social criticism and are not easily offended or embarrassed. They are very practical and people of action. They act before they think and are less emotional. Doctors, engineers, actors, salesmen, advertising agents and social workers belong to this type.

(b) *Introverts*: Generally introverts are those people who share characteristics such as shyness, social withdrawal and a tendency not to talk much. Introversion is a combination of "intro" and "verson" which means "*energy turning inside*". *These persons are more interested in their own thoughts and ideas than in t*he immediate social environment. They always want to remain in solitude. They are lovers of seclusion. These people get satisfaction from their mental imagery.

Introverts are shy, reserved, indecisive and socially sensitive. They magnify their failures too much. On every occasion, they become extremely self-analytical and self-critical. They remain moody most of the times and have few friends. These people are not very practical. They worry too much over trivial matters.

But critics say that it is not wise to classify people into extroverts and introverts, since a large number of people fall between the two extremes, having the characteristics of both the types.

Later, C.G. Jung stated that type differences can be modified, as when a natural-born introvert is forced by circumstances into extroversion, but he believed that such transpositions are rather superficial.

Observation reveals that most people lie between these two types and display both extroversion and introversion. They are called "ambivert". The personality of ambivert include the characteristics of both the extroverts and introverts in some proportion. So these people are midway between the extrovert and introvert. The majority of the people in the society are ambivert (Fig. 2.1).

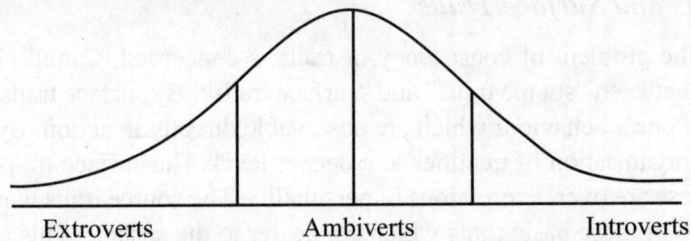

Fig. 2.1: *Distribution of Personality by C.G. Jung (1914)*

Jung said that a particular individual's response to the world and to himself or herself might be said to be typically or characteristically in one or the other modality, which does not imply an absence of the other features. Which of these extremes one should strive for is a question of norms and values.

However, critics nullified the classification of Jung on many grounds. According to them, this classification is based on personal observation and clinical experience. But attempts have proved that it is not appropriate to classify people into definite types. On the whole, the typological division of personality does not give a complete picture about individuals. When an individual is classified into a type, his or her uniqueness of personality is lost. So it is better to study the person as a total individual, considering his or her different traits and to see how these traits are related to each other. It is also very pertinent that typological classification of personality ignores the fact that personality is multidimensional in character and consists of many attributes.

Trait Theory of Personality

The word "trait" refers to any relatively enduring, consistent way of behaving in which people differ from one another. A trait is a generalised tendency towards action. These traits are dynamically interrelated and each trait is influenced by the other which is more or less permanent. Intelligence, anxiety, aggressiveness, prejudice, aptitude, honesty, sensitivity, seriousness and friendliness are all examples of traits. The traits that people possess and the degree to which they possess them are part of their psychological makeup. Traits are more or less permanent. Traits remain with a person for a longer span of time.

Traits are not items of concrete reality. They are concepts, shorthand expressions which summarise the patterns of behaviour that set one person apart from another. Allport and Odbert (1936) cited about 17,953 trait names. Later on, Warren (1963) developed 40,000 trait descriptive terms.

While describing personality in terms of traits, Cattell, Allport and Eysenk faced three problems:

(i) One can not deal with so many traits: there are as many as 40,000 traits.

(ii) Whether these traits are independent or interdependent?

(iii) How far are these traits are consistent or permanent?

Source Traits and Surface Traits

So far as the problem of consistency of traits is concerned, Cattell (1965) found a difference between "source traits" and "surface traits". By surface traits, he meant the qualities of one's behaviour which are observable directly in action. By source traits, he meant, organisation of qualities at a deeper level. The surface traits are so called because these are overt expressions of personality. The source traits were obtained by isolating 16 of these basic traits which are nearer to the surface. This was developed into a self-administered personality questionnaire, called the 16 personality factor questionnaire (16 P.F.).

The source traits are more or less permanent whereas the surface traits may not be consistent to the same degree. Cattell has administered this 16 P.F. test on different types of people and obtained many interesting information.

Allport's Trait Theory

Gordon Allport (1961) counted almost 18,000 trait-like terms in English language. He designated these terms as "distinctive and personal forms of behaviour". These terms are mostly adjectives and they describe how people act, think, perceive and feel. He believed that this rich collection of trait-like terms provided a way of capturing the uniqueness of each individual. According to him, this uniqueness could be described well in terms of the individual's traits or "personal dispositions", at three levels of generality:

(a) *Cardinal Traits*: Cardinal traits are dominant to the maximum extent. These highly influential traits are often called by the names drawn from key historical figures. For example, an individual might be described as Gandhian, Christlike, Nixonian, etc. Here each term describes a trait so broad or so deep in its impact that it overshadows the influence of other traits in that individual.

Allport believed that most people have no true cardinal traits, but when someone does have a cardinal trait, it shows itself in virtually all of that person's behaviour.

(b) *Central Traits*: Most people have no cardinal traits, for them the "central traits" are important. Central traits describe and characterise an individual's behaviour to some extent, but not in such a complete way as cardinal traits. Allport stated that central traits are just like recommendations in a letter or just outstanding characteristics of an individual.

(c) *Secondary Traits*: The least generalised characteristics of a person are "secondary traits", according to Allport. These are traits, such as "likes tea" or "prefers coffee", etc. These traits are influential, but only within a narrow range of situations.

In his theory, Allport stated that people can be described in terms of traits which capture their uniqueness. He was subscribing to the "idiographic approach". This approach involves the psychological study of the individual. It makes efforts to understand, explain, and sometimes predict an individual's behaviour in different situations.

He also valued another contrasting approach called "nomothetic or dimensional approach". This approach is aimed at the discovery of personality principles which apply to people in general. On the whole, the idiographic approach involves a search for consistencies within particular individuals; but the dimensional approach involves a search for consistencies and general principles which apply across individuals.

Single-Trait Research

Allport's trait theory involved multiple traits. But later on, researchers and other trait theorists were not interested in such a broad net. They tried to focus carefully on one single trait.

Many of them studied "locus of control" or the degree to which we believe that we cause or control the events of our lives. If we believe that we are the cause of most events, then we have a highly internal locus of control. But when we believe that most events are caused by luck, fate, etc., we have a highly external locus of control.

This idea was first developed by Julian Rotter in his social-learning theory (1954). In this theory, he placed the importance of expectations in motivating behaviour. Expectation of a future occurrence is based on our post-reinforcement history, which in turn has helped us develop a personal sense of locus of control or the origin of one's life influences.

A locus of control orientation is a belief that the outcomes of our actions are contingent on either what we do (internal control) or on events outside our personal control (external control).

Julian Rotter (1966) developed a questionnaire to measure internal versus external locus of control. It required people to choose between pairs of alternatives such as given in Table 2.5.

Table 2.5: Typical Statements under Pair

1.	(a) People's misfortunes result from the mistakes they make. (b) Many of the unhappy things in people's lives are partly due to bad luck.
2.	(a) Students who try their best should have little difficulty getting good grades in most classes. (b) Grades in most classes are strongly influenced by teacher bias and other factors beyond the student's control.
3.	(a) I am the master of my fate. (b) Most of the things that happen to me in life are caused by forces more powerful than I.
4.	(a) What happens to me is my own doing. (b) Sometimes I feel that I don't have enough control over the direction my life is taking.

Locus of control was a topic for research in relation to different type of therapy, need for achievement and frustration. Though it describes several specific behaviours, it is not comprehensive enough to explain all or even most of an individual's behaviour.

Both type and trait theories invited many questions which are methodological and philosophical. One of the most basic questions about methodology concerns reliability. If the observers are not properly trained, then the question of reliability arises. Problems of inter-judge reliability also arise, when the procedures for inferring traits are not clear or when very subjective judgements are involved.

The other question concerns the validity of trait assessments and whether the assessments mean what they are supposed to mean. From our experience, it is obvious that people may give answers in tests and questionnaires to present themselves in a certain light. Some individuals may try to make themselves "look good". Others may try to make themselves look troubled in order to get help from others. Such responses like social desirability or help-seeking influence the scores on traits or type measures.

Another methodological question concerns type and trait consistency. Generally, we think that types and traits are stable. But it was found that people who are honest in one situation are often not-so-honest in another. Findings like these have led some to conclude that type and trait theories may be a bit misleading and that they claim more consistency in human behaviour than really exists. So psychologists placed importance on situations, but not on enduring "person" characteristics like traits or types.

Another question about trait and type theories is philosophical in nature. Very often, the question arises: Is it really adequate to think of our personality as the sum of our traits or as the particular type we fit? Many experts think that personality can best be described not as a set of traits or types, but as a set of processes by which people cope with life.

Assessment of Personality

An individual's personality includes his or her characteristic ways of thinking, feeling or behaving. Personality tests are conducive for the evaluation of individual personalities. Cronbach (1970) has rightly said that while aptitude and achievement tests are of "maximum performance", personality tests are tests of "typical performance". In the former type of tests, people try to do their best, whereas in the later type of tests, the responses are typical to each individual. Further, there is no right or wrong answer in personality tests.

Now more than 500 personality tests of different types are in use. Also, the techniques of personality tests have become more scientific, refined and comprehensive. All these tests are classified under two broad categories: (a) Psychometric Tests and (b) Projective Techniques. The main difference between these two tests is that while the psychometric tests detect the surface traits, the projective techniques measure the source traits.

Psychometric Tests

The psychometric tests include Case history, Paper pencil tests, Rating scale, Behaviour tests and Interviews. Briefly, these tests are described as follows:

(a) *Case History*: Case history method is generally used to collect information about an individual's home environment, relatives, friends, parents, relation with parents, siblings, classmates, teachers, etc. This method seeks to obtain all informations about the individual which can throw light on his personality factors. It is specifically used by clinical psychologists for the diagnosis and treatment of behaviour disorders.

Case history method involves making observation for a considerable period of time to trace the cause and development of a particular behaviour pattern. No doubt, it is a very comprehensive and useful method. But it requires specialised skill for collection of information.

There are certain limitations of this method. Firstly, it is highly subjective. Unless trained and competent investigators conduct the interview or collect case history, it may lead to erratic and erroneous findings.

Secondly, case history is retrospective in nature. It is based on the contemplation of an event after it has occurred. Thus many valuable events are forgotten. According to Kimble (1980), in the preparation of case history, even the assembly of material can be modified after the knowledge of a person's later life. Further, the case history emphasises the unusual, and less striking facts tend to be overlooked.

In spite of all these limitations, the case history method also has its advantages. In the hand of a trained, qualified, competent person and with a specific format for collecting information, it proves wonderful in understanding the dynamics of human behaviour and a person's problems.

(b) *Paper-Pencil Tests*: The traditional paper-pencil tests are most convenient to administer, less time consuming, less costly and can be used to measure the surface traits of personality. There are various type of paper-pencil tests. Questionnaires and Minnesota Multiphasic Personality Inventory (MMPI) are the prominent ones. These tests are often conducted thorough computer-based forms now.

A questionnaire contains a set of standard questions or statements (to be marked as "Yes", "No" and "Doubtful"). This may be regarding a particular issue or particular trait to be measured. Through such statements or questions, the subject (S) is required to provide information about himself or herself. A uniform key is used for scoring and the numerical results are tabulated.

Questionnaires are often used to obtain information about personal difficulties, attitudes, prejudices, stereotypes and interests of a person.

Questionnaires are otherwise known as self-report inventories. They are extensively used for collecting information about individuals.

The MMPI is a practical test of personality assessment with empirical validity. It is an objective test consisting of 550 items to which an individual has to respond in "True", "False" and "Cannot Say". Practically, MMPI scales are useful in measuring anxiety, hostility, hallucinations, phobias and suicidal impulses.

However, this test is not free from criticisms. The important objections against this test are:

(i) Subjects make responses which are acceptable to others and these responses may not be true. This tendency of subjects may reduce the validity of the scores obtained.

(ii) Since the test items may not provide uniform meaning to all individuals, it may produce different profiles of the same person from time-to-time.

In spite of these limitations, MMPI is widely used as a paper-pencil (or computer-based) test throughout the world. Its clinical value deserves commendation. It has been discovered that computers are capable of arriving at better MMPI assessment than clinicians.

Besides the above two tests, other paper-pencil tests include California Psychological Inventory, Allport Vernon-Lindzey scale and Edwards Performance Schedule.

(c) *Rating Scale*: The rating scale is generally used for infants and adults. The problems and behaviours of children like temper-tantrum, thumb sucking, bed-wetting, etc., are rated on a 5, 7 or 11-point scale. Children are rated as overactive, active and underactive. Students and children are often rated by teachers, supervisors, parents and child psychologists. In some situations, the rating scale is particularly useful in assessing social stimulus value.

Rating scales are of two types: Relative and Absolute. These scales are usually used in connection with an interview or to record subjective impressions based on longer period of contact. The data obtained from both these scales can be quantified.

Usually a relative rating scale is used when several subjects are considered. The order of merit method is applied here. The judge ranks the subjects in order. But in the absolute rating scale, the judge assigns a score to each individual on each trait being rated. The judge compares each subject with some standard or norm established independently of the particular group of individuals being considered. He or she may rate each subject on a 5, 7 or 11-point scale. Undoubtedly, this method is quicker than the first one.

But the absolute rating scale method is subject to more errors arising out of personal equations of the judges. Some judges give high scores, whereas some give very low scores. The standard of individual judges also fluctuates.

Rating scales are subject to relatively less errors of judgement in comparison to interviews, but they are inferior to psychological tests. Their success also depends upon the ability of judges to evaluate others. However, with a skillfully constructed scale, both these limitations can be minimised.

Very often, all subjects are rated near the top of the scale. This is called "Leniency Error". To eliminate this error, a Forced Choice Rating Scale has been developed. In this technique, the rater has to choose between two equally favourable descriptive statements. But in actual practice, the forced choice method does not reduce leniency in rating. Further, experience indicates that most raters do not like to use forced choice scales.

In a study at Bhubaneswar, Puhan, Rath and Das (1991) reported that in personality testing, self report inventories have been shown to suffer from social desirability effect. The researchers described a projective inventory (PI) approach combining classical projective and self report inventory approaches as a possible solution. A critical evaluation of these studies suggests that it allows flexibility and is less susceptible to social desirability effect. Thus, the researchers emphasised upon the need for indigenous tests and measuring techniques in India.

(d) *Behaviour Tests*: In this technique, the behaviour of a person is observed in a typical situation. The subject is exposed to certain standard situations and the researcher records his or her reaction in these situations.

Marston (1925) studied the Introversion-Extroversion dimension of the personality of children through this technique. He took some children into a natural science museum. The path followed by each child was traced and the time the child spent on each exhibit was recorded. Slowness in moving from one exhibit to the other and poor attention to exhibits were considered as indications of introversion. On the contrary, spontaneous interest in the exhibits, rapid movement from one exhibit to the other were rated as characteristics of extroversion.

The personality dimension honesty was also tested by this method. Hartshorne and May have done some studies on the trait of honesty. They have made use of a large number of tests on honesty. One of these tests was "Duplicating Technique". In this technique, students were given the usual school-type of examination. After the examination was over, their papers were taken away and the answers were noted. After a time gap, the original papers were returned to the students who were told the correct answers and they were allowed to evaluate their own papers. The amount of cheating was noted by comparing with the duplicates.

Concluding results indicated a high correlation between honesty and socioeconomic status. It was also found that honesty was not a unitary trait. If a person was honest on one occasion, he may not be so in another. Later on, psychologists studied leadership ability, persistence, caution, cooperation and speed of decision-making through this technique.

However, the behaviour tests are not free from limitations. The main problem with this test is that it has a highly limited scope. It can only be used for children successfully. For adults, it is a complete failure. Because the adults can guess the intention of such tests. Further, one or two behaviour tests may not be the representative of all situations, may not be honest in another situation, because so many factors are responsible for it.

(e) *Interviews*: Truly speaking, certain aspects of personality cannot be assessed objectively by the questionnaire technique or rating scale. For example, how much an individual loves his or her spouse or hates the father cannot be assessed by rating scale or questionnaire technique. An interview is a face-to-face conversation between the researcher and the subject on same specific problems. The interview technique is largely used for selection for different jobs. The main purpose of the interview is to estimate the personality of the interviewee through face-to-face conversation.

This technique is also used for the diagnosis and treatment of behaviour problems. The interviewer creates congenial atmosphere for the subject. As a result, the subject talks freely about his or her problems, difficulties, worries and anxieties. In the course of conversation, the interviewer not only records the statements of the subject, but keenly observes the behaviour. The body language, sentiments and emotions are keenly observed by the interviewer.

Besides its use for the selection of persons for different vocations, the interview technique is also used for the purpose of diagnosis. For the first purpose, unless the questions of the interviews are standardised, they prove to be unreliable in comparing different candidates. In a standardised interview, a set of questions are first prepared for the interview. The order of questions is also fixed. So an equal scope is given to every person to be compared on the same basis.

The judgement of the interviewer definitely plays a major role in assessing the personality of the interviewee. There is a chance of projection by the interviewee. This is the main objection against this technique. It is more subjective compared to rating scales, inventories and behaviour tests.

Further, the judgements of the interviewer can not be standardised. Still, interviews have clinical and therapeutic value. They provide informations particularly in non-directive and client-centred interviews.

Besides all these methods and techniques, some psychoanalytical approaches are also available for the assessment of personality. These are Free Association and Dream Analysis. Sigmund Freud and his followers used these methods to assess the depth of personality of a person. By analysing dreams, a lot about the person's personality can be sensed. Likewise, through free association, the person expresses his or her underlying suppressed and repressed desires, wishes and urges and from these the areas of complexes are spotted.

Projective Techniques

Some of the potentially most powerful techniques for measuring personality come from the evaluation of imaginative productions of various kinds. Collectively, these methods are called the projective techniques (Kimble and Germazy, 1980). Projective tests are theoretically aligned with the psychodynamic perspectives on personality, which give more weight than the other perspectives to the unconscious. These tests attempt to get inside of our mind to discover how we really feel and think.

Projective tests are based on the assumption that the ambiguity of the stimulus allows individuals to invest it with their feelings, desires, needs and attitudes. These tests are especially designed to elicit the individual's unconscious feelings and conflicts, providing assessment that goes deeper than the surface of personality (Blatt, 2000; Leichtman, 2004).

Psychologists rely on the human tendency to interpret stimuli in using a particular assessment strategy in which a respondent projects inner concerns on to a stimulus that has no single meaning. A projective test is an assessment technique in which a respondent is asked to interpret ambiguous stimuli.

Two of the most common projective techniques in use today are the Rorschach Test and the TAT (Thematic Apperception Test).

(a) *Rorschach Test*: Rorschach Inkblot Test was developed by Swiss psychiatrist Hermann Rorschach in 1921. The test contains ambiguous stimuli which are inkblots (Rorschach, 1942).

A total of ten inkblots are shown, one at a time, to the subject: five black-and-white, two with some red ink and the remaining three with different pastel colours. The inkblots are symmetrical in design with a specific shape or form.

The subject or respondent is first shown an inkblot and asked: "Tell me what you see, what it might be to you (Fig. 2.2). There are no right or wrong answers."

The tester first records verbatim what the subject says, how much time he or she takes to respond, the total time taken per inkblot and the way he or she handles the inkblot card.

The second phase is called an "inquiry". Here the respondent is reminded of the previous responses and asked to elaborate on the items.

Assembling the subject's scores into a coherent portrait of personality dynamics is a highly complex process. It is a highly subjective process which relies on clinical expertise and skilled intuition. Good clinical judgement is essential to place all of a subject's responses, even for children (Goldfried, Striker, Levitt, 1972). Skilled interpretation is particularly critical for this test.

Fig. 2.2 Rorschach Inkblot Test

Rorschach's soundness as a testing instrument has often been questioned, because it is based on theoretical concepts (such as unconscious motives) which are impossible to prove. However, some clinicians feel that it can be systematically applied to provide insights as part of a broader personality assessment (Exner & Weiner, 1982). Now-a-days, many researchers find this test useful, but they also recognise that its validity has not been fully established or accepted.

(b) *Thematic Apperception Test (TAT)*: The Thematic Apperception Test (TAT) was developed by Henry Murray and Christina Morgan in the 1930s. This test is designed to elicit stories which reveal something about an individual's personality. TAT is more structured than the Rorschach test. It consists of black-and-white pictures depicting one or more people in a variety of situations. Here

Fig. 2.3: Sample card from TAT

the subjects are asked to tell a story describing the situation presented in the picture – what led to the situation, what will happen in the future and what the people are thinking and feeling.

Here the subject perceives the elements in the actual picture and further apperceives (fills in) personal interpretations and explanations, based on his or her own thoughts, feeling and needs. In addition to being used as a projective test in clinical practice, this test can be administered in research about people's need for achievement (Cramer, 1999; Brilliant, 2001). Many TAT cards can stimulate the telling of achievement- related stories (McClelland and others, 1953).

The psychologist administering the TAT evaluates the structure and content of the stories as well as the behaviour of the individual telling them. He or she makes attempts to discover some of the respondent's major concerns, motivations and personality characteristics. As mentioned earlier, the test can be used with clinical patients to study emotional problems or with normal individuals to study dominant needs, such as need for power, affiliation, achievement, etc.

A standardised procedure is available for scoring TAT responses. Norms and most frequent responses to each card are also available. The test has been modified for children (Bellack, 1975) and for the aged (Wolk & Wolk, 1971). TAT is very useful in examining an individual's characteristic way of dealing with others and the needs that govern his or her interactions with the world.

However, TAT has some limitations. It has the potential of being a valuable aid in studying personality although it is as yet a dull tool (Ruch, 1965). Some experts viewed that TAT lacks objectivity and scientific validity. They said that the interpretations are not quantified and hence it is unscientific.

(c) *Word Association Test (WAT)*: As a projective technique, the Word Association Test (WAT) was first devised by Galton who made use of this test in scientific and systematic ways. The procedure was followed by Galton, Wundt and Cattel. Later on, C.G. Jung used this method for clinical and diagnostic purposes.

The WAT consists of a 100 words prepared by C.G. Jung and subsequently by Kent and Rossoneff, out of which 80 per cent words are normal words and 20 per cent are emotional words scattered randomly in the test.

In the test, the subject is instructed to respond with the first word which comes to his or her mind, after hearing the stimulus word, without any resistance or apparent relevance of propriety of the response to the word.

Normally, the WAT is usually used for four purposes:

(i) Clinical diagnosis differentiating a normal person from psychotic

(ii) Determination of area of complexes

(iii) Detection of guilt

(iv) To investigate into the internal patterns and attitude of the individual.

If the subject takes long reaction time, asks for repetition of the stimulus word, shows physical signs of embarrassment, blushing, expressive gesture, misunderstanding of the stimulus word, very short reaction time, complete failure to respond due to emotional blocking and inability to hear the stimulus word, it is considered as having some significance for the subject's personality.

The critical words are selected on the basis of an index. After the selection of critical words, free association of the subject with these words are taken and interpreted. These interpretations help in finding out of the four purposes of WAT mentioned earlier.

This test is extensively used as a technique to diagnose complexes and centres of emotional loading in the subject's personality. The use of this test is further extended for detecting guilt and insanity to some extent. Disturbances in the personality and various other complexes of emotion are revealed by analysing the critical response words of the subject.

Self-Report Tests of Personality

Self-report tests are otherwise known as objective tests or inventories. These tests do not attempt to assess an individual's hidden and unconscious personality. These tests directly ask people whether items describe their personality traits or not. Self-report tests include the items such as:

- I am easily embarrassed
- I love to go to parties
- I like to watch cartoons on television

A large number of statements are used in this type of test. The respondent has a limited number of answers to choose from (Yes/ No, True/False, Agree/Disagree).

Experts who believe in the trait perspectives of personality have strong faith on self-report tests. They point out that self-report tests have produced a better understanding of an individual's personality traits than what can be derived from, for example, projective techniques.

Still, some critics, especially psychodynamic theorists, believe that the self-report measures do not get into the underlying core of the personality and its unconscious determinants. The behaviourists and social cognitive theorists believe that the self-report measures do not adequately capture the way personality changes as the individual interacts with the environment.

Assessment of the Big Five Factors

Paul Costa and Robert McCrae (1992) constructed a test to assess the big five factors – openness, conscientiousness, extroversion, agreeableness and neuroticism (emotional stability). It is popularly known as the Neuroticism, Extraversion Openness Personality Inventory – Revised, or NEO-PI-R for short.

Costa and McCrae believe that the test can improve the diagnosis of personality disorders and help therapists understand how therapy might influence different type of clients. For example, clients who score high on extraversion factor might prefer group over individual psychotherapy, whereas introverts might do better in individual psychotherapy.

How Useful Is Personality Assessment?

We cannot measure the personality of a person with precision. Personality tests do not measure how much personality we have. Rather, these tests assess the measurable qualities of that personality. That is, the goal of personality instruments is description, not evaluation. For this reason, many psychologists and experts prefer to call personality tests "techniques" or "personality assessment instruments".

But the most effective and useful personality assessments are based on one or more major personality theories. A theory is a collection of explanatory principles and concepts which help to understand and predict natural events. It is important to note that psychologists are able to interpret and apply information from the personality tests more precisely and fairly than if they had to rely only on impressions, hunches and intuitions about people.

No single test can provide all the necessary informations about a person and about his or her personality. To describe overall psychological functioning better, many psychologists administer a battery of tests which often include the MMPI, an intelligence test such as the WAIS-R (Wechsler Adult Intelligence Scale-Revised) and projective tests such as the TAT or Rorschach. Several other tests are used to assess more specific aspects of functioning of a person. These include tests of vocational interests, special abilities, brain dysfunction, motor coordination, anxiety and sexual functioning. More confidence can be placed in the data obtained from several tests than in those from a single test.

Self and Personality

What Is Self?

Self is an organised cognitive structure. It is based on the experience of our being. The characteristic patterns of behaviour constitute 'personality' for a given individual. Each one of us has a unique personality. Our personalities can be assessed by others.

The concept of self is frequently used in everyday life. A lot of time is spent pondering over our own selves. We are not born with the notion of our own self as distinct from others' self. Child psychologists say that children start showing some ideas of self around two years of age. In the beginning, they learn about own self from parents, friends, teachers, etc. The social interaction with them provides the basis of the experience of self. The structure of self is open to modification in the light of our experience in the world.

On the whole, self refers to the totality of an individual's thoughts and feelings having reference to himself or herself as an object.

Self as Subject and Object

Very often, we talk about self by using two expressions: 'I' and 'Me'. Thus self appears to have been expressed in two ways, namely, as a "subject" and as an "object". The "I" who represents the self is known is the subject. Here, "I" is an active observer. The self as an object is said to be represented by "Me", which is observed and known. In everyday life, self is usually understood in terms of meanings attached to self as an object. This is otherwise known as "empirical self".

Different Aspects of Self

Understanding the notion of self and its different aspects has been the concern of thinkers for a long time. The idea has led to the development of different theoretical perspectives. In the course of studies, many aspects of self have been uncovered. For example, we not only hold a self-concept, but also value ourselves.

(a) *Self-esteem*: Our judgement about our own worth is called self-esteem. It has been observed that people with high self-esteem are active, successful and optimistic. They are self-confident. Those who have low self-esteem are often found depressed and feel discouraged. The impressions and evaluations of others about us play an important role in determining our self-esteem.

(b) *Self-efficacy*: Another aspect of self concept is that of self-efficacy. It refers to people's perceptions about their capabilities to produce the desired effects by their own actions. It denotes what a person believes he or she can do with the skills under certain circumstances.

Thus, if an individual believes that he or she can successfully execute the behaviour required by a particular situation, then that individual is considered to have self-efficacy.

(c) *Self-consciousness*: A related aspect of self-concept is that of self-consciousness. We are not always self-conscious, when we behave. When we are conscious of self, we pay attention to self. We are self-focused. On other occasions, we are engaged in focusing on others.

(d) *Self-monitoring*: Self-monitoring is another facet of self. It refers to our ability or monitor our self. Many people take cues from the external environment and change their behaviour accordingly. These people are known as high self-monitoring people. On the contrary, the low self-monitoring people are guided by internal cues and awareness.

(e) *Self-disclosure*: Self-disclosure is an aspect of self functioning. It is the honest sharing of information which is of very personal nature. Very often, it works with a focus on problem-solving. It is a central means by which people develop friendships.

People expect genuineness and the potential for intimacy in their friends. They want their friends to accept their help, to share a common interest and to hold similar attitudes and values. Some individuals talk freely about themselves without any inhibition while others have difficulty in talking about themselves. The former are high on self-disclosure, whereas the latter have low self-disclosure.

(f) *Self-Presentation*: Individuals also learn techniques of self-presentation so that they may relate to others, perform various activities and gain favours from others.

Self-Regulation

The challenges of life are many and at every moment, life demands that we should resist situational pressures and show control over ourselves. The role of our "will" plays a key role here. We can intentionally control and interrupt our behaviour. We can choose to delay or defer the gratification of our needs. Learning to defer gratification is self-control.

Self-regulation is a goal of socialisation. It is the individuals' ability to regulate their behaviour on their own. Self-regulation develops as the self-esteem of the child begins to emerge. Self-esteem depends on expanding cognitive abilities.

As mentioned earlier, the ability to control the behaviour by individuals on their own is self-regulation. Life is full of temptations, traps and tugs that try to pull the individual away from socially acceptable courses of action. An individual's ability to resist these forces is a consequence of both his own emerging cognitive and representational capacities as well as the guidance other socialising agents provide.

Here the question arises: How does this capacity develop to monitor and regulate one's behaviour? According to Kopp (1982, 2002), during the growth and development of a child, he or she passes through a self-regulation phase. Here children become able to use strategies and plans to direct their behaviour and to aid them in resisting temptation and in the delay of gratification. The development of self-control is influenced not only by the child's own efforts, but by actions of parents and other caregivers as well.

Self-control may be regulated by temperament. According to Kochanska (1993, 1995), the process of internalisation through which children develop self-regulatory capacities involves two particular aspects of temperament – the passive and active inhibition systems.

The passive inhibition system is driven primarily by fear and anxiety and often operates outside of awareness. The active inhibition system, on the other hand, is expressed in conscious and effortful control by which an individual regulates his or her behaviour, particularly when desirable behaviour requires giving up or postponing pleasurable outcomes (Kochanska, 2001). Children who are high in effortful control show more internalisation of rules of conduct than children who display little control over this sort. Kochanska has also found that effortful control increases with age and is a stable individual difference among children (Kachanska and Thompson, 1997, 2002).

Techniques for Self-Regulation or Self-control

Self-control can be possible using the following psychological techniques:

(a) *Observation of Own Behaviour*: A person can organise his or her understanding of self by noting down their own behaviour systematically. As a result, they will get necessary information to change, modify or strengthen certain aspects of self.

(b) *Stimulus Control*: This technique involves an attempt to learn to do a set of activities under the presence of certain stimuli and not to preform certain activities in the presence of other stimuli.

(c) *Self-reinforcement*: People find certain behaviours pleasant or unpleasant. Sometimes they reward the pleasant behaviours and thus increase their probability of occurrence. This results in change in self-concept.

(d) *Self-instruction*: Very often, we talk to ourselves. This has been systematically used in changing one's ideas about self and behaviour pattern. If someone gives instruction to himself or herself, naturally they assert and move to behave in that direction.

Self in the Indian Tradition

The idea of self also develops in a cultural context. Of course, the culture in India has elements of continuity as well as change. It is characterised by both modernity and tradition. The role of Vedic hymns, rituals and incidents narrated in the epics cannot be obliterated from the minds of the people. The affiliations with other cultural groups like Aryans, Dravidians, Muslims and Western people cannot be ignored. The impact of science, technology and Western education has also influenced the Indian mind.

From all these sources, we come across concepts like "atman" and "ahankar". The atman represents the independent, non material realisation of the real self, whereas the concept ahankar' refers to the inflated sense of personal worth. This is the consequence of ignorance of one's true being. The individual soul or atman is a part of the Absolute or Brahman. The Indian concept of self encompasses the physical, social, mental and spiritual aspects of human existence. For Western people, the boundary drawn between the self and environment is fixed, but for Indians, the boundary is not static.

❏ Key Terms

1. Ambiverts
2. Asthenic
3. Athletic
4. Behaviour sets
5. Case history
6. Choleric
7. Dynamic organisation
8. Endomorphy-Viscerotonia
9. Extroversion
10. Interview
11. Introversion

12.	Mask approach	29.	Self-Presentation
13.	Melancholic	30.	Self-consciousness
14.	Mesomorphy-Somatonia	31.	Self-disclosure
15.	Minnesota Multiphasic Personality Inventory (MMPI)	32.	Self-efficacy
		33.	Self-esteem
16.	Paper-pencil test	34.	Self-instruction
17.	Personality	35.	Self-monitoring
18.	Personality assessment	36.	Self-regulation
19.	Phlegmatic	37.	Self-reinforcement
20.	Projective techniques	38.	Source trait
21.	Psychometric tests	39.	Stimulus control
22.	Psychophysical	40.	Substance approach
23.	Pyknic	41.	Surface trait
24.	Questionnaire	42.	Thematic Apperception Test (TAT)
25.	Rating scale	43.	Trait
26.	Rorschach Inkblot Test	44.	Typology
27.	Sanguine	45.	Unique
28.	Self	46.	Word Association Test (WAT)

❑ Chapter Summary and Review

1. The literal meaning of the term personality is derived from the term "persona" which means a mask used in make-up by actors in the Roman theatre.

2. Personality refers to a person's unique and relatively stable qualities that characterise behaviour patterns across different situations and over a period of time.

3. G.W. Allport has defined personality as the dynamic organisation within the individual of those psychophysical systems that determine his or her unique adjustment to their environment.

4. Personality is dynamic and unique. It is not static. Every individual has his or her own set of personality characteristics. Personality refers to persistent qualities of an individual. It represents a dynamic orientation of an organism to the environment.

5. Pre-scientific classification of personality was made by Hippocrates. He divided personality by taking body humours into consideration. According to him, there are four types of personality: (a) Sanguine (b) Phlegmatic (c) Choleric and (d) Melancholic.

6. The sanguine personality, having a surplus of blood, is quick, gay, cheerful and active. The phlegmatic personality, having surplus of phlegm, is slow, dull and calm. The choleric, having surplus of yellow bile, is irritable, quick-tempered and angry. The melancholic, having more black bile, is sad, depressed and pessimistic.

7. Kretschmer (1925) classified individuals in terms of their physical form and structure. The tall, long-limbed and sickly individuals are called Asthenic; the tall, well-built and muscular individuals are called Athletic; the short, fatty individuals are called Pyknic.

8. Sheldon's classification of personality has much in common with that of Kretchmer. It is called the Somato type theory of personality by Sheldon (1942). He classified personality into three types: Endomorphy, Mesomorphy and Ectomorphy.

9. C.G. Jung classified personality into two types: Introverts and Extroverts. Extrovert people are outgoing, mobile, lively and inclined towards direct action. They are gregarious and sociable. But the introverts are more interested in their own thoughts and ideas than in the immediate social environment.

10. The personality of ambiverts include the characteristics of both the introverts and extroverts in a balanced manner. The majority of people in our society are ambiverts.

11. Trait theorists tried to describe personality on the basis of traits. A trait is a generalised tendency towards action. It is a stable and enduring attribute of a person which is revealed consistently in a variety of situations.

12. Warren (1963) has developed 40,000 trait descriptive terms. But one cannot deal with all these traits. Cattell (1965) found a difference between Source and Surface traits. By surface traits, he means the qualities of one's behaviour which are observable directly in action. By surface traits he means organisation of qualities at a deeper level.

13. The measurement and evaluation of individual personalities by the help of tests is called personality assessment. The personality tests are classified under two broad categories: (a) Psychometric Tests and (b) Projective Techniques.

14. Psychometric tests include Case History, Paper-Pencil Tests, Rating Scale, Behaviour Tests and Interview. Three projective techniques are important and these are: (a) Rorschach Test (b) Thematic Apperception Test (TAT) and (c) Word Association Test (WAT).

15. The characteristic patterns of behaviour constitute the personality of a particular person. But "self" is an organised cognitive structure based on the experience of our being.

16. Our judgement about our own worth is called self-esteem. The sense of identity is the perception of our self as distinct from other people and other things, as related to our self or allowed to our self.
17. Self-efficacy is a related aspect of self-concept. It refers to people's perceptions about their capabilities to produce the desired effects by their own actions. This term represents what an individual believes he or she can do with the skills under certain circumstances.
18. Another important aspect of self-concept is self-consciousness. While behaving, we are not always self-conscious. When we are conscious of self, we pay attention to self. We become self-focused.
19. Some people talk about themselves freely, while others have difficulty in talking about themselves. This is known as self-disclosure. Self-monitoring refers to our ability to monitor ourselves. Some people in the society take cues from the external environment and change their behaviour accordingly. These people are high self-monitoring people. On the other hand, low self-monitoring people are guided by internal cues and awareness.
20. The techniques for self-presentation include the strategies to relate to others, perform various activities and gain favours from others.
21. Learning to defer gratification is self-control. The techniques enhancing self-control are observation of own behaviour, stimulus control, self-reinforcement, self-instruction, etc.
22. The development of self is related to culture also. The Indian notion of self encompasses the physical, social, mental as well as spiritual aspects of human existence.

QUESTIONS

1. What is personality? Discuss the nature and characteristics of personality.
2. Define personality. Discuss Allport's definition of personality in detail.
3. What do you mean by personality typology? How are personalities classified?
4. Give a critical description of the classification of personality.
5. Examine the type and trait theories of personality. Which theory, according to you, is most acceptable and why.
6. Briefly discuss various techniques of assessing personality.
7. What do you understand by psychometric tests of personality? Describe some paper-pencil tests of personality.
8. What is a projective technique? Discuss the advantages and disadvantages of two projective tests which assess personality.
9. What are the two projective tests that are famous? How are they administered and interpreted?
10. Write brief notes on the following:
    (a) Rating Scale
    (b) Behaviour Test
    (c) Thematic Apperception Test (TAT)
    (d) Introversion–Extroversion
    (e) 16 P.F. Questionnaire
    (f) Hippocrate's Classification of Personality

UNIT II
SOURCES OF POWER

CHAPTER - 3

THEORIES OF PERSONALITY

> ❑ *Personality: Uniqueness and consistency in the behaviour of individuals.*
> ❑ *Personality: The unique and relatively stable ways in which people think, feel and behave.*
> ❑ *Personality: Individual's unique and relatively stable patterns of behaviour, thoughts and feelings.*

❑ **This chapter covers:**
- Meaning of personality
- Theories of personality
    (a) Sigmund Freud and psychoanalysis
    (b) The behaviouristic view of personality
    (c) Social-cognitive view of personality
    (d) Humanism and personality
    (e) Trait theories: who are you?
    (f) The biology of personality: behavioural genetics
    (g) Geert Hofstede's four Dimensions of cultural personality
- Key Terms, Summary and Questions

❑ **After you go through this chapter, you will be able to:**
- Understand the meaning of personality
- Get a thorough knowledge about Freudian theory of personality
- Come to know about behaviouristic and humanistic views on personality
- Gain a preliminary knowledge about trait theories and social-cognitive view of personality
- Know about behavioural genetics and four dimensions of personality
- Have a thorough knowledge about personality assessment
- Evaluate different theories of personality

- *The Psychoanalytic Perspective: Begins with Freud and focuses on the role of unconscious mind.*
- *The Behaviourist Perspective: Based on the theories of learning, focuses on the effect of environment.*
- *Humanistic Perspective: Focuses on the role of conscious life experiences.*
- *Trait Perspective: Trait theories are more concerned with the end result – the characteristics themselves. Some trait theorists assume that traits are biologically determined, but others make no such assumption.*

Introduction

Personality is the individual's unique and relatively stable patterns of behaviour, thoughts and emotions. It is a combination of psychological forces which make people uniquely themselves (Nelson, Miller, 1995; Friedman and Schustack (1999). In other words, personality is the unique and relatively stable ways in which people think, feel and behave throughout their life-span.

Very often, personality is confused with character. Character refers to value judgements made about a person's morals and ethical behaviour. It should not be confused with temperament. Temperament is the enduring characteristics with which each individual is born, such as irritability, kindness, adaptability, etc. The vital parts of personality are temperament and character.

Personality	Character	Temperament
Individual's unique and relatively stable patterns of behaviour, thoughts and feelings.	A person's value judgements of moral and ethical behaviour. (A part of personality)	The enduring characteristics with which each individual is born. (A part of personality)

Ancient philosophers, writers and learned people speculated about why individuals were unique and why they differed from one another. Emergence of scientific psychology initiated systematic research on personality during 20th century. Since then, there has been a continuing discussion among psychologists about whether personality is actually real or not. The question was whether people show enough consistency in behaviour over time and across situations to make studying personality worthwhile.

Research findings of Walter Mischel (1985) said that individuals show so much variability across situations that we cannot make enough predictions about their behaviour from study of personality. He said that various traits show only modest correlations with the overt behaviour of a person.

Anyhow, personality is an arena which is still young in psychology. There are several ways in which the characteristic behaviour of human beings can be explained. Till now, there is no single explanation of personality which can include every aspect of a person's behaviour. It is still difficult to assess personality precisely and scientifically.

Perspectives in Personality Theory

At present, there are four viewpoints or perspectives of personality theory:

(a) *The Psychoanalytic Perspective*: It has emerged with Freudian Psychoanalysis. It exists today. This perspective focuses on the role of the unconscious mind in the development of personality. Biological causes of personality differences are given priority in this perspective.

(b) *The Behaviouristic Perspective*: Behaviouristic perspective is based on the theories of learning. This approach highlights the effects of environment on behaviour.

(c) *The Humanistic Perspective*: The humanistic perspective includes the reactions and criticisms against psychoanalytic and behaviouristic perspectives. It focuses mainly on the role of each individual's conscious life experiences and choices in the development of personality.

(d) *The Trait Perspective*: The above perspectives – Psychoanalytic, Behaviouristic and Humanistic – seek to explain the process which causes personality to form into its unique characteristics. But trait theories state that traits are biologically determined. Other theories have no such assumptions.

Sigmund Freud and Psychoanalysis

Sigmund Freud (1856–1939) was born in Austria. His family moved to Vienna when he was only four years old. He lived there until 1938, when Germany occupied Austria. Having a Jewish background, Freud moved to England to escape the Nazis. During this time, Europe was in what is commonly known as Victorian Age, named after Queen Victoria of Great Britain. As we know, the Victorian Age was a time of sexual repression. People believed that the sexual act should be performed only after marriage and enjoyment of sexual intercourse was considered a sin. All this was propagated by the Christian Church. Upper class women were not supposed to have sexual urges. Men were presumed to be unable to control their "animal" desires. It was found that some wealthy women were Freud's patients with problems stemming from unfulfilled sexual desires or due to sexual repression.

Freud founded of the psychodynamic movement in psychology. He believed that there were layers of consciousness in the mind of every person. His views were published in his book Psychopathology of Everyday Life in 1901. This book shocked the Victorian world at that time.

Freud believed that the mind was divided into three parts: preconscious, conscious and unconscious (Freud, 1904). Preconscious mind is that level of mind where all information, events and thoughts of an individual remain, but he or she is not aware of all these things. These bits of the mind can be easily brought into consciousness. What Freud has said about this layer of mind is similar to the explicit long-term memory proposed by modern psychologists and researchers.

Conscious mind is all of the things of which an individual is aware of at any given moment. Whatever is the uppermost in one's mind is the conscious mind. This is similar to short-term memory. The terms used by Freud may be different, but the concepts are basically same as those used by cognitive psychologists to talk about memory.

> **PRECONSCIOUS, CONSCIOUS AND UNCONSCIOUS MIND**
> - *Preconscious Mind: It is that level of mind in which information is available but not currently conscious. It can easily be brought into conscious awareness, when the need arises.*
> - *Conscious Mind: It is that level of mind which is aware of immediate surroundings and perceptions. Whatever is uppermost in a person's mind is the conscious mind. It is similar to STM (short-term memory).*
> - *Unconscious Mind: It is that level of mind in which thoughts, feelings, memories and other information are kept, but they cannot easily or voluntarily be brought into consciousness.*

There is a part of mind which remains hidden all the times. In this area of mind, thoughts, feelings, memories and other information are kept. These are not easily or voluntarily brought into consciousness. This is the unconscious mind.

According to Freud, the unconscious mind is the most important determining factor in human behaviour and personality. Although some thoughts, desires and impulses have always been unconscious, Freud believed that much of it was once conscious but has been actively repressed. The fact that we are not aware of them, however, in no way prevents them from affecting our behaviour.

Experts feel that to understand the views of Freud regarding personality, four topics are important: levels of consciousness (which we have discussed), the structure of personality, anxiety and defence mechanisms and psycho-sexual stages of development.

The Structure of Personality: Id, Ego and Superego

Freud stated that personality consists largely of three parts: Id, Ego and Superego. These approximately correspond to desire, reason and conscience.

Id is the first and most primitive part of the personality. Id is a Latin word which means "it". The id is completely unconscious. It is that part of personality which is concerned with immediate gratification of primitive needs. It is the amoral part of personality which exists at birth, containing all of the basic biological drives: hunger, thirst, sex and self-preservation. Id operates in accordance with the pleasure principle. Pleasure principle requires immediate gratification of needs without regard for the consequences. This principle can be summed up simply as "if it feels good, do it."

When the drives are active, the individual feels an increase in not only physical tension, but a psychological tension, what Freud called the libido. Libido is an instinctual energy and may come into conflict with the demands of the society's standards of behaviour. When Freud talked about sex drives of babies, it outraged and shocked the Victorians. By "sex drive", Freud really meant "pleasure drive". Babies seek pleasure sensations routinely.

Individuals are pleasure-seeking creatures. Infants seek pleasure from sucking and chewing on anything they can get into their mouths. Infants want their needs satisfied immediately. They do not care about anyone else's needs or desires. But the unfortunate fact is that this world offers few opportunities for instant pleasure. We invite trouble when we attempt to gratify our innate urges immediately. It is in response to these facts that the second structure of personality, the ego, develops. Ego operates in accordance with the reality principle.

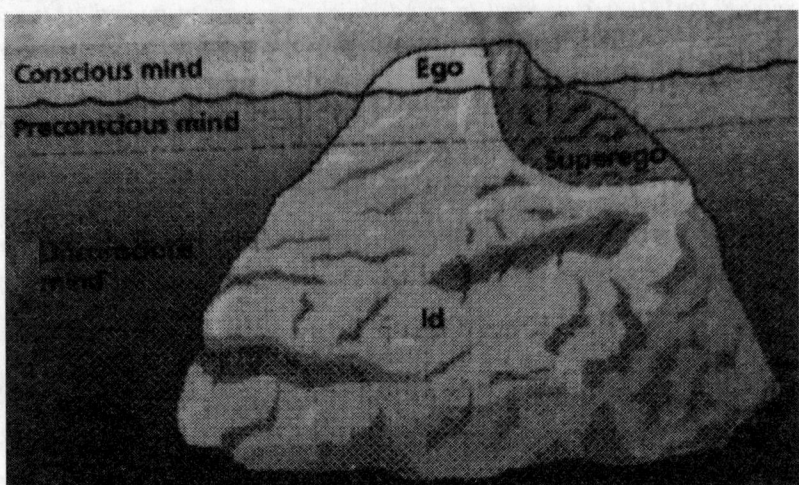

Fig. 3.1: Freud's conception of personality. This iceberg represents three levels of mind: Preconscious, Conscious and Unconscious

The external conditions and the consequences of different actions are taken into account by the ego. It directs behaviour so as to maximise pleasure and minimise pain. The ego is partly conscious, but not fully. Some of its internal struggles with the id are outside our conscious knowledge and understanding.

The word "ego" comes from the Latin word "I". It is far more rational, logical and cunning than the id. The ego works on the reality principle. It reduces the needs of the libido only in ways which will not lead to negative consequences. A simple way of stating the reality principle is, "if it feels good, do it, but only if you can get away with it" (Ciccarelli, 2002).

The superego is the final aspect of personality described by Freud. It is that portion of personality which represents conscience. The Latin word "superego" means "over the self". There are two parts of the superego: the ego ideal and the conscience. The ego ideal is a kind of measuring device. It is the sum-total of ideal, correct and acceptable behaviours which a child learns from his or her parents and other members of the society. All behaviour is held up to this standard and judged by the second part of the superego called the conscience. It is not until the conscience develops that children have a sense of right or wrong.

Superego represents our internalisation of the moral teachings and norms of our society. According to Freud, the constant struggle among id, ego and superego plays a significant role in personality development and in many psychological disorders. The struggle is very often visible in our everyday behaviour, through actions or words which are popularly known as Freudian slips.

> *How the Three Parts of Personality Work Together According to Freud*
>
> - *Id makes demands, the superego puts restrictions on how those demands can be met and the ego has to come up with a plan that will quieten the id and satisfy the superego. Sometimes the superego or id do not get their way, resulting in a great deal of anxiety for the ego itself. The constant state of conflict is Freud's view of how personality works. It is only when the anxiety created by the conflict gets out of hand that disordered behaviour arises.*
>
> —S.K. Ciccarelli (2005)

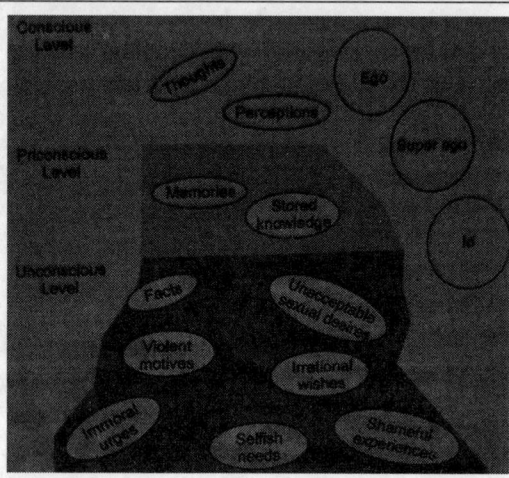

Aspect of Personality	Level of Consciousness	Description/ Function
Ego	Mostly conscious	Mediate between id impulses and superego inhibitions; reality principle; rational
Superego	All levels, but mostly preconscious	Ideals and morals; conscience; incorporated from parents
Id	Unconscious	Basic impulses (sex and aggression) pleasure principle seeks immediate gratification; irrational, impulsive

Fig. 3.2 : Freud's views about Levels of Consciousness and the Structure of Personality, Source: Psychology by Robert A. Baron, 2002

Self-protection by Ego: Defence Mechanisms

When the id and the superego dominate the ego, harmony is broken and the ego applies various defence mechanisms to maintain a balance. Ego adopts measures to control the unconscious desires and resolve the conflicts in an economical fashion. The use of ego defences is a common phenomenon and is used normally by everyone.

Defence mechanisms are the conscious and unconscious processes whereby the inner situation of conflict is eliminated or reduced in severity. Even anxiety is reduced through defensive fantasies, especially by children. The defence mechanisms are classified into successful and unsuccessful defence mechanisms. Most of the defence mechanisms used by the ego are unsuccessful in nature. Most of the defence mechanisms operate unconsciously although they do not belong to the system of unconscious.

Sublimation is considered as the most complete and successful of all defence mechanisms. It is not a defence, but full use of a tamed and channelled drive. One example of this is the transformation of sexual and aggressive urges into creative work in socially acceptable directions. Sexual and aggressive urges are sublimated in art, painting, literature, sports, adventures, etc.

Repression is the major mechanism for managing conscious conflict. Conversion, regression, sublimation, reaction formation, sublimation and rationalisation are the major mechanisms for the solution of unconscious conflict. Repression is a topographic dynamic concept. It refers to purposeful forgetting of wishes, urges and impulses associated with objectionable, aggressive and sexual demands. Rationalisation refers to the substitution of a socially approved motive for a socially disapproved one. Rationalisation functions both at conscious and unconscious level. Regression literally means going back. It constitutes flight from controlled and realistic thinking.

By projection, an individual transfers the blame of his or her own shortcomings, mistakes and misdeeds to others and attributes to others his own unacceptable thoughts. When the ego dislikes its own id and superego desires, it throws the blame on somebody else. It works both at conscious and unconscious level. In identification, an individual wants to be like the object or person while in introjection he or she considers the object as a part of himself or herself. Identification is very often used by normal people.

Displacement is another defence mechanism which is commonly used to avoid anxiety. It involves the discharge of an unconscious impulse by shifting from the original object to a substitute object. For example, displacement is found when a parent shifts his or her anger towards the children at the slightest provocation. In displacement, sometimes the aggressive impulses are redirected to the self, leading to depression and feelings of worthlessness.

Development of behaviour opposite to the unconscious desires of the id is known as reaction formation. It plays a significant role in the symptom formation of obsessional neuroses. Like repression, reaction formation has adjustive value in helping us to maintain socially approved behaviour and to avoid facing unacceptable desires with the consequent self-devaluation that would be involved. When an individuals fails to fulfil their desires, they get frustrated and develop many fantasies and try to gratify their frustrated needs in imagination. When fantasy is used for constructive purposes, such as solving an immediate problem, it is called productive fantasy.

Psychosexual Stages of Development

The concept of psychosexual stages of development is the most controversial aspect of Freud's theory of personality. Before analysing these stages, we must consider the meaning of "libido" and "fixation".

Libido refers to the instinctual life force which energises the id. Release of libido is closely related to pleasure. Focus of pleasure and expression of libido change as we develop. When excessive amount of libido energy is tied to a particular stage, fixation results.

According to Freud, three parts of personality develop in a series of stages. He believed that the stages were determined by the developing sexuality of children. An area of the body which produces pleasurable feelings becomes important and can become the source of conflicts at each stage. This is called an "erogenous zone". Conflicts which are not fully resolved can result in fixation or getting "stuck" to some degree in an earlier stage of development. Children may grow into adults, still carrying emotional and psychological baggage from that fixated period. Since the personality or psyche develops as a result of sexual development. Freud called these periods as the psychosexual stages of personality development.

The first stage of personality development is the oral stage which lasts up to 18 months. Up to this period, the child seeks pleasure mainly through the mouth. If too much or too little gratification occurs during this stage, an individual may become fixated at it. Too little gratification invites a personality which is overdependent. Excess gratification results in a personality which is excessively hostile.

Next stage is the anal stage in which the process of elimination becomes the primary focus of pleasure. At this stage, fixation stems from harsh toilet training. Fixation at this stage leads to excessive exhibitionistic and narcissistic behaviour. The child, in future, will want to be a teacher, actor, singer, etc.

As the child grows older, the erogenous zone shifts to the genitals. This is the phallic stage (at around 3 to 7 years age). They are engaged in perfectly normal self-stimulation of the genitals or masturbation. The word "phallic" comes from the Greek word "phallos" which means "penis".

The boy in this stage loves the mother and the girl identifies with the father. This simultaneous action for love and identification invites a different structure of personality. Extreme love towards mother is called "Oedipus complex". The development of Oedipus complex leads to castration anxiety. The boy apprehends that if he is sexually attached to his mother, his sexual organs will be castrated or removed. Due to castration anxiety, the boy represses his incestuous desire for his mother and his hostility for his father. Ultimately, the identification leads to the formation of superego. The superego is said to be the heir to the Oedipus complex.

In the phallic stage, the girl gradually comes to know that she does not possess the external genitals of the males. She feels that she has already been castrated. She blames her mother for her condition. At that time she hates her mother and loves her father. This is known as Female Oedipus complex or "Electra complex". The girl's love for her father is however mixed with envy because the father possesses something that she does not possess. This is popularly known as "Penis envy".

By the time the phallic stage ends, two things are pertinent to deal with anxiety – the boy represses his sexual feelings for his mother and identifies with his father. As we know, identification is a defence mechanism which is used to combat anxiety. The boy wants to be like his father, taking on the father's behaviour mannerisms, values and moral beliefs as his own. Girls go through a similar process with their mothers. Superego develops as a result of identifying with the same-sex parent. In his psychoanalytic theory, Freud said that if a child does not have same sex parent with whom to identify or if the opposite-sex parent encourages the sexual attraction, fixation occurs. Fixation in the phallic stage usually involves immature sexual attitudes as an adult. Men with this fixation may be "mama boys" who never quite grow up and women may look for much older father figures to marry.

BOX 3.1: FREUD'S ASPECTS OF MIND

Topographical aspects of mind by Freud	*Dynamic aspects of mind by Freud*
• **Conscious**: It is concerned with immediate awareness. It is the sum total of an individual's experience at any given moment. One-tenth of the mind deals with conscious experiences. • **Subconscious or Preconscious:** Readily recallable segment of mind, marginally conscious. • **Unconscious:** About 90% of the mind is unconscious. The process of unconsciousness is not static, but remarkably dynamic. Daily activities cannot be explained without the unconscious mind.	• **Id:** The pleasure principle which stands for antisocial and immoral wishes, desires, motives and strivings. It acts as a reservoir for libido. • **Ego:** Ego is the self or the conscious intelligence. It is the executive division of personality. • **Superego:** Superego is popularly known as the conscience or the moral principle. It is partly conscious and mainly unconscious. It is also the moral and judicial branch of the personality and embodiment of all social restrictions, moral and ethical values.

Children enter the "latency stage" after the resolution of the Oedipus complex. Here the sexual urges are at a minimum. Children push their sexual feelings for the opposite sex into unconscious after they are about seven years old in another defensive reaction called "repression". This stage is called "latency" because in this stage, from the age 6 to 7 to the onset of puberty, children have hidden and latent sexual feelings. During this period, children grow and develop intellectually, physically and socially, but not sexually. In this period, the boys play with boys and the girls with other girls and each one thinks the opposite sex is pretty awful. According to Freud, infantile sexuality is repressed and reaction formation is strengthened. The libidinal urges are sublimated in the process of education. Rapid formal learning takes place for both boys and girls. Superego is fully established during this span. Eroticism and narcissism get reduced in this period.

During this stage, the girls are generally more affectionate than boys, because girls accept their castration whereas the boys still fear of being castrated.

With the onset of puberty, again sexual feelings emerge. The body becomes attractive and sexual urges are once more allowed into the consciousness, but these urges will no longer have the parents as their targets. During this stage, the pleasure is again focused on the genitals. Lust is blended with affection and people become capable of adult love.

BOX 3.2 DEFENCE MECHANISMS AND THEIR BASIC NATURE

Defence Mechanism	Major Defense Mechanisms And Its Basic Nature
• Repression	• Pushing or forgetting unacceptable thoughts or impulses from conscious to unconscious.
• Rationalisation	• Making up socially acceptable reasons for thoughts or actions based on unacceptable motives.
• Displacement	• Redirecting an emotional response from a dangerous object to a safe one.
• Projection	• Transferring unacceptable motives or impulses to other.
• Regression	• Responding to ta hreatening situation in a way appropriate to an earlier age or level of development.
• Sublimation	• Threatening unconscious impulses channelled into socially acceptable forms of behaviour.
• Reaction Formation	• Development of a behaviour opposite to the unconscious desires of id. One instinct is hidden from awareness by its opposite.

Progression to this final stage is possible only if serious fixation has not occurred at the earlier stages. If such fixation exists, development is blocked and different disorders result. This is the longest stage which lasts from 12 to 20 years. This period is characterised by objective choices rather than by narcissism. It is a period of socialisation, group activities, marriage, establishing a home and raising a family. At this stage, the society allows the real outlets of the sexual urges. Since Freud tied personality development into sexual development, the genital stage represented the final process in Freud's personality theory as well as entry into adult social and sexual behaviour.

BOX 3.3 FREUD'S PSYCHOSEXUAL STAGES

• ORAL	Upto 18 months	• Oral activities (Sucking, feeding etc.)	• Weaning
• ANAL	1½ to 3 years	• Bowel and Bladder control	• Toilet Training
• PHALLIC	3 to 6 years	• Genitals	• Identification with parent of same sex of the child
• LATENCY	6 yrs. to Puberty	• Social skills (Such as ability to make friends) and intellectual skills	• School, play, Same-sex friendships
• GENITAL	Puberty to Death	• Social Behaviour	• Sexual relationship with the partner

Theories of Personality

Freud's ideas and writings have exerted a large impact on society. But many aspects of his personality theory were not accepted by most psychologists later. The reasons and criticisms are as follows:

(i) The first reason is that a theory which cannot be tested is largely useless. This criticism applies to many of Freud's ideas. His theory is not scientific. Many aspects cannot be observed or measured.

(ii) Several proposals of Freud are not consistent with the findings of modern research.

(iii) Freud relied heavily on a few wealthy and sophisticated patients for constructing his theory. They were not representative of human beings generally.

(iv) Freud's theory of personality contains so many different concepts that they can explain virtually any pattern of behaviour.

However, his several insights like levels of consciousness and about the importance of anxiety in psychological disorders have contributed to our understanding of human behaviour and personality. Freud made a profound and lasting impact on modern thought.

Theories of Personality by Neo-Freudians: Other Psychoanalytic Views

We mentioned that most of the Freud's ideas were with met later with resistance and ridicule. The Neo-Freudians or "new" Freudians psychoanalysts took different views and differed from Freud in many aspects.

C.G. Jung, a student of Freud, viewed the nature of unconscious differently. He believed that there is not only a personal unconscious as described by Freud, but a collective unconscious as well. With this view, he questioned Freud's assumptions. According to Jung, the collective unconscious holds experiences shared by all human beings. These experiences are a part of our biological heritage. The contents of collective unconscious reflect the experiences our species has had since it originated on earth.

BOX 3.4: STRIVING FOR SUCCESS OR PERFECTION

- *The striving for success is innate and remains present at birth. Therefore, it precedes the feelings of inferiority rather than springing from them.*
- *Although the striving for success is innate and its presence at birth is felt, its development is sure because it exists in the form of potentialities at birth, not in the form of actuality. Therefore, it continues throughout life.*
- *The striving for success is not a confluence of motive. It is a single motive which shapes other drives.*
- *In both normal and neurotic individuals, the striving for superiority is found. But the path adopted by these two types of people in arriving at goal differs. The neurotic individuals adopt the path of exaggerated personal superiority whereas the mentally healthy people adopt the path of "social interest" or perfection for everyone.*

Collective unconscious contains a kind of racial memory, memories of ancient fears and themes which seem to occur in many folk tales and cultures. These collective, universal human memories were called "archetypes" by Jung. Of course, there are many archetypes, but two of the more well known are the "anima/animus" (the feminine side of a man and the masculine side of a woman) and the "shadow" (the dark side of a personality, called the "Devil" in Western cultures).

According to Jung, these archetypes are the manifestations of the collective unconscious which express themselves when our conscious mind is distracted or inactive, for example, in sleep, in dreams or in fantasies (Nehar, 1996). Jung said that in looking for a mate, we search for the person on to whom we can best project these hidden sides (anima or animus) of personality. Attraction occurs when there is a good match between such projections and the other person.

In his theory, Jung said that we are born with innate tendencies to be concerned primarily either with our inner selves or with the outside world. The first category persons are called introverts and the second category, extroverts.

Introvert people are hesitant, cautious and do not make friends easily. They are lovers of seclusion, want to stay alone and are not sociable. They always prefer to observe the world rather than become involved in it. Extrovert persons are open, confident and make friends easily. They enjoy high levels of stimulation and a wide range of activities. These people are gregarious and exchange their ideas very often.

BOX 3.5 FOUR GENERAL LIFE STYLE ATTITUDES

- *Ruling Type: The ruling type of people have dominating attitude towards others and have little social interest.*
- *Getting Type: The getting type of people have interest in getting as many and as much as possible from others. These people are dependent upon others. These individuals become neurotic under stressful situations.*
- *Avoiding Type: These people are characterised by having attitudes of general avoidance and withdrawal which are accompanied by little social interest.*
- *Socially Useful Type: A socially useful individual is one whose behaviour is useful for the society. Such individuals are active and they have high social interest.*

BOX 3.6 THREE FAULTY STYLE OF LIFE

- **The Inferior Style:** *Individuals having an inferior style of life suffer from some organ inferiority and they are unable to make adequate compensation for it.*
- **Pampered Style:** *People having a pampered style are too self-centred and selfish and they lack social interest.*
- **Neglected Style:** *Individuals having a neglected style of life are like pampered style persons and they want to be spoiled.*

Subsequently, Jung's concept of archetypes was vehemently opposed by experts, but his dimension of extroversion–introversion was included by trait theorists.

Alfred Adler (1870–1937) also differed from Freud over the importance of sexuality in personality development. In particular, he emphasised the importance of the feeling of inferiority which he believed we experience as children because of our small size and physical weakness. Adler tried to explain that people having some kind of organ inferiority such as poor vision, poor hearing, etc., try to compensate for it by developing excellence in other fields. An individual may try to compensate the loss or may keep himself or herself satisfied by having only defensive measures. Adler extended his concept of inferiority and reported that inferiority feelings are innate, and therefore universal in nature.

His concept of "masculine protest" is related to the concepts of compensation and inferiority. By masculine protest he meant a striving to be strong and powerful as a compensation for feeling of being inferior and unmanly. To be masculine means to be superior and to be feminine means to be inferior.

The use of masculine protest is similar to the Freudian concept of penis envy. Women's lib movement in which women strive for greater equality can be interpreted as the expression of masculine protest.

Later, Adler said that aggression was the dynamic power behind all motivation. In 1912, he replaced the concept of masculine protest with the concept of "striving for superiority" because he thought that masculine protest did not explain human motivation in a satisfactory way. This term was again modified by Adler as "striving for success or perfection".

In this theory, Adler said that social interest and striving for success are closely related. It is the social interest which motivates the person to strive for success in a healthy way. It can be defined as an attitude of concern for humanity in general as well as showing an empathy for others. It guides human behaviour throughout the life. Like striving for success, social interest is inborn, but it also needs to be developed as the child grows. In the society, there are some people who never develop social interest and among them, exaggerated personal superiority dominates. In this world, the people who lack social interest are criminals, sex perverts, neurotics and drunkards.

Adler added that social interest of an individual develops in accord with the "style of life". By style of life he meant an individual's unique way of arriving at a particular goal as well as his or her self-concept, feelings towards others and attitude towards the world. The style of life is the product of several forces like heredity, environment, social interest and goal of success.

BOX 3.7 IMPACT OF BIRTH ORDER ON PERSONALITY (ALFRED ADLER)

- *First-Born Child: This child gets undivided attention and care from parents, experiences a traumatic experience of dethronement when a new baby is born to the parents, develops over-protective tendencies and high anxiety.*
- *The Second-Born Child: This child is highly competitive, cooperative and has wider social interests. His or her style of life tries to prove that he or she is better than the older sibling.*
- *The Last-Born Child: The last-born child is unique and he has a great risk of being a problem-child. He or she has strong feelings of inferiority and lacks independence. The child is highly motivated to surpass the older siblings. He or she is achievement-oriented and competitive-minded.*
- *The Only-Child: This child has no siblings to compete with the attention of the parents, has inflated self-concept and exaggerated sense of superiority.*

Adler considered "style of life" as a major governing force and similar to the concept of ego of Freud. But style of life includes no forces like id and superego. It always refers to the whole personality plus the attitude which makes a person unique. Usually, style of life does not change, but it may change if the individual clearly recognises the errors or faults and deliberately change the style. According to Adler, four general lifestyle attitudes are: the ruling type, the getting type, the avoiding type and the socially useful type.

Subsequently, Adler recognised three faulty styles of life: the inferior style, the pampered style and the neglected style.

Individuals having an inferior style of life suffer from some strong organ inferiority and they are unable to make adequate compensation. Persons having a pampered style are too self-centred and selfish. Individuals having a neglected style of life are much like pampered style persons and they always want to be spoiled.

"Creative power" develops the style of life of a person to a great extent. According to Adler, each person possesses the freedom to create his or her own style of life. Each person is solely responsible for who they are and how they behave. For Adler, creative power is a dynamic concept because it implies free movement towards a goal. Adler was of the view that people are motivated more by the subjective perception than by external causes. One aspect of such subjective perception is expectation of future.

BOX: 3.8: DIFFERENCES BETWEEN FREUD AND ADLER

Sigmund Freud	*Alfred Adler*
• Freud emphasised upon the biological nature of human beings. His theories were based on the instincts, motives and sex.	• Adler emphasised upon the social nature of individuals and considered social forces to be an important determinant of behaviour.
• Freud emphasised upon the impact of past experiences on present behaviour.	• Adler was basically a teleologist who emphasised on future aims that determined present behaviour.
• In his psychoanalytic theory, Freud has over-emphasised upon sex. For him, sex drive was the most important drive for human beings.	• Alfred Adler considered aggression and striving for power as the major drives for shaping behaviour and personality.
• Freud over-emphasised upon the unconscious mind for shaping our behaviour and personality.	• Adler emphasised on conscious processes rather than unconscious processes for shaping personality.
• Freud did not give emphasis on uniqueness and indivisibility of a person. He did not think that personality was a unique system which can not be divided into sub-systems.	• Adler's Individual Psychology placed more emphasis upon uniqueness and indivisibility of a person. He considered personality as a whole and unique system.

Adler believed on the impact of birth order on personality development. His study covered four types of birth order: First-Born, Second-Born, Last-Born and the Lone Child.

The first-born child gets undivided attention and care from parents. But the child has a traumatic experience of dethronement when a new baby is born. This creates a feeling of hostility and resentment in the first-born child towards his or her younger brother and sister. This child has also overprotective tendencies and high anxiety.

The second-born child starts life in a better environment. Such children are highly competitive, cooperative and have wider social interests. Their style of life constantly tries to prove that they are better than the older siblings. So the second-born child is achievement-oriented. It is a matter of interest that Adler was himself a second-born child.

The position of the last-born child is unique. The child has a great risk of being a problem child. He or she has a strong feeling of inferiority and lacks independence, but is highly motivated to surpass the older siblings. He or she has a competitive mind and is also achievement-oriented.

The only child has no siblings to compete with, hence has to compete with parents. He or she has an inflated self-concept and exaggerated sense of superiority. This child is dependent upon others and lacks the feeling of cooperation and social interest.

Adler's "Individual Psychology" was considered more optimistic and realistic. He recognised the impact of social forces in shaping human behaviour.

Some of the major criticisms against Alfred Adler are as follows:

(i) Adler has several unstable concepts in his theory. One such concept is creative power. Nobody can claim that a conclusion can be drawn from such untestable concepts. Everything relating to them has to be taken on guesswork.

(ii) Most of the terms used by Adler lack precise operational definitions. Terms like "style of life", "social interest", "striving for superiority" and "creative power" have no operational definitions. The term "creative power" is a highly illusory one.

(iii) Adler's concept of the impact of birth order on personality development and behaviour cannot be studied or experimented. No research evidence has confirmed the correlation between personality traits and different birth orders of individuals.

Alfred Adler's Individual Psychology

- *Alfred Adler, a student of Sigmund Freud and a member of Vienna Psychoanalytic Society, developed his own theory of personality, which he called "Individual Psychology". Adler (1917, 1927) argued that the foremost human drive is not sexuality, but a striving for superiority. He viewed striving for superiority as a universal drive to adapt, improve oneself and master life's challenges. Early inferiority feelings motivate individuals to acquire new skills and develop new talents. According to Adler, everyone has to work to overcome some feelings of inferiority. Compensation involves efforts to overcome imagined or real inferiorities by developing one's abilities. He believed that compensation is entirely normal. However, in some people inferiority feelings can become excessive, resulting in what is widely known as an inferiority complex – exaggerated feelings of weakness and inadequacy.*

> **Dream Analysis**
>
> - *In dream analysis, the therapist interprets the symbolic meaning of the client's dreams. For Freud, dreams are the royal road to unconscious, the most direct means of access to the patient's innermost conflicts, wishes and impulses. Clients are encouraged and trained to remember their dreams, which they describe in therapy. The therapist then analyses the symbolism in dreams to interpret their meaning.*

Adler's Individual Psychology, despite all these criticisms, converts different explanations of human behaviour into a meaningful framework.

Another neo-Freudian, Erich Fromm (1900–1980) has also given a different view of personality development. Being a social analyst, Fromm was much concerned with social influences, particularly a person's relationship to society. Freud said that the relationship was constant, whereas Fromm believed that it was constantly changing. According to Fromm, personality is the sum of both inherited and acquired characteristics. He made a distinction between temperament and character.

According to him, temperament refers to the mode of reaction that is inherited, constitutional and unchangeable. Character is different from temperament and is formed through life experiences through different kinds of social influences. Character is determined by both physical constitution and temperament, as well as by social and cultural influences acting upon the individuals.

Character is considered a relatively permanent form in which two processes – assimilation and socialisation – play important roles. These two together are called "orientation" by Fromm. This orientation forms the core of character.

BOX 3.9: DISTINCTION BETWEEN FREUD, JUNG AND ADLER

Sigmund Freud	Carl G. Jung
- *For Freud, the origin of psychic energy was instinct, particularly the sex instinct.* - *Freud overemphasised on the unconscious mind.* - *Freud has given priority to the past experiences which play major roles in present behaviour. So he was called a determinist.*	- *For Jung, the origin of psychic energy arises from different bodily processes which tend to form basic drive for life.* - *Jung emphasised on the unconscious mind in a different way, i.e., racial unconscious.* **Alfred Adler** - *Adler has given emphasis on the role of future on the determination of present behaviour. Jung believed both views and held that an individual's behaviour is guided by future goals and past experiences. Jung maintained independence from the orthodox Freudian psychoanalysis.*

Erich Fromm has distinguished five types of individuals bearing different characters. These are:

(i) The receptive character (ii) The hoarding character
(iii) The exploitative character (iv) The marketing character
(v) The productive character

In short, Fromm tried to present an optimistic view of humans by giving emphasis to social and cultural factors encountered by individuals in their lifetimes. Critics said that the viewpoints enumerated by Fromm in his theory were extremely idealistic and, therefore, unrealistic. He failed to provide empirical data in support of his theory. Later, he was known as an "ethical philosopher" rather than a psychologist.

Karen Horney (1885–1952) was a female psychoanalyst at the Psychoanalytic Institute at Berlin and New York and differed from Sigmund Freud. She was born in Hamburg, Germany, studied medicine and started here career as an orthodox Freudian. In 1923, she challenged some of the Freudian concepts and looked at different view of personality development.

Horney tried to explain the fundamentals of psychoanalysis by placing emphasis upon social and cultural forces. She tried to show that human behaviour is governed not only by biological and instinctual forces, but environmental forces. Her approach to explain personality was holistic rather than instinctual.

Karen Horney

- *Basic Anxiety: Rather than focusing on sexuality, Horney focused on the child's sense of basic anxiety – the anxiety created in a child born into a world that is so much bigger and more powerful than him or her. While people whose parents gave them love, affection and security would overcome this anxiety, others with less secure upbringing would develop neurotic personalities and maladaptive ways of dealing with relationships*

Fromm's Different Characters

- *The Receptive Character or Receptive Type: These persons expect help from others. They are always the "receivers", but not the "givers". They do not want to give love, material possessions, etc. These individuals become too anxious when the supply is withheld.*
- *The Hoarding Character or Hoarding Type: These people are very selfish and orderly. They always expect threats from outside. They feel secure only when they save and keep something.*
- *The Exploitative Character or Exploitative Type : These persons are very aggressive. They always use strategies to acquire things by force. They are clever people.*
- *The Marketing Character or Marketing Type: For these individuals, success depends on how well they can sell themselves. This type of persons consider themselves as a commodity which can be bought and sold like something in the market.*
- *The Productive Character or Productive Type: These type of persons are always wanted by the society. Such a personality is the combination of previous four types, but it is always guided by genuine love, care, responsibility and creativity. The most important characteristic of these persons is their productive activities and devotion to the well-being of others.*

She stated that a child is the product of both heredity and environment. She rejected the undue emphasis on sex on the development of personality. The concept of "basic anxiety" was basic to Horney's psychoanalysis. Basic anxiety occurs in childhood when the child feels helpless and is isolated from the world which appear hostile and threatening. There are three components of basic anxiety: feelings of helplessness, hostility and isolation. All these components grow out of lack of genuine warmth and affection at home, and ultimately play a vital role in personality development. She said that each normal and healthy individual has some creative and positive potential. When the person gets love and affection in the environment, he or she expresses those potentials and develops confidence in the self. On the other hand, if this basic potential is not fulfilled and expressed, anxiety results.

Horney recognised only two types of defence mechanisms which help individuals in reducing their basic anxiety. These are rationalisation and externalisation.

Rationalisation is used in Freudian sense by Horney with the only difference that it is used with the whole organism and is not related to specific instinctual components as Freud had proposed. The concept of externalisation is more or less equivalent to projection. In this defence mechanism, the individual attributes every motive or action to some external agents and not only to the undesirable and weaker ones.

The main criticism against Horney was that she concentrated upon basic anxiety as well as upon basic needs and neurotic needs. She attempted to explain even a normal personality with the help of these concepts, which was unscientific.

H.S. Sullivan (1892–1949), born in New York state, is another neo-Freudian who has given priority to social and cultural forces in the development of personality. He was a doctor by profession. In 1921, he was appointed to St. Elizabeth Hospital in Washington DC, where he worked with mentally-ill people. His experiences in the hospital were vital for the formulation of his theory of personality.

In 1931, he moved to New York city for starting a private practice. During his stay for eight years there, he came in contact with Karen Horney and Erich Fromm. In 1936, he returned to Washington DC where he founded the Washington School of Psychiatry. Until his death in 1949, he was the director of the institute.

Sullivan's theory was influenced by non-psychoanalytical sources. Therefore, he deviated from Sigmund Freud in many aspects. He dropped most of the Freudian concepts such as ego, id, superego and sex theory. Despite these concepts, there were enough elements which were taken from Freudian psychoanalytic theory and included in his theory. He stressed the importance of several distinct periods in the development of personality.

Sullivan's theory is popularly known as the "interpersonal theory of psychiatry". It states that "Personality is the relatively enduring pattern of recurrent interpersonal situations which characterise a human life (Sullivan, 1953)."

According to Sullivan, right from the day we take birth, we make interactions with others. These interactions shape our behaviour. Our personality is something that develops in the context of such interpersonal behaviour. Sullivan's contributions towards the development of personality can be enumerated under three headings: Dynamics of personality, Enduring aspects of personality and Developmental stages.

(a) *Dynamics of Personality*: For Sullivan, a human being is basically an energy system that seeks to reduce tension created by needs. Our tensions are divided into two: tensions created by needs and tensions created by anxiety.

Tensions due to need potentialities call for integrating actions. Tensions due to anxiety produce disintegrative behaviour. Need satisfaction always reduces tension. If needs are not satisfied for a longer span of time, it may lead to apathy. Anxiety is transmitted to an infant by the mother. When the mother herself becomes anxious, she expresses these disturbances in voice, actions and looks. Gradually, the baby picks up these signals and become anxious.

In his theory, Sullivan presented three levels or three modes of cognition: Prototaxic, Parataxic and Syntaxic.

Prototaxic experiences are the primitive experiences of an infant. Such experiences are undifferentiated, presymbolic, momentary and incapable of being conceptualised. Therefore, these experiences are non-communicable. In short, the prototaxic experiences are the primary mode of cognition of a neonate.

Parataxic experiences are prelogical, personal and can be communicated only in distorted form to others. Such experiences are more differentiated than prototaxic experiences.

Syntaxic experiences are meaningful interpersonal communication. These are meaningfully communicated through language, gestures and words. Throughout the life-span of an individual, these three modes of cognition occur. After the sixth year of a child, syntaxic experiences start dominating.

Dynamics of Personality by Sullivan

- *Prototaxic Experiences: Primitive experiences of an infant: undifferentiated, presymbolic, momentary and therefore non-communicable; They are the primary mode of cognition of the neonate.*
- *Parataxic Experiences: Parataxic experiences are prelogical, personal and can be communicated only in distorted form. They begin very early in infancy.*

(b) *Enduring Aspects of Personality*: In his system, Sullivan emphasised several aspects of personality which have stability over time. The important aspects are: dynamism, personification and self-system.

The concept of dynamism is equivalent to the trait theory of personality. Dynamism is considered to be the relatively consistent patterns of action which characterise the persons throughout life. Sullivan divided dynamism into two classes: dynamism related to a particular zone of the body and dynamism related to tension.

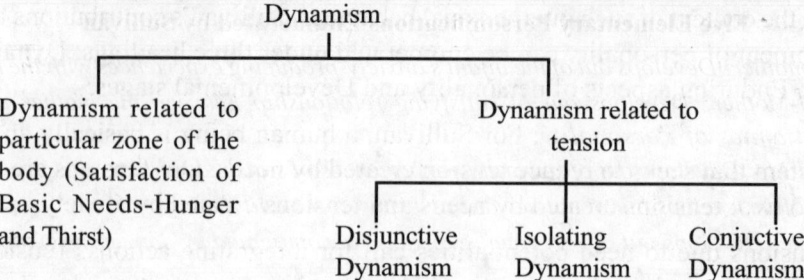

The former type of dynamism tries to satisfy the basic needs of persons such as need for hunger and thirst. The second type of dynamism consists of three categories: Disjunctive dynamism, Isolating dynamism and Conjunctive dynamism.

Disjunctive dynamism includes destructive patterns of behaviour. It refers to a behaviour pattern which is characterised by attitude that people are evil and harmful and this world is a bad place to live in. Isolating dynamism includes dynamism of lust, which is a biological phenomenon. It is particularly produced by tensions either directly or indirectly related to the genitals. Heterosexual and homosexual patterns of behaviour are involved in it. Conjunctive dynamism includes beneficial behaviour patterns, particularly found in intimacy and self-system. Self-system is a very important dynamism among them. This is a complex system which tries to protect persons from anxiety by maintaining interpersonal security.

Self-system is called an anti-anxiety system because it contains those dynamisms which tend to reduce anxiety. This system begins to grow with interpersonal relationships of the child when he or she is about two years old. Though self-system tends to reduce anxiety, it simultaneously also interferes with the ability to live constructively.

Explaining this fact more elaborately, Sullivan said that when a child has more experience with anxiety, his or her self-system becomes more inflated and separated from the rest of personality. It prevents the individual from taking a realistic view and objective judgement of the situation.

Personification, according to Sullivan, is another vital enduring aspect of personality. It refers to an image of the self. The image of personification is built out of experiences with anxiety or need satisfaction. Sullivan stated in his theory that during infancy five elementary personifications are built. These are: (i) Bad-mother (ii) Good-mother (iii) Bad-me (iv) Good-me and (v) Not-me.

Five Elementary Personifications Enumerated by Sullivan

- *Bad-mother: Develops out of the infant's anxiety-producing experiences with the mother*
- *Good-Mother: Develops out of satisfying relationship between the mother and the infant.*
- *Good-Me: Develops out of rewarding experiences of satisfied feeding.*
- *Bad-Me: Develops out of not-rewarding experiences and anxiety.*
- *Not-me: Develops out of very intense anxiety; accompanied by dangerous emotions.*

The Bad-mother personification develops out of an infant's anxiety-producing experiences with the mother. The Good-mother personification develops out of satisfying relationship of an infant with the mother. The personifications of bad-me and good-me develop in a similar way with rewarding experiences or rejection. The not-me personification develops out of very intense anxiety and represents the dissociated aspects of the self.

(c) *The Developmental Stages*: Sullivan described seven stages or epochs of personality development. These are: Infancy, Childhood, Juvenile era, Pre-adolescence, Early adolescence, Late adolescence and Maturity. Changes in personality can take place during any stage of development. Usually, the changes take place during transition from one stage to the other. Perception to others and reaction to others are basic to the development of personality. The main pillar is the interpersonal relationship.

(i) Infancy period extends from birth to the development of articulation of speech, usually about 18 to 24 months of age. The neonate is just like an animal during birth. Gradually he or she becomes human through tenderness and affection by mothering. During this span, the infant develops a dual personification of mother: good mother and bad mother.

She is perceived as a good mother, when the baby satisfies his or her baby needs. She is perceived as bad-mother when she arouses anxiety of the baby. Gradually, the baby makes the transition from the prototaxic mode of cognition to parataxic mode of cognition during this state.

(ii) Childhood period begins from the articulation of speech and learning to the appearance of the need for peer relationship, i.e., to the age of five or six. As the baby grows up, the development of language leads to fusion of different images or personifications developed at infancy stage. For example, personification of good-mother and bad-mother are fused together into one image called "mother".

This time is a period of rapid acculturation because besides learning language, the child also learns cultural patterns like toilet training, eating habits and sex role-expectancies. Two prominent learning processes which are dominant at this stage are dramatisation and preoccupation.

Dramatisation refers to the efforts of a child to act like the father or mother or any other significant figure. Preoccupation refers to strategies by which a child avoids his or her anxiety by keeping engaged in some work which was earlier proved to be rewarding.

(iii) Juvenile era begins at the age of five or six and continues up to eight or nine years of age, i.e., when a strong need for an intimate companionship develops.

There are three basic characteristics of juvenile era: competition, compromise and cooperation. Three negative developments during this period are stereotypes, ostracism and disparagement.

Ostracism is forcible isolation which a child may experience if he or she falls out of any group. Disparagement refers to putting other people down and it is learned from parents who often speak about the people whom they dislike and hate.

(iv) Pre-adolescence marks the beginning from the appearance of need for intimacy until puberty. It is characterised by developing interest in one particular person of the same sex. In previous stages, the interpersonal relationships were based upon personal need satisfaction. But during this span, this relationship is based on intimacy and love. Intimate relationship with the same sex is called the "chum". Without this chum, the pre-adolescents may suffer from a desperate loneliness which is worse than anxiety.

(v) Early adolescence starts with puberty and ends with the need for love with an individual of opposite sex. During this period, the adolescents develop genital interest and lustful relationship. Here, many problems grow out of three basic needs: need for security, need for intimacy (with someone of opposite sex) and need for sexual satisfaction. These three needs collide with one another and produce many kinds of stress and strain during this stage. Sullivan has rightly depicted that adolescent period is the turning point of personality development.

(vi) Late adolescence begins with the stabilisation of genital activities and ends with establishing a lasting love relationship in adulthood. Syntaxic mode of cognition dominates during this stage. The most important characteristic of this period is the fusion of intimacy and lust. The end result of this stage is self-respect which is prerequisite for giving respect to others.

(vii) Maturity is otherwise known as adulthood. Sullivan has said little about this stage, because it is beyond the scope of his system. The significant achievement of each of the previous stages manifests in a mature personality. In his words, "Mature people are quite sympathetically understanding of limitations, interests, possibilities, anxieties and so on of those among whom they move and with whom they deal."

Sullivan's Developmental Stages and Personality Development

(i) *Infancy: Its period extends from birth to development of speech articulation, i.e. upto 2 years; develops dual personification of mother – good mother and bad-mother.*

(ii) *Childhood: Articulation of speech upto appearance of the need for peer relationship, i.e., the age of five or six. Fusion of different images and rapid accultaruton.*

(iii) *Juvenile era: From age 6 to 9; competition, cooperation and compromise develop. Three negative developments are: stereotypes, ostracism and disparagement.*

(iv) *Pre-Adolescence and Early Adolescence: Relationship with the same sex and stabilisation of genital activities.*

(v) *Late Adolescence and Maturity: Syntaxic mode of cognition, manifestations of achievements during last stages.*

Sullivan has presented a systematic theory of personality development which has achieved wide acceptance among psychologists. Interpersonal relationship has been one of the basic principles of Sullivan's system. A major criticism against him is that he has incorporated some hypothetical constructs like personification and self-system.

Erik Erikson (1902–1982) was another neo-Freudian who advanced a different theory of personality development. He was born to Danish parents in Frankfurt, Germany. His parents separated before his birth. At Vienna, Erikson met Freud and his family members at the age of 25. Then he joined Vienna Psychoanalytic Institute as a student and began a personal analysis with Anna Freud, the daughter of Sigmund Freud.

Taking a broader view of Psychoanalysis of Freud, Erikson emphasised on ego, but not on id and superego. According to him, ego possesses creative qualities and tries to provide creative solutions to each new problem. Ego is determined not only by inner forces but by social and cultural influences.

Erikson has built his developmental stages on the Freudian system. He accepts Freudian Oral, Anal, Phallic, Latent and Genital stages and added three more stages – early adulthood, middle adulthood and old age.

The basic features of these stages are as follows:

(i) Each stage has its own developmental characteristics and has a typical crisis. By crisis, he means a turning point in personality and is brought about by interaction of increasing physical maturity on one hand and by demands placed upon the person by parents, society and teachers, etc., on the other hand.

(ii) This crisis is normally resolved by the ego qualities of the concerned period.

(iii) All these stages have both psychosexual and psychosocial aspects of growth and change.

Erikson has enumerated eight stages of personality development. A brief analysis of these stages is discussed as follows:

(a) *Infancy:* Erikson's first stage of psychosocial development is infancy. This corresponds to the Freudian Oral stage which covers approximately the first year of life. Under proper maternal care, the child develops a sense of "basic trust". When maternal care is inadequate, rejecting and unreliable, this produces a crisis in the form of mistrust. When the baby is able to solve the trust–mistrust conflict, the first psychological strength called "hope" emerges. With time, the child learns to focus on meaningful hope and give up useless hope.

(b) *Early childhood:* This stage covers the second and third years of life. It corresponds with Freudian Anal stage. In this period, the neuromuscular maturation, verbalisation and sense of social discrimination of the child become more developed. As a result, the child wants to explore and interact with the surroundings more independently.

(c) *Play Age:* This is the third stage of personality development. It corresponds to Freudian Phallic stage and extends to the age six or seven. At this time, the social environment of the child makes him or her more active and the child learns more skills. One negative point is that at this stage the child develops a guilty feeling. In his theory, Erikson adapts Freudian concept of Oedipus and Electra complex, although his own interpretation is different and more social than Freud.

(d) *School Age:* This stage continues up to 11 years. This period corresponds to the Freudian Latency period. According to Erikson, this stage is "only a lull before the storm of puberty". Socially, it is the most decisive stage. The child gradually learns to control his or her imagination and utilises it in learning rudimentary skills.

(e) *Adolescence:* This stage of psychosocial development extends until 19 years. During this period, the adolescents try to consolidate different types of knowledge which they have acquired and integrate them into a personal identity. They try to establish themselves in the society. This is called "ego identity".

(f) *Young Adulthood:* This stage approximately covers the period of the twenties. In this stage, the young adults are genuinely ready to make social and heterosexual intimacy with other persons. A true sense of intimacy develops only in those persons who have already developed a sense of personal identity. The only danger in this stage is the "sense of isolation". The individual may become self-absorbed or avoid personal contacts.

(g) *Middle Adulthood:* This stage covers the age of 30 to 65. It is marked by "generetivity", which refers to a concern of a person regarding not only the welfare of the next generation but also for the future of the society in which the people of that generation will live. Generetivity is related to the attempts of older generations to establish and guide the persons who are going to replace them in near future. The sense of generetivity is found not only in parents but also in those who have a strong sense of wanting betterment of younger persons. When an individual fails to develop the sense of generetivity, he takes a risk to develop what is called "stagnation".

> **Erikson's Ideas on Socio-cultural Aspects of Personality Development**
> - *Ritualisation: Ritualisation is a cultural pattern and a way of doing something in an interaction between at least two individuals. It has adaptive values for both individuals.*
> - *Ritual: Each stage of personality development revealed by Erikson is characterised by ritualisation. In adulthood, this ritualisation becomes the ritual which refers to an activity done by a community.*
> - *Ritualism: When there occurs distortion in ritualisation, it results in ritualism. In this, people become concerned with their own achievements.*

Stagnation is defined as a stage of self-absorption in which the person cares for the satisfaction of his or her own personal needs. The satisfactory resolution of generetivity versus stagnation leads to the development of the virtue of "care" which refers to the need to look after others as well as to teach them. Care and teaching are required for our cultural progress.

(h) *Maturity:* This is the eighth and last stage of psychosocial development enumerated by Erikson. It gives signals for old age. This stage starts at the age of 65 and extends up to death. During this period, the ego quality of integrity appears. This is called "ego integrity" where the person takes a glance back on his or her life and tries to summate, integrate and evaluate past accomplishments. He or she says silently, "On the whole, I am satisfied".

In this stage, according to Erikson, true maturity and practical sense of wisdom spring up. The person thinks that he or she is near death and is no longer afraid of death. This is because he or she perceive their existence through their offsprings. The danger of this stage is "despair". When they think of the ups and downs throughout this life, they develops the sense of despair.

Sometimes, these old persons think that they have ruined their life and lost a large number of opportunities. When the "integrity" and "despair" crisis is resolved, they develops the virtue of "wisdom". It is this wisdom which maintains and transmit the integrity of accumulated knowledge.

Later, Erikson elaborated his psychosocial stages of development in terms of socio-cultural aspects of personality development. He enumerated three socio-cultural phenomena: ritualisation, ritual and ritualism.

These three phenomena give a new shape and dimension to the development stages of Erikson. According to him, ritualisation is a cultural pattern and a way of doing something in an interaction between at least with two persons. It has adaptive values for both individuals. Each stage is characterised by this ritualisation.

During adulthood, this ritualisation becomes the "ritual" which refers to an activity done by a community of adults for marking an important event of recurring nature. In India, some examples are Holi, Durgapuja and Ramanavami.

Distortion in ritualisation leads to "ritualism". Here the individuals become more concerned with their own achievements rather than with their relationship with others.

> **Erikson's Identity versus Role Confusion**
>
> - *The psychosocial crisis which is faced by adolescents is that of "identity vs role confusion". In this stage, the teenager must choose from the many options for values in life and beliefs concerning things such as political issues, career options and marriage (Feldman, 2003). From those options, a consistent sense of self must be found. On the whole, in this fifth stage of personality development, the adolescent finds a consistent sense of "self".*

Some psychologists and experts prefer Erikson's system because he placed emphasis upon the psychosocial development of personality rather than psychosexual development enumerated by Sigmund Freud and others. Many psychoanalysts praised Erikson for his sensible interpretations and meticulous observations of human behaviour and personality.

In spite of these positive points, Erikson's works have been criticised on many grounds. These are :

(i) Critics have pointed out that Erikson's theory has also included the basic ideas of ego, superego and conscious mind enumerated by Freud.

(ii) Most of the Erikson's concepts on personality development are based on his personal observations. His ideas and concepts lack experimental support.

(iii) Some critics consider that Erikson was too optimistic while providing explanation of human behaviour and personality.

(iv) Some psychologists consider that most of the Erikson's ideas are purely theoretical and unverified. Examples are "hope", "purpose" and "will".

Despite all these criticisms, Erikson's system was accepted by most of the later psychoanalysts and contemporary psychologists. His meticulous observations, particularly upon problems of adulthood, aging and adolescence, have been proved valuable for modern behavioural and social experts. Like Freud, Erikson's concepts on personality development are being used by many psychiatrists and counsellors.

If we take up critical evaluations of Sigmund Freud and Erikson's works, we find that there are some points of similarities and differences between them when they view personality development.

Similarities between Freud and Erikson

Erikson's Psychosocial Adolescent and Adult Stages				
Age	State	Developmental Crisis	Dealing with Crisis (Successful)	Dealing with Crisis (Unsuccessful)
Adolescence	5 (Five)	Identity vs Role Confusion – Children decide about occupations, beliefs, attitudes and behaviour patterns.	Develop a strong sense of identity.	Confused and wants to blend with the crowd inconspicuously

Early Childhood	6 (Six)	Intimacy vs Isolation Individuals want to share with another person a close committed relationship.	People who succeed in this task will have intimate relation-ship.	Unsuccessful adults become isolated and suffer from loneliness.
Middle Childhood	7 (Seven)	Generetivity vs Stagnation The challenge is to be creative, productive and nurturant of the next generation.	dults who succeed become creative, productive and nurturant.	Adults became passive and self-centered.
Late Childhood	8 (Eight)	Ego Integrity vs Despair The issue is whether an individual will reach wisdom, spiritual tranquility, and have a sense of wholeness and acceptance of his or her life.	Elderly people who succeed in addressing this issue will enjoy life and not fear death.	Elderly people who fail will feel that their life is empty and will fear death.

We have discussed the contributions of both Erikson and Sigmund Freud. There are some points of similarities as well as contrast between Freud and Erikson. First, we will discuss the similarities.

(i) Both psychoanalysts have explained development of personality in terms of some invariant stages.

(ii) Freud and Erikson both considered stages of personality development as determined by past experiences.

(iii) Erikson has accepted the biological and sexual foundations of motivational and personal dispositions of Freud.

Despite all these similarities, there are some points of distinction between Freud and Erikson.

Distinctions between Freud and Erikson

The major differences between Freud and Erikson are:

(i) Freud, in his psychoanalytic theory, emphasised upon id, ego and superego, which were considered primary forces in determining human behaviour. But Erikson, in his psychosocial development theory, has emphasised upon ego and undermined the functions of id and superego in determining human behaviour. Erikson has made ego the master rather than the slave of id and superego. Erikson is a true ego psychologist who has regarded ego as an autonomous structure of personality.

(ii) For personality development of children, Freud emphasised only upon the influence of parents. Erikson has given stress upon social forces and value systems which dominate and influence the emergence of the personality of a child, besides parental influence.

(iii) In his psychosocial development theory, Erikson has enumerated eight stages starting from infancy to maturity or old age. The whole life-span was included, the ego was emphasised and the functions of id and superego were nullified. Freud's theory of psychosexual development of personality included only the childhood experiences which never went beyond genital stage.

(iv) Another difference between Erikson and Freud is on the nature and resolution of psychosexual conflicts. In his psychoanalytic theory, Freud said that the major abnormalities in adulthood were related to the childhood experiences lying in the unconscious mind. But Erikson has given priority to ego qualities or virtues which emerge at different levels of psychosocial development. These ego qualities play vital roles in resolving the psychosocial conflicts called crisis.

Distinction between Freudians and Neo-Freudians	
• *In his psychoanalytic theory, Freud emphasised biological instincts, especially sex instincts, as major determinants of human behaviour.* • *Freud emphasised two major complexes: Oedipus and Electra, which are universal and were due to sexual jealousy.* • *Freud described anxiety as the ego function. When ego is threatened by id and/or superego, anxiety emerges.*	• *Neo-Freudians have emphasised social and cultural forces to be the major determinants of human behaviour.* • *Neo-Fraudians like Sullivan, Horney and Fromm explained that those are neither universal nor loaded with sexual jealousy.* • *Neo-Freudians, particularly Karen Horney, in her theory described that basic anxiety is formed in childhood when a child feels that he or she is an isolated organism or when they realise that they are helpless in this world which seems to be full of threats and hostilities.*

From this discussion, it is clear that despite some similarities, Erikson and Freud differ from each other in many ways. These differences show that Erikson was strictly an "ego psychologist", because throughout his psychosocial development theory, he emphasised upon the important role of ego during the life-span of a person.

Adler and Jung were two rebels of Freudian psychoanalysis. They have countered the over emphasis upon sex by Sigmund Freud. Adler made significant contributions by way of formulating concepts like organ inferiority, compensation, striving for superiority, social interest, style of life, creative power, fictional finalism, birth order, etc.

Carl Jung also rejected the over emphasis on sex in Freudian psychoanalytic theory. Among his significant contributions are the conscious and unconscious, attitudes and functions, psychic energy and personality development. Other neo-Freudians like Horney, Fromm and Sullivan did not rebel against Freud, but they have formulated their own theories of personality development, giving emphasis upon different aspects and concepts.

Horney was well-known for her concepts like basic anxiety, neurotic trends, neurotic needs, idealised self-image, rationalisation, externalisation, etc. Fromm explained personality as various types like receptive type, exploitative type, marketing type and productive type. Sullivan's personality theory encompassed understanding dynamics of personality as well as its different developmental stages.

Erikson was a popular ego psychologist who accepted Freudian stages of psychosexual development and added three more stages covering the total life-span of a human being. Throughout his eight stages of psychosocial development, Erikson emphasised upon certain ego qualities which have been considered as basic for personality development.

Current Thoughts on Freud and Psychoanalysis

Freud's psychoanalytic theory seems less relevant in today's sexually saturated world. However, many of his concepts remain useful and still form the basis of many modern personality theories. For example, the ideas of defence mechanisms and the unconscious have research support. Many psychoanalysts believe that there are influences in human behaviour which exist outside of normal conscious awareness.

In his psychoanalytic theory, Freud based much of his interpretations of a patient's problems on the interpretation of dreams and results of the patient's free association. These sources are often criticised as being too ambiguous and without scientific support for the validity of his interpretations. Another significant drawback of Freudian psychoanalysis is that the clients and patients of Freud hailed from Austrian wealthy families and most of them were frustrated women living in the Victorian era of sexual repression. Basing his theory on observations made regarding such a group of clients promoted his emphasis on sexuality as the root of all problems in personality, as the women of that social class and era were often sexually frustrated.

Freud's influence on the modern world is significant, although some experts view his theory with a great deal of scepticism. Still, he was the first theorist who emphasised upon the importance of childhood experiences on personality development. But it is a fact that he never studied children.

Humanistic Psychology

Humanistic psychology was regarded as a third force of psychology, the other two being Psychoanalysis and Behaviourism. Humanistic psychology was not a system, but a movement. It took its shape in early 1960s. Abraham Maslow was the founding father of this movement. He was regarded as the spiritual father of humanism in USA.

Humanistic Psychology

- *Humanistic psychology was regarded as the third force in psychology and it was developed by founding fathers Rogers and Maslow in the early 1960s. This movement was considered as an important theoretical alternative to Behaviourism and Psychoanalysis. It is a movement in psychology which is the collection of a number of lines and thoughts of different schools. It is not a system or school of a single individual or a group of individuals. Humanistic psychology has tried to present a radically different picture of human nature.*

Humanistic psychology describes a person as a whole. It explains behaviour in terms of the entire life-history of an individual. The propounder of self-theory, Rogers, was an important contributor to humanistic psychology. Maslow's self-actualisation theory was another innovation which has given personality a new shape. According to him, human beings are considered basically good and worthy of respect and self-actualisation. With a favourable environment, individuals will readily move towards realisation of their underlying potentialities and abilities.

Of the many humanistic theories, two theories are very significant and influential: Rogers's self-theory and Maslow's self-actualisation theory.

Rogers's Self Theory: Becoming a Fully-Functioning Individual

Carl Rogers was born in Illinois in 1902. He graduated from University of Wisconsin and received his PhD degree from Columbia University in 1931. Among his important publications are Counselling and Psychotherapy (1942) and Client Centred Therapy (1951). Rogers's self-theory was based upon his experiences as a client-centred psychotherapist or as a non-directive psychotherapist.

Basic Tenets of Humanistic Psychology

(i) *Humanistic psychology is not a single organised theory or system. It is a movement which incorporates psychologists of different lines and thoughts.*

(ii) *It describes an individual as a whole – an integrated, unique and organised whole. Humanistic psychologists emphasise upon understanding rather than explaining human behaviour.*

(iii) *Humanistic psychology is concerned with collecting knowledge of the person's entire life history, self-realisation and self-actualisation, the person's inner nature, creative potentiality, psychological health, etc.*

(iv) *Maslow said that mental illness can not be properly understood without understanding the mental health of persons.*

(v) *Humanistic psychology gives overall emphasis upon "healthy functioning of human beings", the "modes of living" and "goals of life".*

His method of treatment for abnormal people is called client-centred therapy. In this method, the patient (called client) makes interaction with the therapist in such a way that the client gradually becomes aware of the conflict and his or her wishes. Here the role of the therapist is passive. The therapist does not give any advice directly, but simply reflects the feelings of the client.

Taking this idea into consideration, Rogers developed his self-theory of personality which is also known as person-centred theory. It is a holistic theory. The following three constructs are significant in Roger's theory:

(a) *Organism*: Organism refers to a biological being which responds to various stimuli in the environment. But Rogers used this term in a different sense. According to Rogers, organism refers to a totality of experiences going on within the whole individual at a particular moment. The organism is considered as a locus of all experiences varying from our own perception of events which occur within our body to our perception of events which occur in the external world.

(b) *Self*: It is pertinent that Roger's organism has a direct reference to the totality of experiences. The totality of experiences constitutes both conscious and unconscious experiences. Such totality of experiences constitute the "phenomenal field".

This phenomenal field is also known as the perceptual field. Although these experiences are inner experiences of the organism, the sources may either be external or internal or both. From this perceptual field or totality of experiences, the self emerges. During infancy, when a portion of phenomenal field becomes personalised and differentiated as "I" or "me" experiences, the self is said to be formed.

The self is just a "fluid" or "changing gestalt" and it may be either in awareness or out of awareness. With the development of self, the infant begins to understand good or bad. The infant tries to evaluate his or her experiences as positive or negative. This self is not a separate dimension of personality. For Rogers, an individual does not possess a self, rather self incorporates the whole organism.

In his personality theory, Rogers mentions about two ideas: self-concept and ideal-self. Self-concept consists of all those aspects of experiences which are perceived by the individual in awareness. Such experiences may not sometimes be perceived accurately. Once this self-concept is formed, change and further learning become difficult, if not impossible. The experiences which seem to be inconsistent with the self-concept are either distorted or denied by the individual. However, self-concept is different from real self or organismic self. Self-concept is limited to only those experiences with which we are aware. But organismic self may also include those experiences which are beyond our awareness.

- *According to Rogers, the larger the gap between an individual's self-concept and reality, the poorer this person's psychological adjustment.*

Ideal-self is another sub-system of the self. It consists of experiences relating to what one thinks one ought to be and what one would like to be. Therefore, it contains all those attributes or characteristics which one aspires to possess. This is almost equivalent to the Freudians concepts of superego. However, a wider gap between the ideal-self and the perceived-self indicates incongruence and a psychologically unhealthy personality.

We have seen that the self emerges out of the organism. To describe the deep relationship between the self and the organism, Rogers said that in a psychologically healthy person, those experiences that constitute self are in line with the experiences with the organism. When these two are not congruent with each other, anxiety results and the individual ultimately becomes defensive.

The two major defence mechanisms are distortion and denial. An individual misinterprets an experiences in distortion. Ultimately it fits well with some aspects of self-concept. But in denial, the experience is not perceived in awareness. Distortion is more common than denial.

In case of high amount of anxiety, the defences of an individual do not work and the personality becomes disorganised. Psychotherapy is necessary in such cases.

(c) *Self-actualisation:* Many psychologists accepted the concept of self-actualisation. Rogers and Maslow shared this common concept. Rogers said that every individual has an inherent tendency to actualise his or her unique potential. He said that self-actualisation is a growth-force and it is a part of the individual's heredity. Potential of an individual not only includes biological potential but also involves a psychological growth. This is essential for maintaining and enhancing the organism.

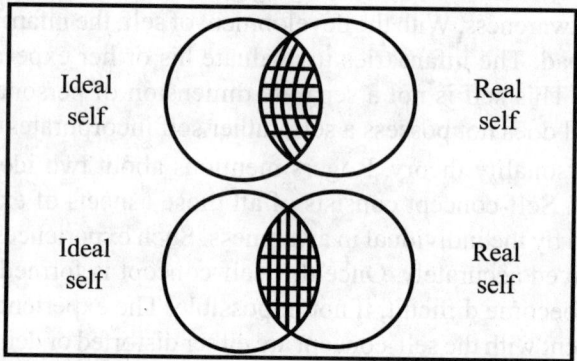

Fig. 3.3: Real and Ideal selves

The self-actualisation gradually develops from simple to complex. When the individual grows richer in his or her experiences, the self can be better actualised which ultimately allows for greater development of creativity. Adequate amount of self-actualisation keeps a person moving forward. Such individuals never like to stop at a particular point.

Rogers recognised two basic needs which are related to self-actualisation. These basic needs are (i) Need for positive regard of others and (ii) Need for self-regard. Both of these needs are learnt during infancy when the baby is loved and cared by the mother.

Roger's personality theory has its own criticisms. His theory has neglected the role of unconscious which plays a vital role in controlling behaviour. Further, Roger's theory is based upon a naive type of phenomenology. However, in spite of all these criticisms, Roger's emphasis on self has invited a lot of research and empirical findings.

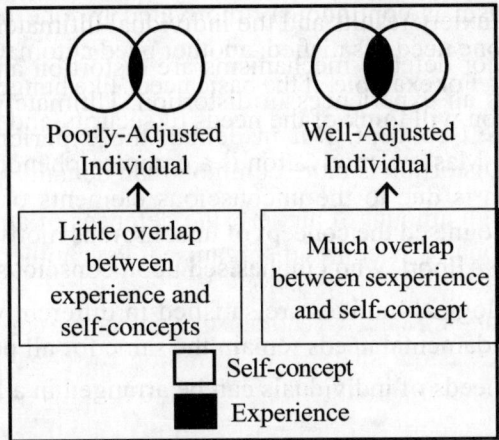

*Fig. 3.4 : Gaps between our self-concept and our experience:
a cause of maladjustment in Roger's Theory*

According to Rogers, the self-concept includes the real-self and the ideal-self. The real self is a person's actual perception of traits and abilities, whereas the ideal self is the perception of what a person would like to be or thinks he or she should be. When the ideal self and the real self are very similar (matching), the person experiences harmony and contentment. When there is a mismatch between the two selves, the person experiences anxiety and may engage in neurotic behaviour.

Maslow's Self-Actualisation Theory of Personality

Abraham Maslow (1908–1970), another founder of humanistic psychology, developed a theory of personality which is popularly known as the "Self-actualisation Theory". He was born in New York in 1908 and received PhD from the University of Wisconsin. During the period 1951 to 1969, Maslow emerged as a leading figure of the Third Force in Psychology. He was considered as the spiritual father of humanistic psychology. He took an optimistic view about human nature. He strongly believed that people have inherent potential and capacity for kindness, love and generosity, which flourish in a suitable environment. But an unfavourable social environment leads to repression of these potentials and capacities.

Maslow's self-actualisation theory has been best explained in terms of motivational processes. He said that human motives are innate and they are arranged in an ascending hierarchy of potency or priority. Before going to evaluate the hierarchy of needs, we have to discuss basic assumptions of motivation.

(i) Maslow's approach was holistic about motivation. For him, the whole individual and not his or her any single part or function is motivated. If we separate motive from the whole individual, it will be an inaccurate and incomplete study. For example, in case of the sex motive, not only the genitals are stimulated, but the brain, some endocrine glands, intestines and finally the whole organism is stimulated.

(ii) Every organism is continuously motivated by one need or the other. If an individual's one need is satisfied, another need automatically arises and guides the behaviour. For example, if the basic needs like hunger and thirst are satisfied, then the person will think of the needs of security and protection.

(iii) According to Maslow, motivation is a complex phenomenon. The complexity of motivation is due to the unconscious elements of the drive. So Maslow indirectly recognised the concept of unconscious motivation. On this point, he differed from Allport, who emphasised upon conscious motivation.

(iv) Different biological motives are satisfied in different ways in many cultures. But these fundamental needs remain the same for all people.

(v) The various needs of individuals can be arranged in a hierarchy of potency of priority.

Five needs are recognised by Maslow, which he depicts in his theory of "hierarchy of needs". These needs in order of their prepotency are physiological needs, safety needs, love and belongingness need, esteem need and need for self-actualisation.

Transcendence
(Spiritual needs for cosmic identification)
Self-actualisation
(Needs to fulfil potential, having meaningful goals)
Aesthetic Needs
(Needs for order, beauty)
Cognitive Needs
(Needs for knowledge, understanding, novelty)
Esteem
(Needs for confidence, sense of worth and competence, self-esteem and respect of others)
Attachment
(Needs to belong, affiliate, to love and to be loved)
Safety
(Needs for security, comfort, tranquility, freedom from fear)
Biological
(Needs for food, water, oxygen, rest, sexual expression, release of tension).

Fig. 3.5: Maslow's Hierarchy of Needs

The concept of needs hierarchy states that human needs exist in a hierarchy ranging from physiological needs, at the bottom, to safety needs, social needs, esteem needs and finally self-actualisation needs at the top. As Maslow depicted, the lower order needs must be satisfied before we can turn to more complex higher-order needs.

Higher-order needs cannot serve as motives until lower-order needs have been satisfied. For example, a hungry person won't be very interested in self-actualisation. Thus, lower-level needs have prepotency over higher-level needs. If the lower-level needs are not satisfied, the higher-level needs will no longer emerge and the individuals will return to unsatisfied lower level needs. These needs are being discussed below in detail:

(a) *Physiological Needs*: These are the basic needs which include need for food, water, oxygen, sex, temperature, etc. If these basic needs are not satisfied, no other higher needs originate. When an individual is hungry, he or she will never think of safety, love and respect for others.

(b) *Safety Needs*: Safety needs arise when physiological needs are satisfied. These needs include need for physical security, protection, stability and freedom from anxiety, danger and chaos. Safety needs are not significant motivators for healthy adult persons. But during emergencies like war, accidents and fire, safety needs become the prime source of motivators.

(c) *Love and Belongingness Needs*: Belongingness and love become effective only when the physiological and safety needs are satisfied. These needs include our need for friendship, for belonging to a group or bonding with our families. The need for having a life partner also comes under this category. Without the fulfilment of love needs, a sound and healthy personality development becomes impossible. People who are deprived of this need in childhood may become cynical and self-defeating in interpersonal relationships.

(d) *Esteem Needs*: Esteem needs come into the front when all the previous three needs are satisfied. Esteem needs includes two sets: the first set includes needs for strength, competence, self-confidence, mastery and independence; the second set includes needs for prestige, fame, dominance, dignity and appreciation. The second set is derived from the first set. In his theory, Maslow categorically pointed out that satisfaction of self-esteem needs produces feelings like self-confidence, capability, strength, etc., and if these needs are not satisfied, it leads to feelings of inferiority, helplessness, weakness, etc. Maslow's esteem needs can be compared with Alfred Adler's striving for superiority and Erikson's need for mastery.

(e) *Need for Self-Actualisation*: According to Maslow, the individuals who are psychologically healthy must have attained high levels of self-actualisation. This need becomes active only when the other needs at lower levels of hierarchy are satisfied. Self-actualisation is a state in which individuals reach their fullest true potential. Self-actualisation refers to the desire for self-fulfilment, to realise all of one's potentials, to become what one wishes to and to be creative in the true sense of the word. To self-actualise means to reach the peak of one's potential.

Self-actualised people accept themselves for what they are; they recognise their shortcomings as well as their strengths. They are well aware of the rules imposed by society. For these people, life continues to be an exciting adventure rather than a boring routine. Need for self-actualisation is an umbrella need which covers seventeen meta-needs. These meta-needs have no hierarchy, but they are equally potent. Examples of meta-needs are need for perfection, wholeness, richness, beauty, goodness and truth. Self-actualised people sometimes have what Maslow describes as peak experiences. These experiences are intense emotional experiences during which individuals feel at one with the universe. These experiences are linked to personal growth, for after them, individuals report feeling more spontaneous, more appreciative of life and less concerned with the problems of everyday life.

Deficiency Needs or D-Needs

The first four needs described by Maslow are called Deficit Needs or D-needs. If you do not have enough of something, then it is said that you have a deficit, that is, you feel the need. But if you get all you need, you feel nothing at all. In other words they cease to be motivating.

Characteristics of Self-Actualised People (Maslow)

Maslow has pointed out that only 10 per cent of the population really becomes self-actualised. He has listed some important characteristics of self-actualised persons. These are:

(i) These people fully understand their self and they lack defensiveness and self-defeating guilt.

(ii) They have efficient perception of reality and they also have freedom from different kinds of prejudice and bias which ordinarily tend to distort reality.

(iii) These individuals are not artificial nor conventional. Therefore, they have the traits of spontaneity, simplicity and naturality.

(iv) They have a stronger need for privacy and autonomy. They maintain proper detachment. They an be alone without being lonely. Such people depend more upon their own feelings for growth.

(v) The self-actualised people have a sense of continued freshness of appreciation. They are always aware of their good fortune, friends and health.

(vi) These people have more frequent peak experiences which means a feeling of complete perfection or ecstasy.

Criticism of Humanistic Psychology

Humanistic psychology has been criticised by many psychologists, particularly by behaviourists. Some of the major criticisms are:

(i) The learning theorist like Skinner has pointed out that humanistic psychology is subjective and dualistic in nature. The viewpoints of humanistic psychology often lack empirical validity. The findings and facts presented in different theories are based on the introspective self-reports which are highly unreliable.

(ii) Experts, very often, feel that humanistic psychologists have regressed psychology back to a vigorous religion. These theorists have tried to pull psychology back from the objective efforts of the experimental psychologists.

Despite these two drawbacks of humanistic psychologists, their contributions are definitely valuable. They have provided a significant theory by emphasising that human nature is basically good. They have opened possibilities for self-realisation. Most of their concepts are based on the fact that we are masters of our own fate and we are not merely a product of environmental forces.

Features of Self-Actualisers

(a) *Reality-centred:* They can differentiate who is fake and dishonest from the real and genuine.

(b) *Problem-centred:* They treat life's difficulties as problems demanding solutions, not as personal troubles to be railed at or surrendered to.

(c) They have a different perception of means and ends. They feel that the ends do not necessarily justify the means.

(d) They have different ways of relating to others. First, they enjoy solitude and are comfortable being alone. Then they enjoy deeper personal relations with a few close friends and family members, rather than shallow relationships with many people.

(e) They want to enjoy autonomy and relative independence from physical and social needs.

(f) These people resist acculturation, i.e., they are not susceptible to social pressure to be "well-adjusted" or "to fit in". In fact, they are non-conformists.

(g) They have an "unhostile sense of humour". These people prefer to joke at their own expense. They never direct their humour towards others.

(h) They always want to change their negative qualities.

(i) They posses qualities like spontaneity and simplicity. They do not like to be pretentious or artificial.

(j) They have a sense of humility and respect towards others – Maslow called it "democratic value".

(k) They are strong in their ethical behaviour.

(l) They have a quality called "human kinship", as Maslow called it, i.e., social interest, compassion and humanity.

(m) They are spiritual, but never conventionally religious in nature.

(n) They have a certain "freshness of appreciation", an ability to see ordinary things with wonder.

(o) They have the ability to be creative, inventive and original.

(p) They tend to have more peak experiences than the average person. A peak experience is one which takes you out of yourself, and makes you feel very tiny. It gives you a feeling of being a part of the infinite and the eternal. Basically, these are called mystical experiences and are an important part of many religious and philosophical traditions.

> **Flaws or Imperfections of Self-Actualised Persons**
>
> Maslow did not think that self-actualised persons were perfect. There are several flaws or imperfections he discovered in them. These are:
> (i) Self-actualised people often suffer from considerable anxiety and guilt.
> (ii) Some people are absent-minded and overly kind.
> (iii) Some individuals have unexpected moments of ruthlessness, surgical coldness and loss of humour.
> (iv) When a self-actualised person does not get his or her needs fulfilled, they respond with metapathologies, i.e., they respond with a list of problems.
> (v) When forced to live without the above values, the self-actualiser develops depression, despair, disgust, alienation and a degree of cynicism.

Can Humanistic Concepts be Studied or Experimented?

This is a big question for modern psychologists: whether research relating to humanistic concepts is possible or impossible.

At a first glance, we may think that like psychoanalytic concepts, these concepts and ideas may not be readily open to scientific tests. But the opposite is actually true. Several concepts which play a key role in humanistic theories have been studied quite extensively. The concept which has received most attention is the Roger's self-concept.

Different aspects of self-concept have been studied – for example, how our self-concept is formed, how it influences the way we think and what information it contains. Research findings also indicate that self-concept is a complex phenomenon and it consists of many different parts, like knowledge of our own traits and beliefs, understanding of how we are perceived by and relate to others and knowledge of how we are similar to and different from others. Many of the research were focused on whether our self-concept is influenced by our culture or not.

Results show that "self-concept" is greatly influenced by the cultures we belong. Part of our self-concept always reflects our culture. For example, Western people are called individualistic because they are known for self-expression and individual accomplishments. These people often express unrealistically optimistic self-evaluations. They think that they are better than they actually are. On the contrary, in Eastern cultures, people are collectivistic. They give priority to cooperation and social harmony. For this reason, people from such cultures do not express over-optimistic self-evaluations.

These findings indicate that Rogers and other humanistic psychologists were correct in assigning self-concept a significant role in personality development. Later psychologists paid serious attention to Rogers view and accordingly some experts engaged in research on his theory.

Humanistic Theories: An Evaluation

Humanistic theories have had a major impact on study of psychology. Later, many psychologists and experts did not lay emphasis on the "free will" concept developed by humanistic psychologists. They felt uncomfortable with some of the ideas developed by Rogers and Maslow. In addition, humanistic theories propose that individuals are responsible for their own actions and can change them if they wish to do so. This is true only to a certain extent and this idea conflicts with "determinism", the idea that our behaviour is a determined by numerous factors and can be predicted from them. The concept of determinism is basic assumption in many sciences. Psychologists cannot ignore it easily. In addition, many key concepts of humanistic theories are loosely defined. These concepts are self-actualisation, peak experience, fully functioning person, etc. Until these terms are clearly defined, it is very difficult to conduct systematic research on them. Despite all these drawbacks and criticisms, the impact of humanistic theories have had a lasting contribution to our understanding of human personality.

Social Cognitive View of Personality

Social cognitive theory is basically a social learning theory. It is based on the ideas that people learn by watching what others do. This view was first developed by Albert Bandura (1989). According to this view, behaviour is governed not by the influence of external stimuli and response patterns but also by cognitive processes such as anticipating, judging and memory, as well as learning through the imitation of models. Social cognitive theorists believe that there is a fair amount of influence on development generated by learned behaviour as a result of interaction with the environment in which one grows up and the individual person is just as important as environment in determining moral development. On the whole, social cognitive theory explains behaviour in terms of a continuous reciprocal interaction between cognitive, behavioural and environmental determinants.

This theory emphasises that people learn by observing others. Three factors are responsible for the development of personality: interaction with the environment, behaviour of others and one's own cognition. These three factors are not static or independent, rather they are reciprocal.

The main tenets of social cognitive theory are :

(a) People learn by observing others. This process known as "vicarious learning". As we know, learning modifies our behaviour. But this is not always true. People do not always apply what they have learned.

(b) Individuals are more likely to follow the behaviours modelled by someone with whom they can identify. When the emotional attachments between the observer and the model are more, there is every possibility that the observer will learn from the model.

(c) The degree of self-efficacy that a learner possesses directly affects his or her ability to learn. Self-efficacy is a fundamental belief in one's ability to achieve a goal. If an individual believes that he or she can learn new behaviours, that would make the person much more successful in doing so.

Albert Bandura's Social Learning Theory

Albert Bandura was born on 4 December 1925 in Northern Alberta, Canada. He received his PhD from the University of Iowa. Bandura has presented his theory in a series of books. In his book *Adolescent Aggression*, social learning principles were used to describe personality development. This was followed by a another book *Social Learning and Personality Development* (1963).

According to Bandura, human behaviour is largely acquired and the principles of learning are sufficient to account for the development and maintenance of behaviour. Bandura has done a great deal of work on social learning throughout his career. He is famous for his "Social Learning Theory" which he renamed as "Social Cognitive Theory". He is seen by many experts as a cognitive psychologist. His focus on cognition differentiates him from Skinner's behaviouristic viewpoint. Bandura's theory of social learning can be explained under three headings: Reciprocal Determinism, Self System and Principles of Observational learning.

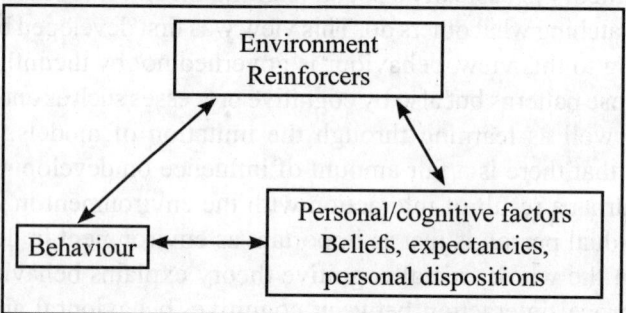

Fig. 3.6: Reciprocal Determinism

(a) *Reciprocal Determinism*: Our behaviour is explained, very often, by one-sided determinism. It is depicted as being shaped and controlled either by environmental influences or by internal dispositions. Social cognitive theory favours a model of causation involving triadic reciprocal determinism. Reciprocal causation does not mean that different sources of influence are of equal strength – some may stronger than others. Reciprocal influences do not occur simultaneously. It takes time for a causal factor to exert its influence and activate reciprocal influences.

Let us discuss the major interactional links between the different subsystems of influence.

The P–B of reciprocal causation reflects the interaction between thought, effect and action. Explanations, beliefs, self-perceptions, goals and intentions provide shape and direction to behaviour. What people think, believe and feel affects how they behave (Bandura, 1986).

The E–P segment of reciprocal causation is concerned with the interactive relation between personal characteristics (P) and environmental influences

(E). Our expectations, beliefs, emotional bents and cognitive competencies are developed and modified by social influences.

The B–E segment of reciprocal causation in the triadic system represents the two-way influence between behaviour (B) and environment. In our daily life, behaviour changes environmental conditions and is changed by the very conditions it creates. Due to this bidirectionality of influence between behaviour and environmental circumstances, individuals are both the products and producers of their environment.

[In Bandura's model of reciprocal determinism, three factors influence behaviour: (i) the environment, which consists of physical surroundings and the potential for reinforcement; (ii) The person (personal/cognitive characteristics that have been rewarded in the past); and (iii) the behaviour itself, which may or may not be reinforced at this particular time and place.

In conclusion, we can say that a complete analysis of behaviour from reciprocal determinism requires consideration of all three sets of behaviour; cognitive, behavioural and environmental influence one another.

(b) *Self System*: From reciprocal determinism, it is evident that all three segments are mutually interactive. Now the question arises: Do they have a starting point?

Bandura answer's "Yes" and says that the starting point is "self-system". It is not a psychic agent that controls behaviour. Rather, self-system refers to cognitive structures which provide reference mechanisms to set functions for perception, evaluation and regulation of behaviour. The three components involved in self-system are self-observation, judgemental processes and self-response.

    (i) *Self-observation*: We look at ourselves and our behaviour, and keep tabs on it.

    (ii) *Judgement*: We compare what we see with a standard. We can compete with others or with ourselves.

(c) *Self-response*: If we do well in comparison with our standard, we give ourselves rewarding self-responses. If we do poorly, than we give ourselves punishing self-responses.

(d) *Self-efficacy*: Over the year, if we find ourselves meeting our standards and life loaded with self-praise and self-reward, we will have a strong sense of self-efficacy. On the other hand, if we find ourselves forever failing to meet our standards and punishing ourselves, we will have a poor sense of self-efficacy. Self-efficacy plays a significant role in the self-system of Bandura's theory.

Role of Self-Efficacy

Every individual in this world wants to achieve his or her goal. They make plans to achieve the goal. But everybody does not succeed. Most people realise that putting a plan into action is not so simple. Bandura (1995) has found that an individual's self-efficacy plays a significant role in how goals, tasks and challenges are approached.

Every individual in this world wants to achieve his or her goal. They make plans to achieve the goal. But everybody does not succeed. Most people realise that putting a plan into action is not so simple. Bandura (1995) has found that an individual's self-efficacy plays a significant role in how goals, tasks and challenges are approached.

People with a strong sense of self-efficacy have the following characteristics:

(i) They view challenging problems as tasks to be mastered.
(ii) They develop deeper interest in the activities in which they participate.
(iii) They form a stronger sense of commitment to their interests and activities.
(iv) They recover quickly from setbacks and disappointments.

People with weak sense of self-efficacy show the following characteristics:

(i) They always avoid challenging tasks.
(ii) They believe that difficult tasks and situations are beyond their capabilities.
(iii) They focus on personal failings and negative outcomes.
(iv) They quickly lose confidence in personal abilities (Bandura, 1995).

Sources of Self-Efficacy

How does self-efficacy develop? It begins from early childhood as children deal with a variety of experiences, tasks and situations. According to Bandura, the growth of self-efficacy does not end in youth but continues to evolve throughout life as people acquire new skills, experiences and understanding.

In his theory, Bandura says that there are four major sources of self-efficacy:

(i) *Mastery Experiences*: An effective way for developing self-efficacy is through mastery experiences. Performing a task successfully strengthens our senses of self-efficacy. On the other hand, failing to deal the task adequately can undermine and weaken self-efficacy.

(ii) *Social Modelling*: Completing a task successfully and witnessing other people who completed their tasks successfully and aptly is another source of self-efficacy. Bandura says that when an individual sees another person or persons similar to himself or herself succeeding by their sustained efforts, it makes the person believe that he or she, too, possess capabilities which could help to perform comparable activities and succeed.

(iii) *Social Persuasion*: Sometimes individuals can be persuaded that they have skills and capabilities to succeed. Very often, we are encouraged by others to achieve a goal. Verbal encouragement may have some positive effects for developing self-efficacy.

(iv) *Psychological Responses*: The individual's own emotional reactions and own responses also play a significant role in developing self-efficacy. Physical reactions, moods, emotional status and stress levels have an impact on how an individual feels about his or her personal abilities in a particular situation. For example, a person may get nervous before speaking in public due to weak self-efficacy.

Principles of Observational Learning

Bandura's theory states that cognitive factors are central to human functioning and learning can occur in the absence of direct reinforcement. In other words, learning can occur simply through observation. According to him, the laws of reinforcement and punishment are more relevant to performance then to acquisition. Learning can occur outside the boundaries of pleasure and pain. This learning may or may not be demonstrated in the form of behaviour. Bandura called this phenomenon as observational learning or modelling and his theory is usually called Social Learning Theory.

In this theory, Bandura says that for learning, first we need to pay attention. The ability to store information is also an important part of the learning process. Once we have paid attention to the model and retained the information, it is time to actually perform the behaviour we observed. Further, unless we are motivated to imitate, the learning is not complete. We must have some reasons for doing it. Reinforcement and punishment play an important role in motivation.

Bandura's Theory

- *Self-efficacy:* The individual's confidence in performing a particular behaviour and his expectations concerning their ability to perform various tasks.
- *Vicarious learning:* It is the process of learning from observing the people's behaviour.
- *Self-system:* In Bandura's social cognitive theory, the set of cognitive processes by which a person perceives, evaluates and regulates his or her own behaviour.
- *Self-reinforcement:* A process in which individuals reward themselves for reaching their own goals.

Vicarious Learning

Vicarious learning is closely related to observational learning. It is another distinctive feature of Bandura's theory. Vicarious learning is otherwise known as the process of learning from other people's behaviour. It is the central idea of the social cognitive theory.

This concept of vicarious learning states that individuals can witness observed behaviours of others and then reproduce the same actions. People avoid making mistakes and can perform better if they see individuals complete actions successfully. People have evolved an advanced capacity for observational learning that enables them to expand their knowledge and skills on the basis of information conveyed by modelling influences.

All learning phenomena resulting from direct experience can occur vicariously by observing people's behaviour and its consequences from them (Bandura, 1986). However, much of social learning occurs either deliberately or inadvertently by observing the actual behaviour of others. Learning by doing requires altering the actions of each individual through repeated trial-and-error experiences. But in observational learning, a single model can transmit new ways of thinking and behaving simultaneously. Another aspect of symbolic modelling magnifies its psychological and social effects, though in our daily lives, we have direct contact with only a small part of the environment. Thus conceptions of social reality are greatly influenced by vicarious learning.

Summary of Bandura's Social Cognitive Theory

Let us sum up Bandura's concepts and ideas:

(i) Social cognitive theory developed by Bandura is based on the idea that individuals learn by watching what others do and that human thought processes are central to understanding personality.

(ii) This theory explains behaviour in terms of a continuous reciprocal interaction between cognitive, behavioural and environmental determinants.

(iii) It identifies human behaviour as an interaction of personal factors, behaviour and environment.

(iv) The starting point of all these three factors is the self-system. A self-system is not a psychic agent which controls behaviour. It refers to cognitive structures that provide reference mechanisms to a set of functions for perception, evaluation and regulation of behaviour.

(v) The three components involved in self-system are self-observation, judgement and self-response.

(vi) Self-efficacy is another important concept in Bandura's theory. Self-efficacy is the belief in one's capabilities to organise and execute the courses of action required to manage prospective situations.

Social Cognitive Theory: A Modern View of Personality

- *In social cognitive theoery, Bandura placed emphasis on self-system – the cognitive processes by which an individual perceives, evaluates and regulates his or her own behaviour.*
- *People do not respond to reinforcements, rather they think about consequences of their actions.*
- *People engage in self-reinforcement when they attain goals.*
- *He emphasised on "observational learning", a form of learning in which individuals acquire both information and new forms of behaviour.*
- *Another concept is self-efficacy, which received much attention reveals about an individual's belief that he or she can perform a given task successfully.*

(vii) There are four major sources of self-efficacy (a) Mastery experiences (b) Social modelling (c) Social persuasion and (d) Psychological responses.

(viii) Bandura's social cognitive theory is different from traditional theories in the sense that cognitive factors are central to human functioning and that learning can occur in the absence of direct reinforcement. In other words, learning can occur directly by observation in the absence of reinforcement.

(ix) Through modelling, people learn the value of a particular behaviour with regard to goal achievement or outcomes.

(x) Bandura proposed a four step conceptual scheme of the processes involved in observational learning. These are:

    (a) The first step is the attention processes which are involved, including certain model characteristics which may increase the likelihood of behaviour being attended to. It also includes sensory capacities, motivation and arousal levels, perceptual set and past reinforcement.

    (b) The second step refers to retention processes including the observer's ability to encode, to remember and to make sense of what has been observed.

    (c) The third step refers to motor reproduction processes, including the capabilities that the observer has, to perform the behaviour being observed. Specific factors include physical capabilities and availability of responses.

    (d) The final step refers to motivational processes including external reinforcement, vicarious reinforcement and self-reinforcement. Motivation is primarily required for imitation.

(xi) Vicarious learning, the process of learning from other people's behaviour, is the central idea of the social cognitive theory developed by Bandura. This idea states that individuals can witness observed behaviour of others and then reproduce the same actions. Thus people can avoid making mistakes and perform behaviours better if they see individuals complete them successfully.

(xii) Vicarious learning is a part of social modelling which is one of the four means to increase self-efficacy. However, social modelling refers not just observing behaviour, but also receiving instruction and guidance of how to complete the behaviour.

Evaluation of Bandura's Theory

Unlike traditional behaviourism, the social cognitive theory developed by Bandura included mental processes and their influences on behaviour. The early behaviourist theories ignored the cognitive factors in human behaviour, but these were included in the modern theories. Bandura's social cognitive approach has been demonstrated to make powerful predictions and has generated useful applications in a large number of areas of human behaviour. Unlike psychoanalysis, the concepts in this theory can and have been tested under scientific conditions (Skinner, 1989).

The terms used by Bandura are very clearly defined. So they lend themselves well to empirical research. Probably the most significant contribution of social cognitive theory is its applied value.

In spite of all the merit in Bandura's cognitive theory, there are some limitations, too. These are:

(i) Behaviour has been found to be more consistent than it represented by Bandura's theory, which focuses on the situation. The theory lacks attention to biological and hormonal processes.

(ii) Some researchers argue that this theory is not unified. Concepts and processes like observational learning and self-efficiency have been highly researched, but there has been little explanation about the relationship among all these concepts.

(iii) Bandura's theory ignores inner conflicts and the influence of unconscious thoughts and impulses on behaviour.

As we can readily see, these are not major criticisms. Social cognitive theories of personality are more in tune with the eclectic sophisticated approach of modern psychology than the earlier theories. Learning approaches are certain to play a significant role in continuing efforts to understand the uniqueness and actions of human behaviour.

Trait Theories of Personality: Seeking the Key Dimensions of Personality

Trait theories are less concerned with the explanation of personality development and changing personality than they are with describing personality and predicting behaviour based on that description. Trait theories include Allport, Cattell, Eysenk and the Big-5 factor model.

According to Allport, the basic principles of behaviour is its continuous flow. Allport's major personality concepts have to do with motivation, i.e., what makes an individual "go". An individual's "stream of activity" has both a variable portion and a constant portion. The constant portion is the trait, the variable portion, according to Allport, is called the "functional autonomy" or the tendency for a behaviour to continue to be performed for reasons that differ from the reasons that originally motivated it. Both trait and functional autonomy are motivational. Many traits have motive power and functional autonomy explains adult motivation. Basing on traits and functional autonomy, Allport talks about "dynamics of personality'.

Cattle's theory explains the complicated transactions between the personality system and the more inclusive socio-cultural matrix of the functioning organism. Eysenk's theory is called both a Type and Trait theory. Type theories are discontinuous, whereas the trait theories are in a continuum. According to Eysenk, the goal of psychology is to predict behaviour. The Big-5 model states that there may be only five key or central dimensions of personality.

Theories of Personality

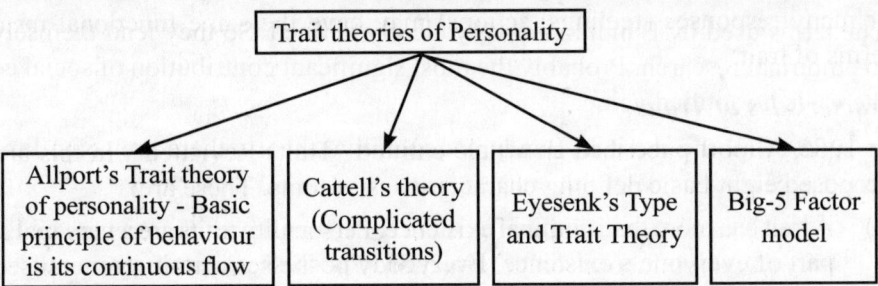

Fig. 3.7: Gordon Allport: A Dispositional Theory of Personality

Allport's Definition of Personality

"Personality is the dynamic organisation within the individual of those psychophysical systems that determine his unique adjustment to his environment" (Allport, 1937).

This definition of personality was widely accepted by later psychologists. We will analyse the components of his definition in detail.

The term "dynamic organisation" denotes that not only is personality constantly developing and changing, but there is within the person some kind of central organisation that holds the components of personality together and relates them to one another. However, personality is dynamic or changeable, it is not constant or static.

The term "psychophysical systems" implies that the individual is not just a hypothetical constant formed by the observer, but a real phenomenon, composed of mind and body elements fused into a personality unity (Allport, 1937).

According to Allport, every person in this world is unique. No two people are the same. Personality expresses itself in some way in virtually all observable human actions. While defining personality, Allport clearly makes a distinction between character and temperament. According to him, character means some code of behaviour in terms of which people or their acts are evaluated, for example, a person may be described having a "good" or a "bad" character. Temperament refers to those dispositions that are closely linked to biological or physiological determinants. Heredity plays an important role in personality development. It is the raw material. Personality is made along with physique and intelligence.

Concept of Trait and Personal Disposition

Allport defines trait as a neurophysic structure having the capacity to render many stimuli functionally equivalent and to initiate and guide equivalent (meaningfully consistent) forms of adaptive and expressive behaviour (Allport, 1961).

Trait is a predisposition to act in the same way in a wide range of situations. If an individual is shy, he or she will tend to be quiet and reserved in many different situations, i.e., sitting in a class-room or eating in a restaurant, etc. Traits are psychological entities which render many stimuli as well as many responses functionally equivalent. In other words, many stimuli may evoke the same response or many responses (feelings, actions) may have the same functional meaning in terms of trait.

Characteristics of Traits

In 1966, Allport published an article entitled "Traits Revisited". In this article, he proposed eight basic defining characteristics of traits. These are:

(i) A trait has more than nominal existence: Personality traits are a very real and vital part of everyone's existence. Everybody possesses certain "generalised action tendencies" (like honesty, aggressiveness, etc.). These personal characteristics are real and actually exist in people. For example, an individual may like to tell the truth even at the cost of losing his best friend.

(ii) A trait is more generalised than a habit: Traits account for the relatively permanent and general features of our behaviour. But habits refer to more specific tendencies and are less generalised in terms of situations which may arouse them or the responses which they may evoke. Brushing the teeth twice a day is a habit for a child. But learning to brush the hair, iron clothes, cleaning the room are traits, not habits. This is learned over a period of time. All these habits woven together may form the trait of personal cleanliness.

(iii) A trait is dynamic or at least determinative in behaviour: Traits are not dormant, waiting to be aroused by external stimuli. Traits motivate people to engage in behaviours which are conducive to express their traits. For example, a gregarious person can not sit idle at a party. He or she tries to prove themselves sociable, so that their sociability trait can be expressed. So traits guide and direct an individual's actions.

(iv) The existence of a trait may be established empirically: It is true that traits cannot be observed directly, but it is possible to verify their existence. We can verify them through the repeated actions of the individual or by collecting case histories or through biographies. We can also use some statistical techniques which determine the degree of coherence among separate responses.

(v) A trait is only relatively independent of other traits: No trait is independent of all the others. They overlap. There is no strict boundary separating one trait from another. The personality consists of a network of overlapping traits, which are only relatively independent of one another.

(vi) A trait is not synonymous with moral or social judgement: Character is not important. But personality is important. Many traits like loyalty or greed are bound by social demands and socio-cultural factors.

(vii) A trait may be viewed in light of either the personality that contains it or its distribution in the population at large: Let us consider an example to clarify this. Suppose "shyness" is a trait. It is both unique and universal. It is unique for an individual because it influences an individual's life; as a trait, it can be studied universally by constructing a reliable and valid "shyness scale" and determining how people score on it.

(viii) Acts or even habits that are inconsistent with a trait are not proof of the non-existence of the trait: Everybody, in this world, does not show the same degree of integration with respect to a given trait. The same person may possess contradictory traits. In some cases, social situations rather than personality traits are the prime movers of behaviour.

Types of Traits

According to Allport, traits are determining tendencies or predispositions to respond consistently over time and across situations. He said that traits may be classified into a three and somewhat overlapping category system according to the degree to which they pervade and influence individual behaviour.

(i) Cardinal Trait: A cardinal trait is extremely pervasive. If almost all of an individual's activities can be traced to its influence, then it is a cardinal trait. The meaning may be grasped by considering many trait activities derived from historical and fictional characters. For example, when somebody is being referred to as being Gandhian, the cardinal disposition of being "non-violent" is inferred.

(ii) Central Trait: According to Allport, central traits are less pervasive but are still quite a generalised disposition of the individual. These are popularly called the building blocks of personality. Central traits are those tendencies that a person often expresses, which people around the person can readily discern. For example, a person may be outgoing or social.

(iii) Secondary Trait: Secondary traits are dispositions which are less conspicuous, less generalised, less consistent and less relevant as compared to cardinal or central traits, for example, the food preferences of an individual. To learn about the secondary traits of a person, the person must be known quite intimately in order to discern the secondary traits.

Common Traits versus Individual Traits

Allport has also distinguished between common traits and individual traits. Common traits are otherwise known as dimensional or nomothetic traits. They include any generalised disposition to which most people within a given culture can be reasonably compared. For example, social attitude, anxiety and values are generalised disposition and the majority of people within the particular culture could be measured and compared with one another on the common traits and dimensions.

Traits never occur in any two people in exactly the same manner. The characteristics which are peculiar to the individual and do not permit comparisons among them are referred to as "individual traits".

Individual traits are otherwise known as "personal dispositions" or "morphological traits". These traits operate in unique ways with each person. This category of traits pinpoints the personality structure of any given individual most accurately, that is, describes the organised focus of his or her life. The true personality of the individual comes out after the examination of individual traits, which can be obtained from the individual's case history, letters, diary and other such documents.

The Proprium: Development of Selfhood

Human beings are motivated by the tendency which satisfies their biological survival needs. This tendency is referred to as opportunistic functioning. This opportunistic functioning can be characterised as reactive, past-oriented and biological (Allport, 1939).

Allport also said that opportunistic functioning was relatively unimportant for understanding most of human behaviour. Most of the behaviour of individuals is motivated by something very different. This different aspect is one which help to express a person's "unique self". This type of something motivating the functioning of a person in terms of expressing the self was termed by Allport as "propriate functioning".

Most individuals think about what they do in their lifetime and who they actually are. Propriate functioning can be characterised as proactive, future-oriented and psychological.

The word "propriate" came from the very word "proprium", which stands for "self", according to Allport. He reviewed hundreds definitions of 'proprium', but found that "self" was appropriate and more scientific. However, "self" continues to be used to represent the individual's unique features that motivate the behaviour of the individual. Doing things in keeping with what we really are, denotes "propriate functioning".

In his theory, Allport put emphasis on proprium or self. He considered proprium from two basic viewpoints: (i) phenomenological and (ii) Functional. Here, phenomenological means the self is considered in terms of what it experiences. He proposed that self has seven functions: (i) Sense of body (ii) Self-identity (iii) Self-esteem (iv) Self-extension (v) Self-image (vi) Rational coping and (vii) Propriate striving.

The propriate functions of personality in order of their sequential appearance in the developing individual are given in Table 3.1:

Table 3.1: Developmental Stages of Proprium by Allport

Stage	Aspects of Personality	Definition
1 (one)	Sense of Bodily self	Awareness of bodily sensations: first aspect of proprium evolves during the first year of life. These recurrent sensations constitute the bodily self.
2 (two)	Sense of identity	Continuity of self occurs despite changes taking place. This second aspect of proprium evolves through language. The child recognises himself or herself as distinct from others.

3 (three)	Sense of self-esteem	It depicts about pride in one's accomplishments. During the third year of life, the child becomes proud of what he or she does and receives praise or reward.
4 (four)	Sense of self-extension	During 4 to 6 years, self includes relevant aspects of social and physical environment. Children learn the meaning of "mine", feel about environmental contributions.
5 (five)	Self-image	The individual's aspirations begins to reflect the goals and expectations. The child's self-image comes at around five years. The child realises what is expected from him or her.
6 (six)	Sense of self as a rational person	This comes between 6 to 12 years of age. Everyday problems are solved by abstract reasoning and logic. Reflective and formal thinking also appears.
7 (seven)	Propriate striving	This comes during adolescence and adulthood. All aspects of self are consolidated. Individuals plan for long range goals. Allport believed that the core problem of an adolescent is the selection of career and other life goals. Pursuing long range goals and imparting a sense of purpose to life are part of propriate striving.

- *Self-esteem*: The favourableness of a person's self-image.
- *Self-image*: The diversity of roles a person plays in order to gain the approval of others and to manage their impressions of who and what the person is.
- *Proprium*: All aspects of a person that make him or her unique. It represents creative, forward moving and positive quality of human nature.

Functional Autonomy

Allport did not believe in looking too much into an individual's past in order to understand the present. This belief is strongly evident in "functional autonomy". This concept reveals that the motives for a certain behaviour today are independent (autonomous) of their origins. This idea of functional autonomy of motives provides the necessary base for a "theory of motivation". For example, an individual might have developed a taste for pizzas due to some reasons. But the past reasons are not important. What is important is that the person likes to eat pizzas now and that it matters.

Functional motives indicate that adult motives are not related to the past. The past is past, it is over. In other words, the reasons why an adult now engages in some behaviour are independent of whatever reasons that might have originally caused him or her to engage in that behaviour.

Types of Functional Autonomy

Two types of functional autonomy were depicted by Allport (1961): (i) Preservative functional autonomy and (ii) Propriate functional autonomy.

The "preservative functional autonomy" is about the repetitious activities in our daily lives. It refers to feedback mechanisms in the nervous system which are governed by simple neurological principles. These mechanisms become neurologically self-maintaining over time and help to keep the organism on track. For example, an individual is habituated to eat and go to bed at a particular time every day.

The second type of functional autonomy is called "propriate functional autonomy". It refers to the acquired interests, values, attitudes and intentions of an individual. It is the master system of motivation. This autonomy imparts consistency to the individual's personality for a congruent self image. It represents striving for values and goals, and the sense of responsibility an individual has for his life.

The Mature Personality

In his theory, Allport said that the emergence of personal maturity is a continuous and lifelong process. The behaviour of a mature person is functionally autonomous and is motivated by a conscious process. On the other hand, the behaviour of an immature person is dominated by unconscious motives stemming from childhood experiences.

Allport said that psychologically mature adults are characterised by six attributes. These are:

(i) They have a widely extended sense of self.
(ii) They have a capacity for warm social interactions.
(iii) They demonstrate emotional security and self-acceptance.
(iv) They demonstrate realistic perception, skills and assignments.
(v) They demonstrate self-insight and humour.
(vi) They have a unifying philosophy of life.

All these attributes are described in the following paragraph:

Mature persons have a widely extended sense of self. They can get themselves "outside". These persons can actively participate in work, family, hobbies, social activities, etc. Secondly, a mature person has a capacity for warm social interactions. There are two kinds of interpersonal warmth – intimacy and compassion. The intimate aspect of warmth is seen in an individual's capacity to show deep love for family and close friends. Compassion is reflected in a person's ability to tolerate differences between the self and others. Thirdly, a mature person demonstrates emotional security and self-acceptance. Mature adults have a positive image of themselves. So they are able to tolerate frustrating and irritating events. Also they deal with emotions, depression, anger, guilt, etc. in such a way that they do not interfere with the well-being of others.

The mature person demonstrates realistic perceptions, skills and assignments. Healthy persons are in direct contact with the reality. They see things as they are not as wish them to be. They always possess appropriate skills and attitude for their work, setting aside there personal desires. Further, mature persons demonstrate self-insight and humour. They have an accurate picture of their own strengths and weaknesses. Humour is an important aspect in self-insight. Lastly, mature persons have a unifying philosophy of life. They have a clear, consistent and systematic way of seeing meaning in their lives.

Application: The Study of Values

According to Allport, the unifying philosophy of a mature person is founded upon values. These "values" denote basic convictions about what is and is not of real importance in life. The meaning of life is governed by values. In his theory, Allport identified and measured basic value dimensions.

Further, Allport tried to develop a personality test: "the study of value". His model is based on the work of Edward Spranger, a European psychologist.

In his book, Edward Spranger mentioned six major types of values. These values are found in varying degrees in all people. Allport said that people construct their lives around them (Allport, 1961). So no person falls exclusively under any one value category. Different value combinations are more or less present in the lives of different people.

Allport believed that these values are best described as deep level traits. They are described as:

(i) The Theoretical (ii) The Economic
(iii) The Aesthetic (iv) The Social
(v) The Political (vi) The Religious

(i) *The Theoretical*: Here the individual is primarily concerned with the discovery of "truth". Such an individual is characterised by a rational, critical and empirical approach to life. This individual is highly intellectual and has a career in philosophy or science.
(ii) The Economic: The economic individual places highest value on whatever is useful or pragmatic. Such an individual is highly "practical" and is keenly interested in making money.
(iii) The Aesthetic: This type of individual places highest value on form and harmony. Every single experience is given importance from the point of grace, symmetry or fitness.
(iv) The Social: This value centres around love towards people. These people love and would regard love as the only suitable form of relationship. Such people view the theoretical, economic and aesthetic attitudes as inhuman.
(v) The Political: "Power" is the main interest of these type of people. They give importance to personal power and influence and want to be renowned within a short span of time.
(vi) The Religious: These individuals are mainly concerned with understanding the world as a "unified whole".

Allport assessed the individual differences in the relative strength of these six values. His study used values scale for this purpose. The test was developed and standardised taking college students as subjects. The test consists of 45 questions and requires 20 minutes to complete. The average scores on these six values differ in the expected directions for different occupational groups. For example, business students scored poorly on aesthetic value and theology students scored poorly on religious value (Allport, 1960). So the test shows that values are an essential part of an individual personality. Allport believed this conclusion.

In summary, Allport provided an explanation of an individual's uniqueness. According to him, personality is the dynamic organisation of those internal psychophysical systems which determine a person's characteristic behaviour and thoughts. He said that trait is the most significant unit of analysis for understanding behaviour. An individual's behavioural consistency over time and across situations is called trait. Traits may be classified as cardinal, central and secondary, according to the degree of pervasiveness within a personality. However, the overall construct that unifies traits and provides direction for the individual's life is termed as the "proprium" or "self". It contributes to an inward sense of unity. The principle of "functional autonomy" reveals that adult motives are not related to the earlier experiences in which they originally originated. There are two types of functional autonomies: preservative functional autonomy and propriate functional autonomy.

Raymond Cattell's Trait Theory of Personality

Raymond Cattell (1905–1998) was educated in Britain and obtained his PhD from the University of London. He came to the US to work with E.L. Thorndike and developed selection methods for officers. Later, he established the Institute for Personality and Ability Testing. He taught at University of Illinois for 30 years and went to Hawaii in 1978. He was teaching at Hawaii until his death in 1998.

Cattell has pointed out that the observations of clinicians had no scientific basis for understanding and classifying personality. He tried to use inductive method of scientific enquiry to develop his theory of personality. He used factor analysis after gathering a large amount of data and looked for clusters within this data.

For Cattell, personality is a prediction of what a person will do in a given situation. The underlying basic factors of a person's personality was termed by him as source traits. To know about source traits, he collected life records, self reports and answers from questionnaires from different people.

Cattell has identified 35 primary traits of which 23 characterised normal individuals and 12 characterised abnormal individuals. A scale called 16 PF was designed to assess 16 different sources associated with normal behaviour.

Further, he distinguished two types of intelligence: Fluid intelligence and Crystallised intelligence.

Fluid intelligence allows the persons to learn new things regardless of past experience, whereas the crystallised intelligence is the ability to solve problems based upon previous experience. Cattell believed that intelligence is an inherited trait. He said that personality is considered in terms of not only traits, but also other variables, including attitudes. He defined attitude as the desire to act in a specific way in response to a specific situation. According to Cattell, environmental factors are considered essential to determine personality and behaviour. "Ergs" are goals created because of hunger, thirst, etc. A person is motivated to get food when he or she is hungry. Those are called ergs.

According to Cattell, socially created goals are called "socially shaped ergs". In his theory, Cattell termed it is "socially shaped ergic manifolds" or SEM. He used SEM to explain the contribution of environment to human behaviour. SEMs are socially acquired and they can satisfy several ergs at one time. Since these are socially acquired, they vary in number and type, by culture.

16 Source Traits which Constitute the Underlying Structure of Personality			
(a)	Warmth	(i)	Vigilance
(b)	Reasoning	(j)	Abstractness
(c)	Emotional Stability	(k)	Privateness
(d)	Dominance	(l)	Apprehension
(e)	Liveliness	(m)	Openness to Change
(f)	Rule Consciousness	(n)	Self-reliance
(g)	Social Boldness	(o)	Perfectionism
(h)	Sensitivity	(p)	Tension

Human beings are innately driven by ergs, which are goals created by curiosity, anger, hunger, fear and many other basic motives. Cattell developed a list of ergs by research. These include food-seeking, mating, gregariousness, parental protectiveness, exploration, safety, self-assertion, pugnacity, narcissistic sex and acquisitiveness.

In his theory, Cattell said that traits are genetically and environmentally determined and the ways in which genetic and environmental factors interact decide the behaviour of the individual. His trait theory of personality tries to explain the interaction between the genetic and personality systems and the socio-cultural milieu within which human beings are functioning. Cattell opined that an appropriate theory of personality must take multiple traits into account, which comprise the personality. He studied personality through multivariate statistics and factor analysis.

Formula for Personality

Cattell (1965) said that personality permits us to predict what a person will do in a given situation. With the help of mathematical analysis of personality, he said that prediction of behaviour can be made by a "specification equation". The formula used by Cattell to predict behaviour with any degree of accuracy is:

$$R = f(S, P)$$

where, R refers to the nature of an individual's specific response, f refers to the unspecified function, S refers to the stimulus situation at a given moment in time and

P refers to the personality structure. Cattell also accepted that it is difficult to predict a person's behaviour in a given situation. The personality theorists must consider not only what traits an individual possesses but also the many non-trait variables such as the person's moods and particular social roles called for the situation and related aspects in order to increase predictive accuracy. However, it is also essential to weigh each trait according to its relevance to the situation in question.

Cattell used factor analysis to investigate structural elements of personality. He said that behaviour is determined by interaction of traits and situational variables. His major organising concept of personality is in his descriptions of the different kinds of traits he has identified. According to him, traits are relatively permanent and pervasive tendencies to respond with consistency from one situation to another and from one time to another.

Categories of Traits

In his theory, Cattell mentioned that traits can be classified in several ways, such as: (i) Surface Traits (ii) Source Traits (iii) Constitutional Traits, (iv) Environmental Mold Traits (v) Ability traits (vi) Temperament (vii) Dynamic Traits (viii) Common Traits (ix) Unique Traits.

Let us take up all these traits in brief and see how they function:

(a) *Surface vs Source Traits*: A surface trait is a set of behavioural characteristics that all seem to "hang" together. For example, there are some characteristics which are observable in human beings. These may be inability to concentrate, restlessness, indecisiveness, etc., which may cluster together to form the surface trait of neuroticism.

Here, the trait of neuroticism is observed by a cluster of overt elements which seem to go together. It does not derive from any single factor or element. Surface traits do not have a unitary basis and are not consistent overtime. Hence, they are not given much value for behavioural accountability.

"Source traits" are the basic, underlying structures which constitute the building blocks of personality. They exist at a deeper level of personality and these traits are the causes of behaviour in diverse domains over an extended period of time.

There are approximately 16 source traits. On these basis, 16 PF (Sixteen personality factor) questionnaire was designed by Cattell. It is a self-report scale which has proved to be quite useful and popular in both applied and research settings.

(b) *Role of Heredity and Environment in Personality Development*: In his personality theory, Cattell tried to determine the relative contributions of heredity and environment to personality traits. He devised a statistical technique for this purpose which is popularly known as "Multiple Abstract Variance Analysis" (MAVA). This particular test estimates not only the presence or absence of genetic influence, but also the degree to which traits are due to genetic or environmental influences. Results from MAVA technique suggest that the importance of genetic and environmental influences varies widely from trait to trait.

(c) *Constitutional vs Environmental–Mold Traits*: Source traits can be divided into two types, depending upon their origin:

(i) Constitutional traits and (ii) Environmental–mold traits.

Constitutional traits derive from the biological and physiological conditions of an individual. For example, recovery from alcohol addiction may cause in individual to be momentarily irritable, depressed and anxious. Cattell argued that these behaviours result from changes in the person's physiology and thus reflect constitutional source traits.

Environmental–mold traits are determined by influences in the social and physical environment. These traits reflect acquired characteristics and styles of behaving. They form a pattern that is imprinted on the personality by the individual's environment. For this reason, an individual who is raised in a rural setting behaves differently from another individual who grows up in an urban area.

(d) *Ability, Temperament and Dynamic Traits*: According to Cattell, source traits can be further classified in terms of the modality through which they are expressed. These traits are: Ability traits, Temperament traits and Dynamic traits.

Ability traits determines the person's skill and effectiveness in pursuing a desired goal, for example, intelligence, musical aptitude, etc. Temperament traits refer to stylistic and emotional qualities of behaviour. For example, people may either work slowly or quickly on a task. In his theory, Cattell considers temperament traits with constitutional source traits which determine an individual's emotionality. Dynamic traits reflect the motivational elements of human behaviour. With these traits, people are activated and directed towards goals. For this reason, an individual may be characterised as ambitious, power-oriented or interested in acquiring material possessions.

(e) *Common Versus Unique Traits*: According to Cattell, a common trait is one which is shared in varying degrees by all members of the same culture. Examples are self-esteem, introversion, intelligence, etc.

Unique traits are shared by few or no other people. These traits are specially observed in the areas of interests and attitudes.

In summary, we can say that Cattell's theory of personality permits us to predict what a person will do in a given situation, as expressed in the equation $R = f(S, P)$. Traits are hypothetical constructs which predispose the person to behave consistently across circumstances and time.

According to Cattell, the essence of personality structure consists of approximately 16 source trait factors. Source traits can be divided into constitutional or environmental–mold traits. His additional trait classification includes ability, temperament and dynamic traits. In his theory, a clear distinction between common and unique traits are crystal clear.

Cattell used three types of data to identify source traits: Life record (L-Data), Self-rating questionnaire (Q-Data) and Objective tests (OT-Data). The 16 personality factor questionnaire (16 PF) was devised by Cattell to measure source traits using self-reported data. He also developed a statistical tool called multiple abstract variance analysis to estimate the relative contributions of heredity and environment to a given trait. He estimated that one-third of personality is determined by genetics and two-thirds by environmental influences.

Hans Eysenck's Trait-Type Theory of Personality

Type theories are slightly different from trait theories. While type theories are discontinuous, the trait theories are in a continuum. Eysenck believed that the goal of psychology is to predict behaviour. It was similar to Cattell's view. Eysenck suggested that not more than three super traits (which are also called types) are needed to account for most of human behaviour (Cattell mentioned at least 16 traits, or 16 PF, of personality).

> - *Hans Jurgen Eysenck (1916–1997) was a British psychologist. He was best known for his theory of human personality. In his personality theory, he suggested that personality is biologically determined and is arranged in a hierarchy consisting of types, traits, habitual responses and specific responses. He considered Freudian psychoanalysis as unscientific. According to him, personality can be studied from either temperamental or cognitive aspects (or both). He focused on the temperament aspect of personality in his PEN model. At the top of the hierarchy are super factors or dimensions of personality such as extraversion (E), neuroticism (N) and psychoticism (P).*

In his theory Eysenck places more emphasis on genetic factors in personality development than does Cattell. But he did not neglect the environmental factors or situational influences.

Eysenck (1916–1997) studied personality from either temperamental or cognitive aspects (or both). Primarily, he focused on the temperament aspect of personality in his PEN (Psychoticism, Extraversion and Neuroticism) model. For better understanding of the PEN model, we should begin with our evaluation of Eysenck's theory with the description or taxonomy of personality or temperament.

Hierarchical Taxonomy

In his theory, Eysenck stated that personality can be studied from either temperamental or cognitive aspects or both. He focused on the temperament aspect of personality in his PEN (Psychoticism, Extraversion and Neuroticism) model. Eysenck stated that in any science "taxonomy precedes causal analysis". By taxonomy (classification), people can be classified into groups. This grouping is based on characters and their relationships.

Eysenck described in plain terms how taxonomy in the study of personality can be achieved using the correlational technique called factor analysis. Since in personality study, the traits of human beings are taken into account, we can safely look at the traits (or people) having the highest factor loadings in order to better identify the trait clusters. According to Eysenck, individual differences in personality or temperament are analysed in terms of traits, which can be defined as theoretical constructs based on covariation of a number of behavioural acts. He states that traits themselves inter correlate and make up higher-order factors or super factors called "types".

Consequently, the PEN model proposes a hierarchical classification of personality containing four levels. At the bottom level of this hierarchy are behaviours such as talking with a friend on a single occasion. At the second level are habits such as talking with friends on multiple occasions, which consist of recurring behaviours. Sociability constitutes the third level of hierarchy. At the top level of hierarchy are super factors or dimensions of personality such as extraversion, which are inter correlated sets of traits or factors. The PEN model is based on the principle of "aggregation".

When there are many items, then higher reliability is found (Eysenck, 1990). Each super factor in the PEN model consists of many different factors, habits and behaviours, so reliability is increased. The super factors like extraversion, neuroticism and psychoticism are somehow stable, whereas behaviours such as talking with a friend on a single occasion at the bottom of the hierarchy are changeable across time and situation.

Let us look at the distinction between levels for the analysis of personality in the PEN model.

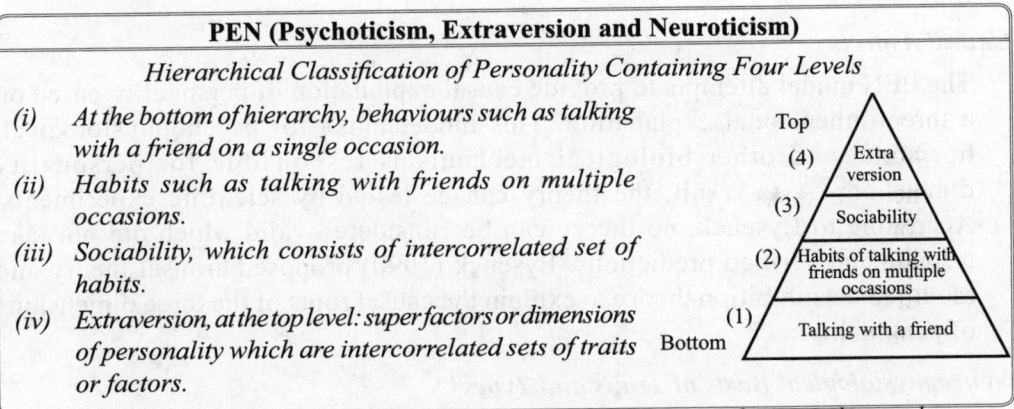

PEN (Psychoticism, Extraversion and Neuroticism)
Hierarchical Classification of Personality Containing Four Levels
(i) At the bottom of hierarchy, behaviours such as talking with a friend on a single occasion.
(ii) Habits such as talking with friends on multiple occasions.
(iii) Sociability, which consists of intercorrelated set of habits.
(iv) Extraversion, at the top level: super factors or dimensions of personality which are intercorrelated sets of traits or factors.

- **PEN:** Such super factors of personality, according to Eysenck, are orthogonal to one another, i.e., they do not correlate with one another.

Three Dimensions of Personality

Eysenck said that there are only three major dimensions or super factors in the description of personality: (i) Extraversion–Introversion (ii) Emotional stability vs instability and (iii) Psychoticism vs Impulse control.

These dimensions or super factors are based on constitutional, genetic or inborn factors which are to be discovered in the physiological, neurological and biochemical structure of the individual (Eysenck, 1985).

According to Allport, each person does not necessarily have either 100 per cent or zero per cent of extraversion, neuroticism or psychoticism. An individual may show some degree of these super factors on a continuum. He may have high extraversion, moderate neuroticism and low psychoticism.

The following conclusions were presented by Eysenck after studying psychosis:

(i) Psychotic symptoms and illnesses do not form completely separate diagnostic entities.

(ii) Psychosis is not a separate diagnostic entity which is categorically separated from normality.

(iii) The continuum is co-linear with the concept of psychoticism, embodied in the P (Psychoticism or Tough-Mindedness) scale of the EPQ (Eysenck Personality Questionnaire).

On this continuum, an individual with high extraversion is sociable, popular, optimistic, but unreliable, whereas a person with low extraversion is quite introspective, reserved and reliable. An individual with high neuroticism is anxious, worried and moody, but unstable, whereas a person with low neuroticism is calm, even-tempered, carefree and emotionally stable. Lastly, a person with high psychoticism is troublesome, uncooperative, hostile and socially withdrawn, whereas a person with low psychoticism is socialised, empathic, altruistic and conventional (Eysenck, 1985).

Causal Aspects

The PEN model attempts to provide causal explanation of personality based on a three-dimensional explanation. This model looks for psychophysiological, hormonal and other biological mechanisms responsible for personality dimensions. As a result, the theory can be tested by scientific experiments. According to Eysenck, no theory can be considered valid which did not take testable and verified predictions. Eysenck (1990) proposed arousal theory and modified his inhibition theory to explain the causal roots of the three dimensions of personality.

Neurophysiological Basis of Traits and Types

Many studies of neurotic patients indicated that there is a neurophysiological basis of traits and types. Aleksandrov and Schukin (1992) studied 107 patients with different patterns of neuroses and concluded this fact. Analysis of dynamics of neurophysiological characteristics, made during group psychotherapy, supported clinical data. It was found that patients with hysteroid type character accentuation appeared more resistant to psychotherapy. According to Eysenck, the super-trait introversion–extraversion is closely related to levels of cortical arousal as indicated by electro-encephalographic (ECG) recording. Introverts are over-aroused and they are highly sensitive to incoming stimulation. Extroverts are under-aroused and highly insensitive to incoming stimulations.

Eysenck said that individuals high on neuroticism tend to react more quickly to painful, novel and disturbing situations in comparison to stable persons. Eysenck's neurophysiological interpretation of the dimensions of personality is closely related to his theory of psychopathology. The symptoms or disorders of an individual (or patient) are related to combined impact of personality traits and nervous system functioning. For example, an individual who is high on the dimensions of introversion and neuroticism is more prone to develop anxiety disorders such as phobias, obsessions and compulsions. On the other hand, an individual who is high on extraversion and neuroticism dimensions is at a risk of psychopathic (anti-social) disorders. Eysenck said that psychological disorders do not occur automatically as a result of genetic predisposition. When these genetic predispositions interact with the environment or a certain situation, they produce psychological disorders.

After evaluation of the arousal theory, Eysenck provided a biological explanation of extraversion in terms of cortical arousal via ascending reticular activating system (ARAS). According to Eysenck, activity in the ARAS stimulates the cerebral cortex, which, in turn, leads to higher cortical arousal. This cortical arousal can be measured by brain waves, skin conductance or sweating (Eysenck, 1990). Due to different levels of ARAS activity, introverts are characterised by higher levels of activity than extroverts.

In his theory, Eysenck also explained neuroticism in terms of "activation thresholds" in the sympathetic nervous system or visceral brain. The visceral brain is otherwise known as limbic system which consists of the hippocampus, amygdala and aggression. In dangerous situations, it is responsible for fight-or-flight response. Activation levels of the visceral brain can be measured by heart rate, blood pressure, skin conductance, sweating, breathing rate and muscular tension in the forehead. Studies indicated that neurotic individuals have greater activation levels and lower thresholds within the visceral brain. Minor stresses make them easily upset. But emotionally stable people are calm and quiet under stressful conditions because they have lesser activation levels and higher thresholds (Eysenck, 1990).

Psychoticism and Gonadal Hormones

Eysenck (1990) did not forget to provide an explanation of psychoticism in terms of gonadal hormones such as testosterone and enzymes like monoamine oxidase (MAO). According to him, low platelet monoamine oxydase (MAO) was found in psychotic patients. He suggested that low MAO activity may be a marker for vulnerability.

In summary, we can say that, according to the theories developed by Eysenck:

(i) Elements of personality can be arranged hierarchically.

(ii) Some super traits or types of personality like extraversion exert a powerful influence over behaviour.

(iii) These super traits consist of several components of traits and these component traits are either mere superficial reflections of the underlying type dimension or are specific qualities which contributes to that dimension.

(iv) Traits are composed of numerous habitual responses, which in turn, are derived from a multitude of specific responses. The trait of sociability is connected with such response dispositions as liveliness, assertiveness, activity, etc. Taken together, these traits define a super trait or type which Eysenck called extraversion.

Taking Eysenck's hierarchical model of personality into consideration, it should be noted that the word "type" refers to dimensions of personality which he regards as normally distributed along a continuum. This is almost equivalent to traits. The type concept of extraversion is a dimension with a low end and a high end along which people may fall at different points between the two extremes. It is not a dimension on which individuals can be classified as either low or high. He does not imply discontinuity when he uses the word "type".

Basic Personality Types

Different methods were used by Eysenck to gather information about people in order to evaluate their personality. These methods are self-reports, observer ratings, biological information, assessments of physique and physiology and objective physiological tests. Factor analysis was applied to the collected data to determine the structure of personality. Initially, Eysenck found two basic types of dimensions: Introversion–Extraversion and Neuroticism–Stability. Neuroticism–Stability was also called Instability–Stability.

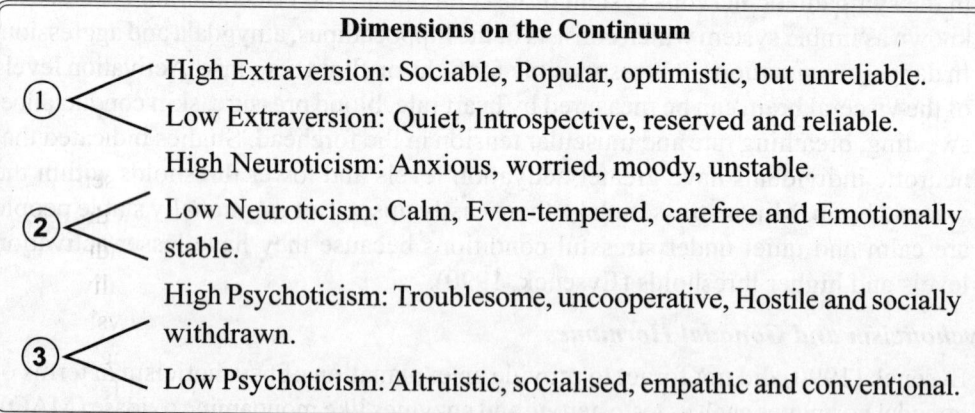

Dimensions on the Continuum

① High Extraversion: Sociable, Popular, optimistic, but unreliable.
　Low Extraversion: Quiet, Introspective, reserved and reliable.

② High Neuroticism: Anxious, worried, moody, unstable.
　Low Neuroticism: Calm, Even-tempered, carefree and Emotionally stable.

③ High Psychoticism: Troublesome, uncooperative, Hostile and socially withdrawn.
　Low Psychoticism: Altruistic, socialised, empathic and conventional.

Later, Eysenck (1976) added a third dimension of personality, which he called Psychoticism–Superego strength. Individuals high on this super trait dimension tend to be egocentric, impulsive, sensitive to others and opposed to social customs. These people are often seen as (i) troublesome (ii) not fitting in well with others and (iii) intentionally upsetting other people. According to Eysenck, psychoticism is a genetic predisposition towards becoming either psychotic or psychopathic. He regarded psychoticism as a personality continuum along which all individuals can be located. This trait is found more commonly in men than in women.

Measurement of Personality

Many self-report questionnaires were constructed by Eysenck to assess individual differences associated with his three super trait dimensions of personality. One popular scale is EPQ (Eysenck Personality Questionnaire). EPQ includes a lie scale aimed at detecting a person's tendency to fake responses to look good. A junior EPQ was also constructed for measuring children between the ages 7 and 15 (Eysenck, 1973).

Differences between Extroverts and Introverts

After employing factor analysis on data collected from questionnaires and laboratory techniques, Eysenck found some individual differences in behavioural functioning among extroverts and introverts. A review of these results indicated that:

(i) Extroverts have a greater tolerance for pain than do introverts.

(ii) Extroverts engage themselves in talking and discussing more than introverts.

(iii) Excitement enhances the performance or extroverts whereas it interferes with the performance of introverts.

(iv) Extroverts prefer people–oriented jobs (e.g., sales and social work) whereas introverts prefer theoretical and scientific vocations (i.e., engineering, science, etc.)

(v) Introverts perform frequent masturbation compared to extroverts, but extroverts engage in sexual intercourse earlier in life and with more partners than do introverts.

(vi) Introverts have higher grades in schools and colleges than do extroverts.

(vii) Extroverts show higher arousal levels in the evening, whereas introverts show higher arousal levels in the morning.

The most striking difference between extroverts and introverts is in their sensitivity to stimulation. This difference can easily be demonstrated by the "lemon drop test" (Corcoran, 1964). When four drops of lemon juice are placed on an individual's tongue, it turns out that introverts secrete almost twice the amount of saliva as do extroverts. Of course, this finding is related to different patterns of physiological functioning in extroverts and introverts. According to Eysenck, ascending reticular activating system in the brain stem is responsible for controlling the differences in response to stimulation between extroverts and introverts.

In summary, we can say that most of the concepts by Eysenck on personality were developed through factor analysis. His hierarchical model of personality structure includes the dimensions of types, traits, habitual responses and specific responses. On the whole, types represent super trait dimensions along which people may be located in various points between two extremes. He said that personality types are dimensional and most people do not fall into separate categories. He said that only two major types or traits are found in personality structure: (i) Introversion–Extraversion and (ii) Stability–Neuroticism.

Later he added another dimension, psychoticism and superego strength. This is related to neurophysiological functioning. Eysenck placed more emphasis on the genetic foundations of traits than Cattell. Interaction between genetic factors and environmental factors produce the requisite behaviours which may be normal or abnormal. Several questionnaires were developed by Eysenck to assess three major super traits underlying his hierarchical model of personality. EPQ is an important tool to assess the differences between extraversion and introversion.

The Big-Five Factors: The Basic Dimensions of Personality

During the last several decades, attempts have been made to reduce the number of trait dimensions to a more manageable number because 16 factors (16 PF) are still quite a lot to discuss when talking about someone's personality. According to some researchers, there may be only five key or central dimensions of personality. Using factor analysis from among a large number of dimensions, the researchers identified clusters of dimensions and these formed the personality factors (Botwin & Buss, 1989). These five dimensions have become known as the Five-Factor Model or the Big-Five (Table 3.2) which represent the core description of human personality.

Table 3.2: Five-Factor Model of Personality

High Scorer Characteristics	Factor	Low scorer Characteristics
• Creative, artistic, curious, imaginative, non-conforming	• Openness (O)	• Conventional, down-to-earth, uncreative
• Organised, reliable, neat, ambitious	• Conscientiousness negligent, spontaneous (C)	• Unreliable, lazy, careless,
• Talkative, optimistic, sociable, affectionate	• Extraversion (E)	• Reserved, comfortable being alone, stays in the background
• Good-natured, trusting, helpful	• Agreeableness (A)	• Rude, uncooperative, irritable, aggressive, competitive
• Worrying, insecure, anxious, temperamental	• Neuroticism (N)	• Calm, secure, relaxed, stable

Source: Adapted from McRae & Costa (1990)

Allport and Odbert's classifications provided initial structure for the personality lexicon. Since taxonomy has to provide a systematic framework for distinguishing, ordering and naming individual differences in individual's behaviour and experience, they took a list of a large number of personality traits used in common parlance. But the size of that list was too big. Cattell began with 4,500 trait items. Later he reduced these 4,500 items to a mere 35 variables. He used these smaller number of variables to identify 12 personality factors which eventually became a part of his 16 PF questionnaire.

> **Contribution of PEN Model to the Study of Personality**
>
> - It combines both descriptive and causal aspects of personality in one theory. This distinguishes the PEN model from most other trait theories such as five-factor model, etc.
> - It provides causal explanations in addition to the description of personality.
> - The PEN model is comprehensive in description by proposing a hierarchy of four levels and by making a clear distinction along those levels.
> - The PEN model becomes most compelling because of its experimental approach to the study of personality. As a result, the PEN model is likely to generate more specific predictions about personality.
> - This PEN model is supported by more credible evidence than purely descriptive models.

The big five personality dimension is the outcome of finding a general taxonomy. These dimensions do not represent a particular theoretical perspective but are derived from people's description of themselves and others in their natural language. Instead of replacing the earlier systems, the big five serves as an integrative mechanism and represents the various and diverse systems of personality description in a common framework.

Differences between Extroverts and Introverts according to Eysenck	
Extroverts	*Introverts*
(i) Greater tolerance to pain.	(i) Less tolerance to pain.
(ii) Engage in more talk, coffee breaks and gregarious.	(ii) Less talk, not sociable and gregarious.
(iii) The performance is increased due to excitement.	(iii) Excitement decreases the performance.
(iv) Prefer people-oriented jobs like sales and social work.	(iv) Prefer theoretical and scientific vocations.
(v) Rare masturbation, but engage in sexual intercourse.	(v) Report frequent masturbation, but less sexual intercourse.
(vi) Lower grades in schools and colleges.	(vi) Higher grades in schools and colleges.
(vii) Students withdraw from colleges for academic reasons.	(vii) Students withdraw from colleges for psychiatric reasons.
(viii) Show higher arousal levels in the evening.	(viii) Show higher arousal levels in the morning.
(ix) Work better in the evening.	(ix) Work better in the morning.

As shown in Table 3.2, these five trait dimensions can be remembered by using the acronym OCEAN, in which each of the letters is the first letter of the five dimensions of personality.

(a) *Openness*: This is also called as Intellect or Intellect/Imagination. It can be best described as a person's willingness to try new things and be open to new experiences. This dimension includes traits like having a broad range of interests and being imaginative and insightful. People who try to maintain status quo and who do not like to change things would score low on openness.

(b) *Conscientiousness*: Conscientiousness includes traits like organised, thorough and painstaking tendencies of an individual. Common features of this dimension include high levels of thoughtfulness, with good impulse control and goal-directed behaviour. Those high in conscientiousness tend to be organised and mindful of details. Someone scoring low on this dimension might always be late to important social events and often borrow belongings and fail to return them. If they, at all, return, they return in poor condition.

(c) *Extraversion*: This term was first used by Carl Jung (1993). He believed that all people can be divided into two groups Extroverts and Introverts. Extraversion is otherwise known as surgency. The broad dimension of extraversion encompasses specific traits such as talkative, energetic and assertive. These include also excitability, sociability, talkativeness, assertiveness and high amount of emotional expressiveness. On the other hand, introverts are more solitary and dislike being the centre of attention.

(d) *Agreeableness*: Agreeableness refers to the basic emotional style of a person. This person may be easy-going, friendly, kind and affectionate, or crabby and grumpy,

(e) *Neuroticism*: Neuroticism is otherwise called emotional stability or emotional instability. This dimension includes traits like tense, moody and anxious. Individuals high in this trait tend to experience emotional instability, anxiety, moodiness, irritability and sadness.

Costa and McCrae (1998) believed that these five traits were not interdependent. In other words, knowing someone's score or extraversion would not give any information about scores on the other four dimensions, allowing for a tremendous amount of variety in personality descriptions. However, these dimensions represent broad areas of personality. Studies have demonstrated that these groupings of characteristics tend to occur together in many people. For example, individuals who are gregarious tend to be sociable. But these traits do not always occur together. Personality is complex and varied. Each individual may display behaviours across several of these dimensions.

The Big-Five Factors: An Evaluation

How basic and therefore how important are the Big-Five dimensions? Although there is far from complete agreement on this point, many researchers believe that these dimensions are indeed basic ones. These dimensions are the ones to which most people in many different cultures refer to while describing themselves (Friedman and Schustack, 1999). There is a large and growing body of evidence suggesting that these dimensions are indeed very basic ones where personality is concerned.

But there are many aspects of personality which are not subsumed within the Big-Five. The term "personality trait" has a special meaning in personality psychology which is narrower than the everyday usage of the term. Motivations, attitudes, emotions, abilities, self-concepts, social roles and autobiographical memories are just a few of the other "units" which personality psychologists study.

Another criticism of Big-Five came from Eysenck (1994). He believed that there are only three basic dimensions of personality: extraversion, neuroticism and psychoticism. Some other experts believe that the methods on which the Big-Five dimensions are based (largely by Factor Analysis) are inadequate. However, many psychologists view the Big-Five as providing important insights into key dimensions of personality.

The Big-Five Theory

Let us examine the difference between the terms Big-Five, Five-Factor Model and Five-Factor Theory.

Collectively, the Big-Five are a taxonomy of personality traits. It is a coordinate system that maps which traits go together in people's descriptions or ratings of one another. It is not a theory of personality, but an empirically based phenomena.

The Big-Five Factors were discovered through a statistical procedure called factor analysis, which was used to analyse how ratings of various personality traits are correlated in humans.

Five-Factor Model is a term which is used for Big-Five. In scientific usage, the word "model" can refer either to descriptive framework of what has been observed or to a theoretical explanations of causes and consequences. It is a model in the descriptive sense only. The term "Big-Five" was coined by Lew Goldberg. It was originally associated with studies of personality traits used in natural language.

The term "Five-Factor Model" is commonly associated with studies of traits using a personality questionnaire. Many perspectives on the concept of Big-Five dimensions have been presented in the past. The Big-Five factors were first discovered in lexical research to provide taxonomy of trait items. Later research showed that the dimensions have external/predictive validity and all five of them show equal heritability. The Big-Five dimensions refer to real individual differences, so one must look for how these differences are conceptualised.

Many theories present the Big-Five as relational constructs. For example, the interpersonal theory emphasises the individual relationships. Sullivan stated that the Big-Five factors describe the enduring patterns of recurrent interpersonal situations that characterise human life. Socio-analytic Theory (Hogan, 1996) projects on the social functions of self and other perceptions and Hogan points out that traits are socially constructed to serve interpersonal functions. The Evolutionary Theory (Buss and Shackelford, 1997) states that humans have evolved "difference detecting mechanisms" to perceive individual differences which are important for survival and reproduction. Buss (1997) stated that personality was one where the Big-Five traits represent the most salient and important dimensions of the individual's survival needs. This theory emphasises both person perception and individual differences. The Big-Five was viewed by McCrae and Costa (1996) as causal personality dispositions. According to them, the Big-Five dimensions have a substantial genetic base and hence derive from biological structures and processes. According to this theory, personality traits are basic tendencies which refer to the underlying potentials of the individual. Comparative Approach (another theory of personality) studies individual differences in humans and non-humans. Thus, there are a diverse theories regarding the Big-Five dimensions from purely descriptive to biologically based causal concepts.

Advantages of Big-Five Structure

The best advantage of the Big-Five factor is that it is easily understood by every person. Extraversion and Neuroticism have been explained both from physiological and mechanistic perspectives. The Big-Five differentiates domains of individual differences that have similar surface manifestations. It captures the communities among most of the existing systems of personality description and provides an integrative descriptive model. Besides all these, the five-factor theory includes a number of propositions about the nature, origins and development of personality traits and about the relations of traits to many personality variables. This theory presents a biological account of personality traits in which learning and experience play little if any part in influencing the Big Five.

However, Five-Factor Theory is not the single account of the Big-Five. Other personality psychologists have proposed that environmental influences, such as social roles, combine and interact with biological influences in shaping personality traits. For example, Brent Roberts has advanced an internationalist approach under the name of Social Investment Theory.

Lastly, it must be noted that the Big Five are used in many areas of psychological research in ways that do not depend on the specific propositions of any theory. For example, in interpersonal perception research, the Big-Five are a useful model for organising people's perception of one another's personalities. Srivastav, an Indian Psychologist said, "I have argued that the Big-Five are best understood as a model of reality-based person perception. In other words, it is a model of what people want to know about one another" (Srivastav, 2010). Researchers feel that it is still quite possible that they will benefit from measuring and thinking about the Big-Five in their research.

Measurement of Big-Five Inventory

The Big Five Inventory (BFI) is a self-report inventory designed to measure the Big-Five dimensions. It is just like a multidimensional personality inventory (44 items in total) and consists of short phrases with a easily understood vocabulary. Besides BFI, there are other ways of measuring Big Five, i.e., BFI is not the only method.

The following are the other ways of measuring the Big-Five:

(i) The International Personality Item Pool (IPIP) developed and maintained by Lew Goldberg.

(ii) Big Five Aspect Scales (BFAS) published by Collin De Young, a 100-item measure which scores not only Big-Five factors, but also two "aspects" of each. The BFAS is in the public domain as well.

(iii) The NEO PI-R (Revised Neuroticism-Extraversion-Openness Personality Inventory) is a 240-item inventory developed by Paul costa and Jeff McCrae measures not only the Big-Five, but also six "facets" (subordinate dimensions) of each of the Big-Five.

(iv) If a short measure of the Big-Five is needed, then the Ten Item Personality Inventory (TIPI), developed in 2003 by Sam Gosling, Jason Rentfrow and Bill Swann can be used.

Trait Theories: An Evaluation

Most research on personality by psychologists occurs within the context of the text approach. Without referring to grand theories offered by Freud, Jung and Rogers, most psychologists now direct their effort to the task of understanding specific traits. This is perhaps due to the success of trait approach of personality and drawbacks of different approaches discussed earlier.

However, the trait approach is not perfect. It can be criticised on several grounds:

(i) The trait approach is largely descriptive in nature. Traits seek to describe the key dimensions of personality, but do not attempt to determine how various traits develop, how they influence behaviour and why they are important.

(ii) In spite of a large amount of research, there is no final agreement concerning the traits that are most important and most basic. Rather, the Big-Five dimensions are widely accepted.

The trait approach to personality has generally been a very valuable one. It helps to understand how people differ and is conducive for understanding the uniqueness and consistency of key aspects of human behaviour.

Best Ways to Describe Personality

What are the best ways to describe an individual's personality? To answer this question, we may use many words, sentences or concepts. We agree that individuals differ from one another. Every language has hundreds of words for different ways to describe individuals. The English language has 20,000 words of this type (for example, gregarious, agreeable, nervous, intelligent, etc.). This "texical hypothesis" is the basis of much modern research on the structure of human personality traits. After a large amount of research conducted in many countries, the Big-Five factor structure has become a scientifically useful taxonomy to understand individual differences in personality traits. Many psychologists view the Big-Five as providing important insights into the key dimensions of personality.

Current Thoughts on Trait Perspective

It was confirmed by many psychologists that personality traits will not always be expressed in the same manner across different situations. The social cognitive theorist named Walter Mischel (1995) has said that there is a "trait-situation interaction" in which the particular circumstances of any given situation are assumed to influence the way in which a trait is expressed. For example, a talkative person will not laugh and talk at a funeral. Cross-cultural studies found evidence about Big-Five trait dimensions in eleven different cultures, including Japan, Philippines, Germany, China and Peru (Digman, 1990). This cultural communality has raised a question about the origins of Big-Five trait dimensions. Two questions are pertinent here:

(i) Are child-rearing practices across all those cultures similar enough to result in these five aspects of personality?

(ii) Could these five dimensions have a genetic component which transcends differences?

These questions invite discussion regarding the evidences for the genetic basis for Big-Five.

The Biology of Personality: Behavioural Genetics

The domain of Behavioural Genetics is devoted to the study of how much of an individual's personality is due to inherited traits. Temperament is, no doubt, determined by biology to a great degree. It is presumed that personality characteristics related to temperament in human beings may also be influenced by heredity (Isabal, 2003; Trut, 1999). When identical and fraternal twins were studied, especially when twins were not raised in the same environment, experts found evidence of possible genetic influences on many traits, including personality. Adoption studies have confirmed what twin studies have shown – genetic influences account for a great deal of personality development, regardless of shared or non-shared environments. Studies have confirmed that the five personality factors of the five-factor model had nearly a 50 per cent rate of heritability across several cultures. The results of Minnesota twin study and other researches confirmed that the studies of genetics and personality which indicated that variations in personality traits are about 25 to 50 per cent inherited (Jang, 1998). This implies that environmental influences apparently account for about half of the variation in personality traits as well.

Although the five-factors have been found across several cultures, this does not mean that different cultures do not have impact on personality. Here Geert Hofstede's four dimensions of cultural personality can be mentioned. In the early 1980s, organisational management specialist Geert Hofstede conducted a huge study of the work-related values of employees of IBM, a multinational corporation. The study was a survey across 64 countries. He analysed the data from his survey and found four basic dimensions of personality along which differed across cultures: (i) Individualism/collectivism (ii) Power distance (iii) Masculinity/femininity (iv) Uncertainty Avoidance.

❑ Key Terms

1. Ability trait
2. Ability source
3. Agreeableness
4. Ambiverts
5. Assessment of personality
6. Basic anxiety
7. Bodily self
8. Cardinal disposition
9. Cardinal traits
10. Case study method
11. Central disposition
12. Central traits
13. Client-centered therapy
14. Conscientiousness
15. Consciousness
16. Consistency
17. Constitutional trait
18. Defence mechanisms
19. Emotional stability
20. Extraversion
21. Factor analysis
22. Factor inventory (16 PF)
23. Five Factor Model
24. Functional autonomy
25. Hierarchy of needs
26. Humanistic approach
27. Hypothesis
28. Id, Ego and Superego
29. Ideal-self
30. Impulse control
31. Introversion
32. MMPI
33. Neo Personality Inventory (NEO-PI)
34. Neurocticism (N)
35. Ocean
36. Openness
37. Persona
38. Personality
39. Physical attractiveness
40. Physical constitution
41. Propriate striving
42. Proprium
43. Psychophysical system
44. Psychoticism
45. Rating scale
46. Reciprocal determinism
47. Reinforcement
48. Reliability
49. Secondary traits
50. Self-actualisation
51. Self-concept
52. Self-efficacy
53. Self-esteem
54. Self-extension
55. Self-identity
56. Self-image
57. Self-report techniques
58. Self-system
59. Situational test
60. Sixteen personality
61. Social desirability
62. Source trait
63. Standardisation
64. Structure of personality
65. Super trait
66. Superego strength
67. Temperament
68. Test norms
69. Thematic Apperception Test (TAT)
70. Trait hierarchy
71. Traits of personality
72. Types of personality
73. Unconscious
74. Validity
75. Vicarious learning

❑ **Chapter Summary and Review**

1. Personality can be defined as the distinctive and unique ways in which each individual thinks, feels and acts, and which characterise an individual's response throughout life. Personality refers to all those relatively permanent traits, dispositions or characteristics within the person that give some measure of consistency to the person's behaviour.

2. Allport defined personality as the dynamic organisation within the person of those psychophysical systems which determine the unique adjustments to one's environment.

3. Development of personality can be explained in terms of the following equation :

   Personality Development = Physical determinants × Psychological determinants × Environmental determinants

4. Allport said that traits are the building blocks of personality as well as the source of individuality. For him, trait was something which exists but remains invisible. Raymond Cattell (1950) considered personality to be a pattern of traits providing the key to understanding it and predicting a person's behaviour. He also said that traits are relatively permanent and broad reaction tendencies of personality. They serve as building blocks of personality. He found 23 source traits in normal persons, 16 of which he studied in detail.

5. British Psychologist Hans Eysenck (1990) believed that personality is largely determined by genes and the environmental factors have very little role to play in it. He opined that personality is more or less stable and enduring organisation of a person's character, temperament, intellect and physique.

6. Guilford defined personality as the individual's unique pattern of traits. For him, traits are any distinguishable, relatively enduring ways by which one person differs from another.

7. The most talked-about trait approach to personality is Five-Factor Model (FFM), also known as Big-Five. According to this model, there are five broad personality factors, each of which is composed of constellation of traits (OCEAN). Goldberg (1992) has developed a questionnaire named Transparent Bipolar Inventory for assessing these five dimensions.

8. The original psychodynamic theory was Freud's psychoanalysis. He described it under three main headings – (i) Structure of personality (ii) Dynamics of personality and (iii) Development of personality. His topographical model represents the configuration of mind. Under the dynamic model, Freud conceived human mind as Id, Ego and Superego. By reformulating Freudian thought, Karen Horney presented a holistic, humanistic perspective which emphasised cultural and social influences. Later Abraham Maslow developed a theory called "theory of self-actualisation" to understand personality. Sullivan placed a lot of focus on both the social aspects of personality and cognitive representations.

9. Albert Bandura developed a social-cognitive theory to understand personality. His approach represented a break from traditional theories by proposing that cognitive factors are central to human functioning and learning can occur in the absence of direct reinforcement. That is, learning can occur simply through observation.

10. Pavlovian conditioning explains how a previously neutral stimulus can come to have a learned effect on someone. Gradually the organism learns to respond to the conditioned stimulus with a conditioned response. The principles of classical conditioning are found effective for the modification of behaviour.

11. Maslow developed a theory of human motivation based on hierarchy of needs. The lower a need in the hierarchy, the more prepotent or dominating that need is. He proposed a simple and intuitive appealing theory of motivation, which explains where such a self-actualising personality comes from.

12. Roger's theory is otherwise known as "self-theory" which is basically phenomenological. It places strong emphasis on the experience of the persons, their feelings, their values and all that is summed up by the expression "inner life". Rogers talked about healthy development in terms of how the individuals perceived their own being. Roger's theory is explained under the three headings: (i) Enduring aspects of personality (ii) Self-actualisation and (iii) Development of self. Organism and the self are of fundamental importance in Roger's theory. His personality theory distinguishes between two personalities: the "real self" which is created and developed through the actualising tendency and the "ideal self", which is created through the demands of society.

13. Gordon Allport explained an individual's uniqueness as the paramount goal of psychology. He defined personality as the dynamic organisation of those internal psychophysical systems which determine a person's characteristic behaviour and thoughts. According to him, trait is the most significant unit of analysis for understanding behaviour. Further, traits account for a person's behavioural consistency over time and across situations. The construct which unifies traits and provides direction for individual life is termed the "proprium" or "self" which contributes to an inward sense of unity. Functional autonomy is a process whereby a given form of behaviour becomes an end or goal in itself despite the fact that it may originally have been adopted for another reason, i.e., what was formerly a means to an end becomes the end itself.

14. Cattell viewed personality as that which permits us to predict what a person will do in a given situation, as expressed in the equation $R = f(S, P)$. Traits are hypothetical constructs which predispose the person to behave consistently across circumstances and time. The essence of personality structure consists of approximately 16 source trait factors. According to him, one-third of personality is determined by genetics and two-thirds by environmental influences.

15. Eysenck's personality theory was based on "factor analysis". He developed several questionnaires to assess three major super traits underlying his

hierarchical model of personality. EPQ is the most important tool to assess the differences between introverts and extroverts.

16. There was a big controversy regarding the number of basic personality traits for over a decade or two. Costa and McCrae have examined all possible personality traits and emphasised upon a set of five factors often called Big-Five factors. These factors include openness, conscientiousness, extraversion, agreeableness and neuroticism (OCEAN). This model represents an important theoretical development in the field of personality. It is considered the most promising empirical approach to the study of personality.

QUESTIONS

1. Define personality. Distinguish between individual traits and common traits.
2. Following Allport, discuss different types of individual traits and their importance in predicting human behaviour.
3. Evaluate viewpoints of Cattell regarding traits as being one of the determiners of human behaviour.
4. Do you find Eysenck's type-trait hierarchy a satisfactory explanation for making prediction about human behaviour?
5. Analyse different trait modalities as outlined by J.P. Guilford for understanding and predicting human behaviour.
6. Discuss the role of Five-Factor Model in understanding human behaviour.
7. Do you think that the trait perspective gives a satisfactory explanation for explaining personality? Give reasons.
8. What role can Five-Factor Model play in resolving the theoretical controversy in personality research?
9. "The cross-cultural issue in personality is difficult to be resolved." Why?
10. "The interactional approach gives a mid-way solution to person-situation controversy." Discuss.
11. Discuss the Nature-Nurture debate in the study of personality.
12. What role does the environment play in moulding an individual's personality? Discuss with examples.
13. Discuss the main features of Freud's psychoanalytic theory of personality.
14. Describe different stages of psychosexual development enumerated by Freud. What role do they play in developing adult personality?
15. Explain the main features of Karen Horney's theory of personality.
16. On what account does Horney's theory of personality differ from Freud's theory of personality?
17. Describe the salient features of Sullivan's personality theory.
18. Discuss the importance of neurotic needs in the formulation of Horney's theory of personality.
19. What do you mean by defence mechanisms? How they tend to reduce anxiety? Illustrate your answer with suitable examples.
20. Distinguish between Sullivan's developmental epochs and Freud's stages of psychosexual development.
21. Discuss the main enduring aspects of personality proposed by Sullivan. Evaluate the concept of personification in detail.
22. Point out the main features of social cognitive theory of personality.

23. What do you understand by "reciprocal determinism"? Discuss its importance in the light of Bandura's theory.
24. Critically evaluate the development of self-esteem as proposed by Bandura.
25. What is observational learning? Discuss the main processes involved in observational learning.
26. What is vicarious learning? What role does it play in Bandura's social learning?
27. What are the main features of Behaviouristic theory of personality?
28. Describe the principles of classical conditioning and discuss how it can be applied in explaining the development of personality.
29. How does the learning theory of personality differ from the psychoanalytic theory of personality?
30. Critically evaluate the main tenets of Maslow's theory of personality.
31. Discuss the characteristic features of Humanistic approach to personality.
32. Discuss the importance of deficiency needs and growth needs in the development of personality.
33. What are the main characteristics of a self-actualising person? Discuss it in detail.
34. On what ground does Maslow's theory differ from Roger's theory of personality?
35. Critically evaluate Roger's theory of personality.
36. Discuss the importance of self in Roger's theory of personality.
37. What do you mean by phenomenal field? Discuss its importance in the light of Roger's theory.

CHAPTER - 4

INSPIRATION TO LIVING

MOTIVATION

> Motivation is any general condition internal to an organism which appears to produce gossal-directed behaviour.

❑ **This chapter covers:**
- Meaning and definition of motives, drives and incentives
- Brief ideas about different types of motives: biological, social and psychological
- Motivational cycle
- Theories of motivation
- Measurement of motives
- Key Terms, Summary and Questions

❑ **After you go through this chapter, you will be able to:**
- Understand the nature of human motivation
- Find out the differences between needs and incentives, motives and needs, drives and motives, etc.
- Explain different types of human motives
- Evaluate different theories of motivation
- Gain an understanding of the measurement of human motives

Introduction

Motivation focuses on the "why" aspect of behaviour. It directs an individual's behaviour towards a goal. Motives are specific conditions which direct an organism towards a goal. Very often, psychologists say that people are motivated; they also say that people are directed to specific goals by specific motives. So, the psychologists use the term "motivation" very precisely. But in everyday life, people use the term to refer to a variety of complex concepts like intentions, desires, wants, etc.

No doubt, human behaviour is affected by motivation. In studying motivation, psychologists examine the internal drives and needs which direct an organism towards a goal.

Motivation cannot be seen directly, but behaviour is observable. To explain the observable behavioural changes, we have to find out the underlying physiological and psychological variables which influence those changes.

Motivation is a driving state. It is also a behaviour-arousal state within the individual.

Motivation has the following three aspects:

(a) A driving state within the organism that is set in motion by bodily needs, environmental stimuli or mental events.

(b) The behaviour aroused and directed by this state.

(c) The goal towards which the behaviour is directed.

Motivation is derived from the Latin word "movere" which means "to move". It is a process which arouses the energy or drive in the individual to proceed in an activity. The aroused activity fulfils the need and reduces the drive or tension. Until it has not fulfilled the need, the drive is not reduced.

Drive is a psychological state. It leads one to activity. Only an unsatisfied need generates a drive.

Needs, Drives and Incentives

The terms such as needs, drives and motives are frequently used interchangeably. But each term has a different connotation.

Motivation is the general term for all the processes involved in starting, directing and maintaining psychological activities.
—*Philip G. Zimbardo and Ann L. Weber*

Motivation is an internal condition initiated by drives, needs or desires and producing goal-directed behaviour.
—*Lester A. Lefton*

Motive: A specific internal condition directing an organism's behaviour towards a goal.
—*Lester A. Lefton*

Aspects of Motivation
1. A driving state.
2. Behaviour aroused by driving state.
3. Goal.
q "Why" aspect of human behaviour:

Human motivation is extremely complex. It is very difficult to understand, interpret, predict and control. Also, it is not possible to bring human beings to the cage or laboratory for experimenting on their drives and motivational processes. It is true that most of the researches on motivation have been done on animal behaviour. Inferences were drawn from animal studies.

Motives refer to any process – internal or external – involved in instigation, direction or termination of behaviour. All voluntary responses involve motivation.

Needs are physiological imbalances which give rise to "drives". An individual is aware of his or her needs when he or she is in a state of deprivation. For example, when individuals are hungry, they need food, when thirsty, they need water and when alone, they needs social companionship.

Drives are the effects of the deficits and deprivations, which define needs. Drives are the tendencies or urges to act in specific ways. For example, during fasting, the need for food gives rise to hunger drive. That is, an unsatisfied need generates a drive.

Intrinsically Motivated Behaviour
Behaviour that a person performs in order to feel more competent and self-determined.

Goal
A "goal" refers to some substance, objects or environmental condition capable of reducing or temporarily eliminating the complex of internal conditions which initiated action.
—Ruch (1970)

Indicators of Motivation
In his book Purposive Behaviour in Animals and Men (1932), the famous learning theorist Edward C. Tolman described motivation as a process that intervenes between stimulus input and response outcome in an organism.
Researchers have found the measurable qualities and events that indicate motivation underlying behaviour.
(a) The more motivated an organism is, the higher will its level of activity be up to an optimal point.

An incentive is a motivator of behaviour. It is also a motivational concept like needs or drives. It is associated with drive-reduction components or subjective value attached to a goal. The value or effectiveness of the goal is a motive for behaviour. On the whole, incentives are conditions or objects which are perceived as satisfiers of some needs. The greater the value of an object, the greater is its perceived incentive. For example, a bonus in a company job or a merit-based promotion in an office serve as incentives for reaching the goal.

Without a need, there cannot be a drive and without a drive, the behaviour cannot be goal-oriented. Finally, without a goal, a motive cannot function successfully. This leads to the learning theorist Hull to say that all learning is purposive.

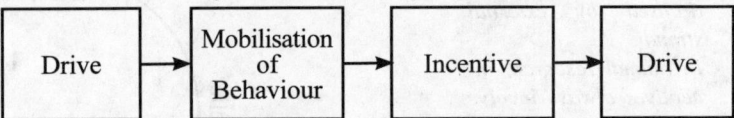

The term incentive refers to the motivational value of the reinforcer. The incentive may be positive or negative, like food and electric shock or reward and punishment. It may be verbal or nonverbal. The incentive may be symbolic, when it does not have direct reinforcing power (Woulfe, 1936 and Cowles, 1937).

A goal may be distant or near. Usually, near goals act as better reinforcing factors than distant goals.

Intrinsic and Extrinsic Motivation

Very often, human beings are engaged in several activities which bring no tangible rewards. For example, children do crossword and jigsaw puzzles, build cities with erector sets and take them down again. These behaviours are performed for no apparent reward except the pleasure of the activity itself. Psychologists call these type of behaviours as intrinsically motivated behaviours.

(b) Strong motivation increases an individual's rate of learning.
(c) Motivation enables one to attain a higher level of performance.
(d) Once learned, a motivated response will be more resistant to extinction.
(e) Being motivated in one task can disrupt efforts in other activities.
(f) Motivation leads an organism to make certain choices among goals, tasks and rewards.
(g) Finally, behaviour that consummates or satisfies a motive will be stronger than less motivated behaviour.

Incentive Motivation

External stimuli that promise rewards are called incentives. Incentive motivation is motivation that is aroused by external stimuli.

In animal research, incentives always involve external stimuli. For humans, incentive motivation may be self-induced by mental imagery.

—*Zimbardo & Weber (1997)*

Effectance Motivation

Effectance motivation plays an important role in human behaviour. The motivation behind competence activities has been called "effectance motivation."

It is a general motive to act competently and effectively when interacting with the environment.

—*White (1959)*

Edward Deci (1975), a psychologist at the Rochester University, suggested that people perform intrinsically motivated behaviour for two reasons: (i) to achieve stimulation and (ii) to achieve a sense of accomplishment, competence and mastery over their environment.

External rewards can strengthen existing behaviours and provide people with information about their performance. Extrinsic motivation is directed towards goals external to the person, such as money or grades in a class. Extrinsic rewards have their uses in guiding behaviour in business and in school. Very often, reliance on extrinsic motivation can stifle intrinsic motivation and impair performance (Condry, 1977). But the delivery of an extrinsic reward does not always decrease intrinsically motivated behaviour or suppress it permanently.

Motivational Cycle

Motivation is said to consist of (a) a driving state (b) the goal directed behaviour initiated by the driving state (c) the attainment of an appropriate goal and (d) the reduction of the driving state and satisfaction and relief when the goal is reached.

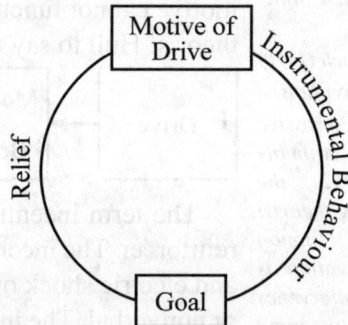

Fig. 4.1: Motivational Cycle

When motives are aroused, they trigger behaviour which leads to a goal and finally, after the goal is reached, they are shut off. The behaviour which is related to drive state is called "instrumental behaviour" because it is instrumental in bringing about the goal or the satisfaction of need.

The first stage of the motivational cycle is the Driving State. When the motive state has a biological or physiological basis, it is called a drive. Drive impels an animal or person to action. Very often, the term "need" is used. The need creates a driving state in the organism.

Motivation

A concept similar to effectance motivation is intrinsic motivation. It is defined "as a person's need for feeling competent and self-determining with his environment.

—*Deci (1975)*

It is called intrinsic because the goals are internal feelings of effectiveness, competence and self-determination.

—*Morgan (1983)*

Stages of Motivational Cycle.
1. *Driving State.*
2. *Goal-directed or Instrumental Behaviour.*
3. *Attainment of an appropriate goal.*
4. *Reduction of the Driving State.*

Positive and Negative Goals

Goals may be positive or negative. Food and sexual satisfaction are the examples of positive goals. The individuals try to reach these goals to get satisfaction. But the organisms always try to escape or avoid negative goals. Dangerous and unpleasant situations are some of the examples of negative goals.

Physiological Equilibrium or Homeostasis

1. *A physiologist, Claude Bernad, coined the word "homeostasis" to explain the stability of the inner environment or physiological equilibrium.*

The second stage of motivational cycle is the instrumental behaviour. It is instigated by the driving state. For example, thirst drives an animal to explore water.

When instrumental behaviour reaches the goal, the need or drive is satisfied and there follows a temporary period of relief. This is the third stage of motivational cycle.

However, drives can also originate when an organism lacks something. They can also be aroused by environmental stimuli such as advertisements from magazines and television, etc. Sex drive can be aroused by seeing a sexy picture in a magazine or newspaper. Some cognitive factors like thoughts and memory can also trigger driving state.

Homeostasis

All human bodies need to maintain a physiological balance. This is necessary for their existence. Restoration of physiological balance or equilibrium is called homeostasis.

In the early part of twentieth century, psychologists were very fascinated by the concept of homeostasis. They borrowed this concept from physiology. The function of all drives is to regulate and maintain the physiological equilibrium of all the organisms. When the internal state of an organism is disturbed, the conditions propel the organism to seek activity. Such activity continues until the equilibrium is restored. This state is popularly known as homeostasis.

Homeostatic processes are automatic and physiological in nature. Maintenance of body temperature is an example of homeostasis.

There are two terms for homeostasis used often by psychologists. For animals, it is known as static equilibrium or static homeostasis. This process involves a limited part of the organism – mostly reflexes or chains of reflexes. Here these activities are controlled by the spinal cord and the brain. But human being are more than a merely biological creature. The psychologists use the concept of "dynamic homeostasis" to explain the complex human behaviour. This behaviour is regulated by the cerebral cortex.

An organism strives to restore its balance when there is a physiological deficiency. It also strives to maintain equilibrium when there is a physiological imbalance. This is basically inferred from the processes of adjustment or coping patterns. The organism may use other methods to resolve conflicts and

2. Homeostatic processes are physiological and automatic in nature.
3. For animals, it is known as "dynamic homeostasis." Dynamic homeostasis explains complex human behaviour.

Homeostatic Activities
1. Maintainance of constant body temperature.
2. Proper balance of oxygen and carbon dioxide.
3. Maintainance of constant level of sugar in the blood stream.

reduce the tension arising out of such conflicts. This state is referred as dynamic equilibrium by Kurt Lewin. On the whole, static and dynamic homeostasis are the key concepts in understanding human motives.

The concept of homeostasis has been borrowed from physics and physiology to explain physiological processes. But often humans exhibit such a variety of behaviour that it can be explained neither by static nor by dynamic homeostasis. A particular behaviour can deliberately upset the equilibrium and destroy it. Bringing about social reforms and revolting against society are the examples here. Often, an individual chooses death to dishonour or prefers aesthetic experiences to satisfaction of hunger. Here homeostasis fails to explain such deviations. However, homeostasis has tremendous evolutionary significance because maintenance of the constancy of the internal environment is necessary for life.

Types of Motives

Motivation explains why we behave as we do. Every behaviour of an organism has motivational causes. What we do is called "performance". Performance is the actual manifested behaviour of the organism. Many performances are learned, not innate.

But there are situations where learning is not reflected directly in performance. Here performance depends on more than learning. It depends on appropriate motivation. Motivation explains the factors that account for actual behaviour. The basis of motivation for different behaviour are many. Important motives have been classified by psychologists into some categories. These are: (a) Biological motives, (b) Social motives and (c) Psychological motives.

Physiological (Biological)	Cognitive Personal Psychological	Social
• Hunger • Thirst • Sex • Sleep • Need for sensory stimulation • Postural changes	• Curiosity • Exploration • Achievement	• Affiliation • Dependency • Competitiveness • Cooperation • Conformity

Fig. 4.2 : Types of Motives

Biological Motives

The biological motives are rooted in the physiological state of the body. Hunger, thirst and sex are the most obvious biological or physiological motives. They are physiological

The living being is an agency of such sort that each disturbing influence induces by itself the calling forth of compensatory activities to neutralise or repair the disturbance.
—**A Physiologist**

Many biological motives are triggered by departures from balanced physiological conditions of the body.
—*Morgan (1983)*

Hunger Drive

Although awareness of hunger under many conditions may have been associated with strong stomach contractions, it is obvious that it is not caused by emptiness of stomach.
—*Mickelson & Taylor (1950)*

Current indications are that hunger sensations have caused more pangs than the emptiness of the stomach.
—*Ruch (1970)*

Psychological Explanation of Hunger

The availability of food, its prominence and other external cues tell obese subjects when to eat. In contrast, normal-weight individuals eat in response to internal physiological mechanisms, such as hunger. Some experts argue that obese people are not necessarily more responsive to external cues than are normal-weight people. It may be simply that their physiological responses are triggered more quickly than those of normal-weight people. Both the internal physiological cues and externally learned cues motivate people to seek food.
—*Schachter (1971)*

because they are associated directly with physiological systems. Other physiological motives include temperature regulation, sleep, pain avoidance and a need for oxygen.

(i) **Hunger:** Earlier experimental literature of hunger states that the source of hunger drive is stomach contractions. The experiments were simple. The observers used subjects who were trained to swallow small balloons with rubber tubes attached. The balloons were inflated in the stomach and the rubber tubes were connected to kymographs recording mechanisms. Each spasm of the stomach muscles would cause a mark on the smoked drum. On different occasions, the subjects were also asked to press a key when they felt hunger pangs. As a result, a mark was made on the drum just below the record of stomach activities. The abnormal breathing of the subjects were also recorded.

The investigator could recognise whether the spasms represented in the record were due to stomach or abdominal movements. It was observed that the hunger pangs coincided with stomach contractions, but these pangs were not related to movements of the abdominal muscles.

But the subsequent work on hunger presents a different story. The conclusions are that the relationship between stomach contractions and hunger is weak. A joint venture of both psychologists and physiologists tried to find some other conditions of the body which trigger hunger. Research also has shown that people report normal feelings of hunger even when the nerves from the stomach have been cut or the stomach has been entirely removed.

Physiologists believe that changes in the metabolic functions of the liver when fuel supplies are low provide the body's stimulus for hunger. The liver can give a signal to hypothalamus that more fuel is needed which triggers hunger drive. Further experiments on the functions of hypothalamus revealed that two regions of hypothalamus are involved in the hunger drive – lateral hypothalamus and ventro-medial area. Lateral hypothalamus is the excitatory area. Animals eat when this area is stimulated. When this area is damaged, animals stop eating and die of starvation.

Cessation of Eating: Satiety

Our stomach contains nutrient receptors which provide satiety – "stop eating" signals.

Another satiety signal may be provided by a hormone called cholecystokinin (CCK). This hormone is involved in the breakdown of fats. It is released when food reaches the part of the intestine immediately below the stomach.

Lateral Hypothalamus: Start-eating centre
Ventromedial Hypothalamus: Stop-eating centre

Psychological Explanation of Hunger

People eat for reasons other than hunger. Obese adults tend to eat not only when they are hungry, but whenever food is present.
—Stanley Schachter (1971)

Double Depletion Hypothesis

The idea that cellular dehydration and hypovolemia contribute to thirst and drinking is called the "double-depletion hypothesis".

The two mechanisms under double-depletion hypothesis work together to regulate water intake of the body. The mechanisms, which explain the intake of water, also seem to be responsible for stopping the intake of water. However, the precise physiological mechanisms underlying the thirst drive are yet to be understood.

The ventro-medial area is located in the middle of the hypothalamus, which is otherwise known as the hunger-controlling area. Experts consider this area as the inhibitory region of the hunger drive.

Studies show that when this ventro-medial area is activated, animals develop voracious appetites. They want to take huge amount of food and they also overeat. Experimental literature also says that cessation of eating or satiety is controlled by a hormone called cholecystokinin (cck), which is released into the bloodstream when food reaches the intestine (Gibbs Smith, 1973). Injections of cck to food-deprived rats who are eating causes them to stop eating and to start grooming and other behaviours which are part of satiety in animals (Smith & Gibbs, 1976).

The role of cck as a satiety hormone has been questioned. It is obvious that both hypothalamus and blood chemistry are responsible for hunger.

(ii) **Thirst:** Thirst serves a strong drive mechanism in both animals and humans. Humans can live for weeks without eating, but they can live only a few days without replenishing their supply of fluid. When human beings experience fluid deprivation, their mouths and throats become dry, sending a message to them to drink.

Previously it was believed that drinking is triggered by a dry mouth. But physiologists discovered that a dry mouth does not result in enough drinking to regulate the water balance of the body. Thirst and drinking are controlled by processes within the body itself. Since maintaining its water level is essential for life itself, the body has a set of complicated internal homeostatic processes to regulate its fluid level and drinking behaviour.

Our body's water level is maintained by physiological events in which several hormones play a vital role. One of these hormones is the antidiuretic hormone (ADH). It regulates the loss of water through the kidneys.

Experts believe that thirst drive and drinking of water are mainly triggered by two mechanisms. The first one is that when the water level of the body goes down, certain neurons located within the hypothalamus begin to give

Sex hormones and Their Activational Roles

(a) *Both male and female sex hormones are present in both men and women – it is the relative amounts which differ.*

(b) *At puberty, the sex organs grow rapidly and the hormone release increases markedly.*

(c) *Secondary sexual characteristics – breast development, body shape, pitch of the voice and amount and texture of facial hair, develop under the influence of estrogens and androgens at puberty.*

(d) *Hypothalamus in the brain is responsible for sexual behaviour, as observed in lower animals.*

(e) *As estrogen levels in the blood rise during the reproductive cycle, the females of many species come into what is called estrus or "heat" and will actively engage in sexual behaviour. When not in estrus, they are generally indifferent to male advances.*

How is the sex drive different from other biological drives?

1. *Sex is not necesary to maintain the life of an individual, although it is necessary for the survival of the species.*
2. *Sexual behaviour is not aroused by a lack of substances in the body.*
3. *In higher animals, sexual motivation is perhaps more under the influence of sensory information from the environment – incentives than are other biological motives.*

—*Morgan (1983)*

out water. The thirst which results from this mechanism is known as "cellular dehydration thirst".

Some experimental results also showed that the loss of water from the cells in the particular region of the hypothalamus might initiate a drinking behaviour. The experimenters observed that the neurons in the preoptic regions of the hypothalamus (known as osmoreceptors) are responsible for controlling drinking behaviour of the organism. Thirst triggered by loss of water from the osmoreceptors is called cellular-dehydration thirst.

The second mechanism which is responsible for triggering drinking behaviour is known as hypovolemia or the condition of low blood plasma volume. Loss of water in the body results in hypovolemia or a decrease in the volume of the blood. When blood volume goes down, so does blood pressure. The drop in the blood pressure stimulates the kidney to release an enzyme called renin. This enzyme is involved in the formation of a substance known as angiotensin which circulates the blood and may trigger drinking.

(iii) **Sex Drive:** Sexual behaviour, in part, depends on physiological conditions. So it may be considered as a biological motive.

But sexual motivation is far more than a biological drive. Sexual motivation is social because it involves other people and provides the basis for social grouping in higher animals. Sexual behaviour is powerfully regulated by social pressures and religious beliefs. Sex is psychological because it is an important part of our emotional lives. It can provide intense pleasure, but it can also give us agony and involve us in many difficult decisions.

Physiologists are still trying to find the exact location of the internal control of the sexual drive. The intensity of sexual urge is dependent upon chemical substances circulating in the blood known as sex hormones. Studies confirmed that this urge is profoundly influenced by the presence of hormones produced by gonads – testes in males and ovaries in females. The male sex hormones is known as testosterone. The ovarian hormones are known as estrogens. But in case of human beings, socio-cultural and emotional factors seem to play pivotal roles.

Estrogens
The female sex hormones from ovaries and adrenal glands. Estradiol is one of the most important estrogens.

Androgens
The male sex hormone is secreted into blood from both the testes and adrenal glands. Testosterone is a major androgen.

Studies show that purely biological processes like hormone secretions seem to play insignificant roles in sex drive. It was also observed that women have greater sexual desire immediately before and after the menstrual period than during the fertile period, which corresponds to the heat period of animals. Sexual behaviour is also influenced by other endocrine glands. Pituitary and adrenal glands are, very often, responsible for sex drive.

Studies also indicate that, in case of humans, sexual drive is primarily stimulated by external stimuli and its expression depends upon cultural learning. One psychologist has advanced a theory that sex is more a learned drive than a biological one.

Scientific investigation of normal human sexual behaviour was first conducted by Alfred Kinsey (1953). William Masters and Virginia Johnson (1979) broke down the traditional sexual taboo and legitimised the study of human sexuality by direct observation and recording. From their study, they have drawn four conclusions :

1. Men and women have similar patterns of sexual responses, regardless of the source of arousal.
2. Although the sequence of phase of the sexual response cycle is similar in the two sexes, women are more variable, tending to respond more slowly but often remaining aroused longer.
3. Many women can have multiple orgasms, while men rarely do in a comparable time period.
4. Penis size is generally unrelated to any aspect of sexual performance (except in the male's attitude about the size of the penis).

Masters and Johnson also found four phases in the human sexual response cycle- excitement, plateau, orgasm and resolution.

1. In the excitement phase, there are changes in the blood vessels in the pelvic region. The penis becomes erect, the clitoris swells and blood and other fluids become congested in the testicles and vagina.
2. A maximum level of arousal is reached in the plateau phase. Rapid increases of heartbeat, respiration, blood pressure, muscle tension and glandular secretions are found.
3. Both males and females experience a very pleasurable sense of release from the cumulative sexual tension in the orgasm phase. Orgasm is characterised by rhythmic genital contractions. It culminates in ejaculation of sperm in men and can involve either clitoral or vaginal sensations in women.

4. During the resolution phase, the body gradually returns to its normal pre-excitement stage with both blood pressure and heartbeat blowing down. After one orgasm, most men enter a refractory period preventing further orgasm for hours together. But with sustained arousal, women are capable of multiple orgasms in fairly rapid succession.

Sexual Cues
For most humans, the goal of sexual activity is "the attainment of a cognitive state: the conscious perception of sexual satisfaction. The state depends upon a combination of experiences originating in experiencer's body and in that of the sexual partner."
—*Davidson (1981)*

Sexual Scripts
Sexual scripts are socially learned programmes of sexual interpretation and responsiveness.
—*Zimbardo (2003)*

Date Rape
Date Rape is a trauma which illustrates devastating conflict between male and female sexual scripts.

The Sleep Cycle
1. *In Stage-1 sleep, the EEG shows brain waves similar to the waking state, if a bit slower.*
2. *During Stage-2, the EEG is characterised by sleep spindles, minute bursts of electrical activity, faster than Stage-1 brain waves.*

Sexual Cues

Sexual activities which may culminate in orgasm can begin with a single unconditioned stimulus but involves an endless variety of conditioned stimuli. The unconditioned stimulus may be tactile stimulation or touch. In the form of genital caresses, touch is a universal component of sexual foreplay (Ford & Beach, 1951). Any stimuli that become associated with genital touch or orgasm can become conditioned motivators. These conditioned motivators may be present physically or only in memory or fantasy. Studies indicate that sensations and fantasy during masturbation provide the primal setting for associating virtually any stimulus with pleasurable arousal. For human beings, sexuality can be less concerned with meeting physiological need than with satisfying cognitive desires.

Sexual Scripts

Very often, the questions are:
1. How do you know you are "supposed" to feel aroused?
2. What do you do when you feel that way?

Our culture provides us with many cues but few helpful lessons. Sexual scripts are socially learned programmes of sexual interpretation and responsiveness. An individual learns the importance of kissing and touching from the images in movies and television. Advertisements and gossip also contribute to many young people's sexual scripts. Different aspects of these scripts are assembled through social interactions over one's lifetime.

Date Rape

Individual rights and responsibilities in the eyes of the society change within short spans of time. As a result, sexual scripts become dangerously confused. Date rape is a trauma which illustrates devastating conflict between male and female sexual scripts.

In a study, one in every three male college students in US said he would rape a woman, if he was sure he would not

3. In the next two stages (3 & 4), we enter a very deep state of relaxed sleep. Brain waves slow dramatically, breathing and heart rate decreases.
4. After Stage-4, electrical activity of our brain decreases. We experience a REM sleep during this period, our eyes move rapidly back and we begin to dream.

The activation synthesis theory states that dreams result when biological activation throughout the sleeping brain is organised into a meaningful pattern.

get caught (Mulamuth, 1984). In another sample of college women, 57 per cent reported having experienced what they thought of as rape. Experts in sexual behaviour suggest that rape may be a result of confusion over sexual scripts.

Sexual Orientation: Homosexuality and Heterosexuality

Human sexual orientation is a complex business. In the early studies of Kinsey, a large percentage of men had homosexual experience. Gradually psychologists became more interested in this important aspect of human sexual motivation. Cultural and historical studies show that human societies vary widely in their attitudes and expressions about homosexuality. In some cultures, it is suppressed, but in other cultures, it is accepted.

Neurobiology studies identified hypothalamus as somehow being responsible for homosexual or heterosexual behaviour. In their studies, Simon Levay (1991) and Hamer (1995) have found that a part of the hypothalamus of homosexuals was significantly smaller than the heterosexuals. Research works in this field also revealed that individual gays and lesbians go through a developmental sequence in experiencing and recognising their sexual orientation. Four stages have been identified in this self-definition process. These are:

1. Until about age 12, boys and girls feel "different" from their peers, not in sexual feelings, but in terms of preferred activities.
2. As adolescents, they recognise their sexual feelings do not match the heterosexual script.
3. By early childhood, they begin to incorporate homosexuality into their self-identity, interacting with other gays and lesbians and dealing with the social stigma attached to their orientation.

Serotonin and norepinephrine are brain chemicals necessary for storing memories. We forget some 95 per cent of our dreams because they are only stored temporarily in our short-term memory. They cannot be printed to more permanent memory because serotonin and norepine-phrine are shut off during dreams.

4. Lastly, they come to see their homosexuality as natural and normal for themselves.

However, human sexual orientation does not have a single cause. Cultural variation plays a vital role in sexual orientation. Some theorists state that the individual's family life or early learning experiences influence the development of a particular sexual orientation.

(iv) **Sleep:** Sleep is the basic necessity of life. About one-third of our life is spent in sleeping. It is a dramatic alteration of consciousness and it also happen spontaneously. The ordinary fluctuations in consciousness are part of the rhythmic in nature.

Sleep Work

- Sleep may be as much a habit as it is a need.
- Sleep duration can be controlled by circadian rhythms.
- Children begin life by sleeping about 16 hours per day, with half that time devoted to REM. Young adults typically sleep 7 to 8 hours, with 20 per cent REM. By old age, people sleep very little, with only 15 per cent of sleep in REM.
- Sleep has definite functions and is not merely a state of being "not awake".
- Dreams are vivid, colourful and nonsensical hallucinations characterised by complex mini-plots.
- Dreams are primarily REM phenomena.

Decoding Dreams

1. Dreams have two levels of meanings: Manifest Content and Latent content (Freud, 1900).
2. The manifest content is the story of the dream. What we dream is the manifest content.
3. But this manifest content is really a "code" or disguise for the latent content.
4. The latent content is the true meaning of the dream, hidden behind the symbols of the manifest story.
5. The manifest content disguises the latent meaning of the dream.

Activation-Synthesis

The proponents of activation-synthesis

All creatures in this world are influenced by nature's rhythms. Human beings are attuned to a time cycle known as circadian rhythms. These rhythms are bodily patterns which repeat approximately in every 24 hours. About one-third of circadian rhythm is devoted to the period of energy-restoring rest called sleep.

The most significant discovery after EEG technology in sleep research was that of rapid eye-movement (REM). These are the bursts of quick eye movements under closed eyelids, occurring at periodic intervals during sleep. The time when a sleeper is not showing REM is known as non-REM or NREM sleep.

Dreams are possible during REM sleep. But NREM reports were filled with brief descriptions of ordinary daily activities, similar to waking thoughts.

Research indicated that over the course of the night, our sleep cycle crosses several stages, each of which shows a distinct EEG pattern. It takes about 90 minutes to progress through the first four stages of sleep (NREM sleep).

The first period of REM sleep last for about 10 minutes. In a night's sleep, an individual passes through this 10 minute cycle four to six times. With each cycle, the amount of time spent in deep sleep (stages 3 & 4) decreases and the amount of time spent in REM sleep increases. During the last cycle, we may spend an hour in REM sleep. If we are deprived of REM sleep for a night, we would have more REM sleep than usual the next night.

REM sleep also plays a key role in the maintenance of moods and emotions. It is also required for storing memories.

There is biological need for sleep. Sleep has two general functions: to conserve and to restore. It enables animals to conserve energy at times when there is no need to forage for food, search for mates or work. Sleep also enables the body to restore itself in several ways. During sleep, the neurotransmitters build up to compensate for the quantities used in daily activities and the neurons return to their optimal level of sensitivity. Sleep and dreams help the brain to flush out the day's accumulation of unwanted and useless information. Research work *theory were J. Allan Hobson and Robert Mc Carley (1977).*

They said that REM sleep furnishes the brain with an internal source of activation, when external stimulation is turned down, to promote the growth and development of the brain.

Instincts
- *Inherited, inborn, unlearned, predetermined behaviour patterns.*

Imprinting
- *The process by which animals form species-specific behaviours during a critical period early in life. These behaviours are not easily modified.*

also indicated that dreams can also serve to reduce fantasy and obsession.

Sleep accomplishes important physical and psychological work. How much time should we sleep? This is an intriguing question, since sleep may be as much a habit as a need. The duration of nocturnal sleep depends upon many factors. There is a genetic need for sleep which is different for each species.

For human beings, volitional determinants are important for sleep. These volitional determinant includes "wanting to sleep." That means, how much time an individual wants to sleep. Human beings can actively control the length of sleep in a number of ways, such as staying up late and using alarm clocks. Studies also indicated that duration of sleep can be controlled by circadian rhythms, so that how long we sleep may depend on our personal peak times for REM. Individuals very in the amount of sleep they need.

People who sleep longer than average are found to be more nervous, worrisome, artistic, creative and nonconforming. Short sleepers are generally more energetic and extrovert people.

Strenuous physical activity does not affect REM time (Orne, 1988). Sleep duration also varies over one's life time. Moreover, sleep has definite functions, it is not merely a state of being "not awake". We, very often, become concerned when our sleep is disturbed or inadequate.

Dreams

Dreams are the most fascinating events of the human minds. They are primarily vivid, colourful and completely nonsensical hallucinations characterised by complex miniplots. The dreams are probably best characterised as the theatre of the absurd – chaotic dramas which appear illogical when analysed in the rational mindset of our waking hours. Dream research received its impetus from sleep laboratory findings which correlated rapid eye-movements, unique EEG patterns, etc. Now dreams have become a vital area of study for scientific researchers.

Dreams are basically REM phenomena. But some dreams of different quality also come out during NREM periods. Dreams in NREM states have less story-like qualities and little sensory images. A comparative study indicated that we can recall a much higher percentage of REM dreams than NREM dreams (Freeman, 1973).

Why do we dream?

Two broad views of dreaming are prominent: Dreaming as Adaptation and Dreaming as an Outcome.

1. Dreaming as Adaptation: In his classic book *The Interpretation of Dreams* (1900), Sigmund Freud said that dream analysis is the cornerstone of psychoanalysis. According to him, dreams are the royal roads to the unconscious. In the Freudian perspective, dreams have two main functions: (a) to guard sleep and (b) to serve as sources of wish fulfilment.

Dreams guard sleep by relieving psychic tensions created during the day and by allowing the dreamer to work through unconscious desires. The wish-fulfilment theory says that the unfulfilled desires are satisfied in dreams.

2. Dreaming as an Outcome: Some experts view dreams as accidental events and the outcomes of biological processes involved in sleep. When we sleep, the brain stem emits random electrical discharges. As this energy activates higher areas of the cerebral contex, the sleeper experiences impression of sensations and movements.

The activation is purely biological and the events are not logically connected. But our brain tries to make sense of the flood of input it receives. Then the brain also synthesises the separate bursts of electrical activation by producing a coherent story – a dream.

(v) *Need for Sensory Stimulation:* Human beings have many sensory organs, such as eyes, ears, nose, skin, tongue, etc. These organs are the gateways of information about both environments and the conditions within. Different studies indicate that human beings are in constant need of some kind of sensory stimulation. When deprived of a normal amount of visual, auditory or tactile stimulation, adults may become irritable and consider their situation or environment intolerable. Lack of sensory experience does not result in physiological imbalance, yet both humans and animals seek sensory stimulation. Studies have shown that animals and humans appear to have an innate desire to explore, manipulate and experience the world.

Early studies indicated that instincts or inborn behaviour patterns are the prime motivators of all organisms. Instincts are inborn, unlearned and predetermined behaviour patterns. Instinctive behaviour is more apparent in animals than in humans. Subsequently, the instinct explanation was abandoned in favour of learning theories, at least for human behaviour.

Instinctive behaviour is more apparent in animals than in humans. The best example of instinctive behaviour is imprinting. It is a process by which a behaviour pattern specific to one species is established in a member of that species through exposure to appropriate stimuli during a critical periods, early in life. Early research on ducks has shown that, if imprinted with a moving object other than their mother during the critical period, they would follow that object as if it was their mother. Such behaviour is clearly biologically determined and instinctive. However, no such process has been shown conclusively to exist in humans.

(vi) *Need for Postural Changes:* Need for postural changes is a physiological need. We need to change our body postures constantly at some time intervals. Photographic evidences indicate that during sleep at night, an individual changes his or her posture more than four hundred times. In the classroom, a student has minute shifts of his or her body position.

Social Motives

Social motives are otherwise known as secondary motives. They are also known as acquired or learned motives. These motives are complex in nature. Social motives are called secondary because they involve interaction with others and are learned due to social conditioning in a social context. They develop due to habit and conditioning. Since they are learned motives, their strength differs greatly from one individual to another.

A social motive which acts on an individual is dependent upon the individual's own social experience. It is unique for the individual and depends upon his or her way of perceiving things. For this reason, it is difficult to arrive at a commonly agreed list of social motives. But this is possible in case of biological motives. Since social motives are inferred from behaviour, it is very difficult to measure these motives.

(i) *Need for Affiliation:* Seeking other human beings and wanting to be close to them both physically and psychologically is called affiliation. It refers to the need that people have to be with others. This motive is aroused when individuals feel helpless or threatened and also when they are happy. Individuals high on this need are motivated to seek the company of others and to maintain friendly relationships with other people.

Research findings indicate that fear and anxiety are closely related with the affiliation motive. Where the degree of anxiety and threat is very high, such affiliation behaviour is often absent. Studies also revealed that early learning experiences influence this motive. The first born or the only child in the family has stronger affiliation needs than those born later. Studies have also shown that children who are brought up to be dependent or raised with closed family ties show a stronger affiliation need than those coming from more closely-knit families which encourage early independence. Cultural differences were also found. Affiliation needs are stronger in some cultures than in others.

Four General Ways of Expressing Power
(a) People do things to gain feelings of power and strength from sources outside themselves.
(b) People do things to gain feelings of power and strength from sources within themselves.
(c) People do things as individuals to have impact on others.
(d) People do things as members of organisations to have impact on others.
—McClelland (1975)

(ii) *Need for Power:* The need for power expresses itself in behaviours which tend to control and influence the course of events including the behaviours of others. Historically, humans have always fought for power. Power was desired by individuals as an instrument to satisfy other motives like aggression, greed, affiliation, etc. Now psychologists consider power motive as an independent motive in itself. This view was proposed by McClelland.

In his theory, David McClelland (1975) has said that power motive can be revealed through four general ways:

1. People do things to gain feelings of power and strength from sources outside themselves. For example, children express power motivation by reading stories. Individuals gain strength by reading the activities of past leaders.
2. People do things to gain feelings of power and strength from sources within themselves. For example, a college student may express power motivation by body-building and by mastering urges and impulses.
3. People do things to have impact on others. For example, an individual may argue with another individual or may have a competitive attitude in order to influence that person.
4. People do things as members of organisations to have an impact on others. For example, the leader of a political party may use the principles of his or her party or an army officer may express the need for power through the chain of command to influence others.

Studies show that for an individual, any one of these ways of expressing power motivation may dominate. But a combination of power motives cannot be ruled out. With age and experience, the dominant mode of expression often changes. Studies have also shown that women seem to have less strong needs for power than men. They choose indirect ways for impact and influence. For example, women prefer to express their power motivation by being counsellors, advisors and resource persons for other people.

(iii) **Dependency Motive:** Dependency refers to interpersonal relationships where an individual behaves in a way in order to gain attention, assistance, comfort and support from fellow persons. For example, children spend more time with parents or intimate friends in difficult situations. People appear to be more dependent on social interactions and approval. Studies show that the girls and women tend to be more dependent and more affiliative than boys. In stress, people want to resort to dependency.

Dependency
It refers to interpersonal relationships where an individual behaves in a way in order to gain attention, comfort, reassurance and support from fellow persons.

Co-operation
It is an acquired motive. It signifies lack of mutual disagreement and opposition among fellow group members and absence of rivalry.

(iv) **Cooperation Motive:** Cooperation is an acquired motive. Moreover, it is a condition manifested when two or more individuals or groups work together to achieve a common goal. It signifies lack of mutual disagreement and lack of opposition among fellow group members and absence of rivalry.

Research indicates that the citizens of Zuni in New Mexico are found to be extremely co-operative. Being wealthy in Zuni brings no status. Status is derived not from power, but from friendship. A happy and successful Zuni has many friends. Different studies on a altruism among children say that helping-behaviour can be fostered through the use of models (Peulson, 1974).

*(v) **Conformity Motive:*** Conformity refers to the tendency to allow one's opinions, attitudes, actions and even perceptions to be affected by prevailing opinions, attitudes, actions and perceptions. Often people act in ways consistent with the majority. This tendency to "go along with the group" is popularly known as "behavioural conformity".

Changes in attitude, belief also take place due to pressures from others. This is known as "attitudinal conformity". There is also conformity of personality traits, i.e., underlying characteristics of a person undergoes changes according to the norms of the society.

With the help of a conformity curve, F.H. Allport (1935) described the conformity motive phenomena. He stated that most people exhibit complete conformity to social norms with few people having deviations. Our submissiveness to social influences is due to conformity motives to the norms of the society in which we live. Norms refer to behaviour that is usual or expected, acceptable and socially prescribed.

Psychological and Personal Motives

(i) ***Curiosity:*** Curiosity is a psychological motive. It is a motivational tendency to act which does not have specific and indefinable goals. Behind any act of exploration, investigation and research, there is a desire to know, which is otherwise known as "curiosity".

Research findings of Dember (1956) and Fowler (1958) say that rats preferred novelty, change and complexity in Y and T mazes. It is not an exclusively human trait. Animal experiments showed that curiosity behaviour is also found in many animals (Buttler, 1954). Curiosity motives for sensory stimulation are also conducive for the motive for exploration.

Evidences indicates that curiosity motive can be unlearned. The need for changing sensory stimulation is closely related to curiosity. It is the basic motive. Exploration and curiosity are just two expressions of it. Very often, we are motivated to master challenges in the environment. This is called "Competence Motivation".

(ii) ***Achievement Motivation:*** The need for achievement causes individuals to strive for bigger and better accomplishments. It is a personal need which directs a person to strive constantly for excellence and success. It is a personality variable which appears to differ from one individual to another. Some people are highly achievement-oriented and competence-oriented and others are not so.

This motive has been a subject of intensive study by a group of Harvard psychologists like David McClelland and John Atkinson. They used projective tests to assess achievement motivation. Many studies have been done to find out the relationship between achievement motivation and performance. Generally, people with a need for achievement seek to accomplish things and to improve performance. The results of these studies say that people who are high in achievement

Need for Achievement
It is a personal need which directs a person to strive constantly for excellence and success.

motivation generally do better on tasks than those who are low. Further studies also state that people high in the need for achievement are motivated to succeed.

Research also indicates that the need for achievement is increased by independence, training and self-dependent attitudes. McClelland has found that the need for achievement is also related positively with higher economic status in the society. Both extrinsic and intrinsic motivation are closely related to achievement motivation.

(iii) ***Self-actualisation:*** A humanistic approach of motive was developed by Maslow (1954). This approach is very important for its practical value. Maslow's humanistic model is popularly known as the "theory of self-actualisation".

Maslow's approach was unique. He attempted to present a total picture of human behaviour. Maslow tried to explain human motives or needs by arranging them in a hierarchy, in the order of potency and priority of unsatisfied human needs.

The most basic aspects of human motivation are physiological needs and at the highest level is the desire to utilise one's personal capacities. Here the individual develops his or her potentialities to the fullest and to engage in activities for which he or she is well-inclined. This level is called self-actualisation.

- **Psychic Energy and Theory of Instincts**
  Freud assumed two types of energy: the physiological energy and the psychic energy. Physiological energy is derived from food and the psychic energy is derived from neuro-physiological states of excitation.
- **Instinct**
  Instinct is a wish to fulfil a physiological need. An instinct is an internal drive which operates as a constant motivational force. It originates from id but comes under the control of the ego.

Maslow's approach reveals that every category of need has a limited capacity to motivate behaviour. Beyond this point of limitation, it is necessary to involve a higher category of need to motivate action. But this humanistic approach has been criticised for being over-optimistic about humankind in general. This has been discussed under Humanistic Theory of Motivation.

Theories of Motivation

In the past, philosophers tried to distinguish between human action and non-human action. Basically, human action is guided by reason and free will, but non-human action is dominated by brute appetites. Later, Darwin's theory of evolution challenged this distinction. He said that both human and animal behaviours are driven by instinct. Five theoretical perspectives are very prominent: instinct theory, drive theory, arousal theory, humanistic theory and social cognitive theory.

(a) ***Instinct Theory:*** Instinct theory states that organisms are born with certain inbuilt tendencies which are essential for their survival. The instinct concept also explains the behaviour of many non-humans. The instinct theorists merely describe instincts in terms of mysterious inner forces that impelled certain activities.

William James (1890) stated that humans rely on even more instincts than lower animals do to guide their behaviour. But Sigmund Freud (1915) had a different view of instincts.

Homeostasis
A state of physiological balance within the body. It is the body's internal balance or equilibrium.

Arousal Theory
A theory of motivation suggesting that human beings seek an optimal level of arousal, not minimal levels of arousal.

Task Difficulty
On some tasks, performance is best when motivation is relatively low. The key to the appropriate level of motivation is "task-difficulty".

The Yerkes–Dodson Law
As arousal increases, performance of difficult tasks decreases and performance of easy tasks increases. (Yerkes & Dodson, 1908)

Maslow's Hierarchy of Needs
Maslow's theory holds that our basic needs form a needs hierarchy. Our inborn needs are arranged in a sequence of stages, a hierarchy, from primitive to advanced goals.

Freud maintained that human beings are complex energy systems. He assumed two types of energy – physiological energy and psychic energy. Physiological energy is derived from the food we consume and it is utilised for purposes like breathing, walking, running, writing, etc. Psychic energy is derived from the "neurophysiological states of excitation".

The id is the mediating point between the psychic energy and physiological energy. Each person has a limited psychic energy and the total amount of psychic energy is expended in those mental activities that attempt to reduce bodily excitation created by the various needs. The psychological or mental representations of these bodily excitations or need is called "instinct".

In other words, instinct is a wish to fulfil a physiological need. For example, thirst instinct is derived from water deficit in the body cells and it is mentally represented as a wish for drinking water. Thus instinct indicates quantity of psychic energy and all instincts taken together constitute the total amount of energy available to the person.

Freud distinguishes two categories of instincts – the life instinct or eros and the death instinct or thanatos.

Life instinct includes all those forces that maintain vital life processes and assure propagation of species. Of the various life instincts, sex instinct was singled out by Freud to include not just the desire for and enjoyment of genital sexual pleasure but also pleasure derived from several bodily areas. Sex instinct is important for the development of personality.

Death instinct is also known as destructive instinct which includes all those forces that underline the manifestation of suicide, murder, aggression and cruelty.

Right from the beginning, life instinct and death instinct constantly interact with each other and both interact with the reality principle.

Subsequently, the learning theorists have criticised the theory of instincts developed by Freud. They demonstrated that much of the seemingly "inborn" behaviour is really learned.

(b) Drive Theory: Drive theory was introduced by Robert Woodworth (1918). He, along with William James, viewed motivation as an inner drive which determines behaviour. He also defined drive in biological terms as energy released from an organism's store.

Clark Hull (1943, 1952) developed a different approach. His drive-reduction theory is homeostatic because it assumes that an organism is driven to maintain homeostasis. Homeostasis is a balance among the systems and processes of the body. But during the 1950s, studies showed that humans and animals often do things in the absence of any apparent deprivation or drive reduction in order to increase stimulation.

(c) *Arousal Theory:* Early research indicated that certain emotions such as fear and rage motivate us for action when we are faced with danger. These arousal reactions are accompanied by measurable bodily changes.

Arousal is a measure of the general responsiveness of an organism to activation of the brain stem's reticular system. EEG measurements revealed about the ways arousal of the brain prepares individuals to respond to stimuli. Some research findings also indicated a particular relationship between arousal and performance.

How does arousal affect performance? Some experimental graphs indicated that as motivation increased, the performance first rose and then later declined over time. This U-shaped graph indicated that either too little or too much motivation can impair performance. This inverted U-shaped curve (of relationship) implies that an individual has a "best level" of arousal for performing a particular task. Such optimal level is the level of arousal at which one best performs tasks of varying levels of difficulty.

It was found that on some tasks, performance is best when motivation is relatively low. The key to the appropriate level of motivation is 'task difficulty'. With difficult or complex tasks, even mild arousal quickly approaches the optimal level for the performer. On the other hand, for simple or easy tasks, the optimal level of motivation required is greater. The Yerkes–Dodson Law reveals the relationship between arousal and performance. According to this law, as arousal increases, performance of difficult tasks decreases and performance of easy tasks increases (Yerkes & Dodson, 1908).

(d) *Humanistic Theory:* Humanistic psychologist Abraham Maslow (1970) developed a theory of motivation popularly known as the theory of self-actualisation.

Transcendence
(spiritual needs for cosmic identification)
Self-Actualisation
(needs to fulfil potential, have meaningful goals)
Aesthetic
(needs for order, beauty)
Cognitive
(needs for knowledge, understanding, novelty)
Esteem
(needs for confidence, sense of worth and competence, self-esteem and respect of others)
Attachment
(needs to belong, affiliate, to love and to be loved)
Safety
(needs for security, comfort, tranquility, freedom from fear)
Biological
(needs for food, water, oxygen, rest, sexual expression, release from tension)

Maslow holds that the basic biological needs, such as hunger and thirst, are at the bottom of hierarchy. They must be satisfied before other needs can begin to operate. When biological needs are satisfied, safety needs motivate us. When we are no longer concerned about danger, we become motivated by attachment needs – needs to belong and affiliate with others. If we are well-fed and safe and if we feel a sense of social belonging, we move up to esteem needs. These include the needs to like oneself, to see oneself as competent and effective and to do what is necessary to earn the esteem of others. Then stimulation of thought invites "cognitive needs". We are motivated by strong cognitive needs to know about our past existence and to predict the future. For this reason, scholars and scientists spend their lives in the quest for new knowledge. The next level of Maslow's hierarchy comes the human desire for beauty and order, in the form of aesthetic needs which give rise to the creative aspect of humanity.

At the top of the hierarchy, is the need for self-actualisation. A self-actualised person is self-aware, self-accepting, socially responsive, creative, spontaneous and open to novelty and challenge. These people move beyond basic human needs in the quest for the fullest development of their potential or self-actualisation.

The hierarchy of needs includes a step beyond the total fulfilment of individual potential. The need for transcendence may lead to higher states of consciousness and a cosmic vision of one's part in universe. Of course, very few people develop the desire to move beyond the self to achieve union with spiritual forces.

Some researchers support Maslow's hierarchy of needs and others rejected the idea of transcendence. Some psychologists feel that spiritual needs are not scientific.

(e) **Social Cognitive Theories:** Social-cognitive theories place importance on subjective motivation. The propounders believe that the higher mental processes control motivation, but not the physiological arousal or biological mechanisms. This idea clearly shows why human beings are often motivated by imagined, future events rather than by genuine, immediate circumstances.

In social-learning theory, Julian Rotter (1954) placed importance on expectations in motivating behaviour. According to Rotter, the probability that someone will engage in a given behaviour is determined by two factors: (i) The person's expectations of attaining the goal following that activity and (ii) the personal value

---

Self-actualisation

The process of realising one's unique human potential or the process of achieving everything that one is capable of achieving.

- *Self-actualised people are those who have achieved their true natures and fulfilled their potential.*
- *According to Maslow, self-actualised people:*
  – *are realistic*
  – *accept themselves for what they are*
  – *are problem centred*
  – *have a need for privacy*
  – *are independent*
  – *have spiritual experiences*

Locus of Control

A locus of control orientation is a belief that the outcomes of our actions are contingent on either what one does (internal control) or on events outside one's personal control (external control).

of that goal. Expectation of a future occurrence is based on our past reinforcement history which, in turn, has helped us feel a personal sense of "locus of control" or the "origin of one's life influences".

A locus of control orientation is a belief that the outcomes of our actions are contingent on either what we do (internal control) or on events outside our personal control (external control).

Unconscious Motivation

Sometimes we perform some action without our knowledge. This aspect of our behaviour can be analysed through Freud's concept of unconscious. Both the concepts of "instinct" and "unconscious", which were developed by Freud at the beginning of 20th century, are main pillars of psychoanalysis. These terms are very important to explain human motivation.

Collective Unconscious
In Jung's theory, this is the portion of the unconscious shared by all human beings.

In his theory of psychoanalysis, Freud said that the unconscious includes ideas, thoughts and feelings which cannot be brought to awareness or conscious level by ordinary means. It is just like an unseen force, which influences conscious thoughts and the actions of the individual. Freud said that unconscious processes guide human behaviour and this can be known by special techniques devised by psychoanalysts. These special techniques are hypnosis, free-association, dream-analysis, etc.

In his analytical psychology, C.G. Jung, a student of Freud, also emphasised human behaviour and its relation with the unconscious mind. He differed from Freud, his teacher, in many ways. According to him, the unconscious is much more complicated. It is made up of two functional divisions: (i) the personal unconscious and (ii) the collective unconscious or racial unconscious.

Personal unconscious is somewhat similar to Freud's concept of the unconscious. But Jung's idea of "collective unconscious" is different and influential. C.G. Jung believed that human behaviour is guided by two potential forces: the unconscious and teleology.

Human unconscious includes everything about our past life and teleology includes everything about the future like one's aims, aspirations and intentions. So the psychic life results from an interaction of the past with the future. C.G. Jung said that the main agency which guides the past and future is the ego. He calls it the "conscious mind" in his psychoanalytic theory. The conscious mind is made up of conscious perceptions, memories, thoughts, feelings, etc. But there is a bigger interacting system which lies beyond our ego. It influences our behaviour. Jung calls it the "personality" of an individual.

In his theory, C.G. Jung presented a fascinating concept called "collective unconscious". According to him, this is the most powerful and influential system of the personality. The collective unconscious is inherited from a person's ancestral past.

Jung also held that an individual always adopts a mask in response to social demands, norms and conventions. He called this "persona". This is the role assigned to the person by the society. The intention of having a mask is to make a definite impression upon others and often to conceal the real nature of the individual. In short, the persona is the public personality, which is different from the private personality.

In his theory, C.G. Jung also said that humans inherit some animal instincts, which indicate the animal side of their nature. This nature can be inferred from the display of violence, aggression and injury to oneself. The concept of "unconscious motivation" was heavily criticised by many psychologists later. This approach was stated to be most unscientific by many experts. Jung's idea of collective unconscious is considered to be absurd and which lacks scientific proof.

Measurement of Human Motives

It is very difficult to measure human motives, because they are a complex phenomena. Earlier, animal motives were measured by the activity wheel and obstruction method. But the idea of measuring human motivation through activity is ridiculous. At the human level, there can be motivated activity as well as unmotivated activity.

Human motivation shows a high degree of complexity. For example, the Freudian concept of unconscious motivation indicates that different forms of activity may spring from the same motive. This has necessitated the development of a variety of tools and techniques for measuring motivation. After consideration, psychologists have developed many different tools and techniques.

Direct and Indirect Measurement of Motives

The two approaches to the measurement of human motives are: (a) Direct Measurement and (b) Indirect Measurement.

When motives or needs are assessed through objective observations, it is called "Direct Measurement of Motives". These measurements include conscious self-reports and administration of questionnaires and inventories to assess specific motives as required by the observer. For the measurement of drives like hunger and thirst, many gadgets have been derived. These gadgets have quantitative measures of the level of deprivation and physiological changes accompanying the drive and some behavioural changes. Here, the tools are structured and responses are classified into predetermined categories.

Subsequently, some experts rejected the concept of direct approach of measuring motivation. They opined that motives cannot be measured directly but can be inferred through certain indirect means. So they use projective techniques for the measurement of motivation. In these measurements the stimuli are deliberately made ambiguous and the individual (or the subject) is free to respond according to his or her own wish. Popular indirect techniques are ink-blots, pictures, incomplete sentences and ambiguous figures.

Chances of faking are somewhat less in these techniques. An individual is more likely to project his or her own needs and motives into responses. The most popular test is the Thematic Apperception Test (TAT) developed by Morgan and Murray in 1935. This test consists of a series of pictures about which the individual is asked to write stories. The collected stories are then analysed and evaluated for motives and needs which are observed to have been projected by the respondent into the characters in the pictures.

But these tests are also not free from criticisms. Despite their flaws, these projective techniques are often used by psychiatrists and psychoanalysts to discover reasons for neurotic and psychotic diseases.

❑ Key Terms

1. Affiliation
2. Androgens
3. Biological motives
4. Cellular Dehydration Thirst
5. Circadian Rhythms
6. Collective unconscious
7. Conformity motive
8. Curiosity
9. Date Rape
10. Dependency motive
11. Dream
12. Drive
13. Drive reduction
14. Dynamic equilibrium
15. Effectance Motivation
16. Estrogen
17. Extrinsic motivation
18. Frustration
19. Goal
20. Hierarchy of needs
21. Homeostasis
22. Homosexuality
23. Hunger
24. Hypothalamus
25. Hypovolemia
26. Imprinting
27. Incentive
28. Instinct
29. Instrumental behaviour
30. Intrinsic motivation
31. Locus of control
32. Motivation
33. Motivational cycle
34. Need
35. Need for achievement
36. NREM Sleep
37. Orgasm
38. Personal Unconscious
39. Postural changes
40. REM Sleep
41. Self-actualisation
42. Sensory stimulation
43. Serotonin
44. Sex
45. Sexual Scripts
46. Sleep
47. Sleep cycle
48. Sleep work
49. Task difficulty
50. Teleology
51. Testosterone
52. Thalamus
53. Thematic Apperception Test (TAT)
54. Thirst
55. Unconscious motivation

❏ Chapter Summary and Review

1. Motivation is an internal condition which involves starting, directing and maintaining physical and physiological activities.
2. The term "motivation" is derived from the Latin word "movere" which means to move.
3. Drive is a physiological state. It leads a person to activity. Only an unsatisfied need generates a drive. Needs are physiological imbalances which give rise to drives.
4. A motive is a specific internal condition directing an organism's behaviour towards a goal.

| Drive | Mobilisation of Behaviour | Incentive | Drive Reduction |

5. Often, the behaviours are performed for no apparent reward except the pleasure of activity itself. Psychologists call these type of behaviours as intrinsically motivated behaviour.
6. Extrinsic motivation is directed towards goals external to the individual.
7. When motives are aroused, they trigger behaviour which leads to a goal. Finally, after the goal is reached, they are shut off. This is called the motivational cycle.
8. Human bodies need to maintain a physiological balance. It is essential for their existence. Restoration of physiological balance or equilibrium is called "homeostasis".
9. The main physiological cause of hunger is the low blood-sugar level which accompanies food deprivation. Studies reveal that hypothalamus is also responsible for hunger and thirst.
10. The sexual responsiveness of lower animals is primarily under hormonal control. In humans, learning plays a significant role.
11. Sexual scripts are socially learned programmes of sexual interpretation and responsiveness. Date rape is a trauma which illustrates devastating conflict between male and female sexual scripts.
12. Human beings are attuned to a time cycle known as "circadian rhythms". These rhythms are bodily patterns which repeat approximately in every 24 hours. About one-third of circadian rhythms is devoted to the period of energy-restoring rest called "sleep".
13. Dream is a REM phenomenon. It is a collection of vivid, colourful and nonsensical hallucinations characterised by complex miniplots.
14. Need for affiliation is a social need. Seeking other human beings and wanting to be close to them both physically and psychologically is called "affiliation".
15. Need for achievement is a personal need. It causes individuals to strive for bigger and better accomplishments.

16. Maslow revealed that the individual has a need to develop his or her potentialities to the fullest and to engage in activities for which they are well-suited. This is called "self-actualisation".
17. The physiological or mental representations of bodily excitations or need is called "instinct". It is a wish to fulfil a physiological need. An instinct is an internal drive which operates as a constant motivational force.
18. Arousal is a measure of the general responsiveness of an organism to activation of the brain stem's reticular system.
19. On some tasks, performance is best when motivation is relatively low. The key to the appropriate level of motivation is "task difficulty".
20. Cognitive theorists believe that higher mental processes control motivation, but not the physiological arousal or biological mechanisms.
21. The outcomes of our actions are contingent on either what we do or on events outside our personal control. This is known as "locus of control".
22. Direct and indirect measurement of human motives can be done. Indirect measures include projective techniques.

QUESTIONS

1. What is a motive? Discuss the relationship between needs and motives.
2. Define motivation. How do motives differ from incentives?
3. What do you mean by motivational cycle? Point out the differences between needs and drives.
4. Discuss different types of motives with suitable examples.
5. Explain the importance of biological motives in human life.
6. Discuss different social and psychological motives with suitable examples.
7. Distinguish between:
   (a) Drives and incentives
   (b) Motives and needs
   (c) Intrinsic and extrinsic motivation
   (d) Biological and social motives
   (e) Need for recognition and need for achievement.
8. Discuss different methods of measuring motives.
9. Critically evaluate different theories of motivation.
10. Write short notes on the following:
    (a) Incentives
    (b) Need for affiliation
    (c) Self-actualisation
    (d) Homeostasis
    (e) Unconscious motivation
    (f) Intrinsic motives
    (g) Achievement motivation
    (h) Role of motivation in learning
    (i) REM and NREM Sleep
    (j) Sex drive

CHAPTER - 5

MOMENTUM OF LIFE

EMOTION

❑ *Emotion is an acute disturbance of the organism, as a whole psychological in origin, involving behaviour, conscious experience and visceral functioning.*
—*P. T. Young*

❑ *Emotions play a vital part in our motivational patterns. Life without emotion would be virtually a life without motion. Emotion has also organising and motivational values. When strong emotions arise, strong motives are satisfied.*
—*Ruch (1970)*

❑ *The very term "emotion" has been derived from the Latin word "emovere", which means "to move", "to excite", "to stir up" or "to agitate". Arousal-behaviour is emotion, which is an affect-laden state of the organism.*
Affect means experience of pleasantness, unpleasantness, excitation, calmness, tension and relaxation.
—*E.B. Titchener*

❑ **This chapter covers:**
- Meaning and definition of feeling and emotion
- Differences between feeling and emotion
- Nature and functions of emotions
- Expressing emotions: physiological changes
- Theories of emotion
- Role of thalamus and cerebral cortex in emotion
- Key Terms, Summary and Questions

❑ **After you go through this chapter, you will be able to:**
- Understand the meaning of emotion and feeling
- Explain the nature and functions of emotion
- Find out the differences between feeling and emotion
- Gain an understanding about organic changes during emotion
- Evaluate different theories of emotion

Introduction

Can we imagine life without emotions – without joy, anger, sorrow or fear? The closer we look into the phenomena, the more complex these reactions seem to be. Emotion is a subjective response that is usually accompanied by a physiological change and is associated with a change in behaviour. There is a general agreement among psychologists who study emotions that emotions invoke three major responses: (i) Physiological changes within our bodies – shifts in heart rate, blood pressure and so on (ii) Subjective cognitive states – the personal experiences we label as emotions and (iii) Expressive behaviours – outward signs of these internal reactions (Tangney et al., 1996).

- *Emotion is a complex pattern of bodily and mental changes including physiological arousal, feeling, cognitive processes and behavioural responses to a personally significant situation.*
  —*Zimbardo (2000)*
- *An emotion is a subjective response that is usually accompanied by a physiological change and is associated with a change in behaviour.*

When researchers study emotional behaviour, they observe that a wide range of emotions, including love, joy, fear, disgust and anger have motivating properties and that they can impel and direct people's behaviour. Over the years psychologists have focused on different aspects of emotional behaviour. The earliest researchers described basic emotions, others tried to discover the physiological basis of emotion. Some psychologists also focused on how people perceive the emotions of others and how they convey emotions to others through nonverbal mechanisms such as gestures or eye contact. Recent studies have investigated the ability to control emotional responses to some extent (Meichenbaum, 1977).

Emotions are complex experiences composed of several processes – physiological and neurological activity, subjectively experienced feelings, behavioural expressions and responses. In a way, the concept of emotion is similar to that of motivation. Emotions move us to experience and express feelings, while motivations move us to action. Then, what is the difference between emotion and motivation?

Emotions are more obvious, recognisable and harder to define and study than motivation. Unlike emotions, the effects of motivation can be measured by overt actions, i.e., by test performance or perseverance in trying to overcome barriers.

What Is Emotion?

Understanding Emotion

Since emotions involve so many aspects of human functioning, the study of emotions has emerged as a central issue in research. For human beings, a broad range of stimuli and personal experiences can trigge r emotions (Hebb, 1980). But many emotions are surprisingly similar among people throughout the world. In some cases, it is easy to bring out a connection between motivations and emotions. But in other cases, the motive–emotion connection is not direct or obvious.

Emotions are subjective experiences. They are distinctive and personal for every individual. The ability to explain emotions is complicated by individual assessments of experiencing emotion.

Development of Emotion

Expression of emotions by human beings develops over time. Some aspects seem to be learned and others seem to be inborn, Harry F. Harlow (1905–1981) has conducted a series of experiments on infant monkeys. His study discovered that emotions like fear, curiosity and aggression are inborn and the brain mechanisms underlying them develop over time and in a specific sequence. He concluded that nature and nurture must interact at specific times for normal emotional and social development to occur. Early isolation from parents or family members causes fearful, aggressive and destructive behaviours in the future.

Human beings need and seek warmth, love and stimulation. When such stimulation is denied, they display definite changes in behaviour, ranging from boredom to aggression. The ability to respond emotionally is present in neonates. It is a part of the developmental process and not learned. Emotion is generally governed by the biological clock of the brain. The environment and its influences at different times can alter the emotional development in children. As they grow, they learn to control and regulate their emotions through the socialisation process.

Emotional patterns develop from the second week after birth. During the first month, the general excitement gets divided into pleasant and unpleasant emotions, having opponent appearance of undifferentiated form. According to Stenberg and Davis (1982), the infants display a wide range of emotional expressions at a very early age.

Children display pleasure emotion through general relaxation of the total body. It is followed by smiling, drooling and laughing response. Learning to walk is a pleasant emotion for children.

One prominent way of the expression of displeasure is crying. Children cry in distress, because of physical discomfort and pain. Besides crying, children also show displeasure by sulking, running away, verbalising their displeasure and hiding. Grown up children express their displeasure through language and also using slangs.

- *Emotion is an acute disturbance of the organism, as a whole, psychological in origin, involving behaviour, conscious experiences and visceral functioning.*
  —*P.T. Young*

Definition of Emotion

Emotions involve many aspects of human functioning. It is a complex pattern of bodily and mental changes including physiological arousal, feelings, cognitive processes and behavioural responses to a personally significant situation.

—(Zimbardo, 2000)

Table 5.1: Developmental Timetable for Infants' Emotional Expression

Age	Expressions of Emotion
At birth	Generalised undifferentiated excitement
• 2 to 4 weeks	Spontaneous pleasant and unpleasant emotions without any specific cause, startle response, close hugging – girls show more spontaneous smile than boys
• 3 weeks	Responding to unfamiliar food, unpleasant taste, smell through disgust
• 3 to 6 weeks	Social smile while responding to voices, faces, moving from one side to the other, hide-and-seek of one's face.
• 1 to 2 months	Calm or excited fleeting smile when they are picked up
• 2 to 4 months	Anger, surprise, sadness corresponding to the nature of stimulation
• 3 months	Distress and delight
• 4 months	In response to facial, tactile, visual, auditory or social stimulus, laughter.
• 5–7 months	Loud sound, animals, displacement, darkness, high places, loss of body support, presence of stranger, fear emotion, undifferentiated jealousy, joy, elation
• 12–18 months	Jealousy, selective affection
• 15 months to 2 years	Affection for other children
• 2 years	Shyness, pride, guilt, self-awareness
• 3 years	Fears of snake, death and ghosts.

(i) The physiological arousal includes neural, hormonal, visceral and muscular changes.
(ii) The feelings include both a general affective state and a specific tone such as joy or disgust.
(iii) The cognitive processes include interpretations, memories and expectations.
(iv) The overt behavioural responses include expressive reactions and action-oriented responses.
(v) Finally, we may perceive the situations as "significant" either consciously or unconsciously.

P. T. Young has provided an operational definition of emotion in the following way: "Emotion is an acute disturbance of the organism, as a whole, psychological in origin involving behaviour, conscious experiences and visceral functioning."

According to Young, during emotional state, the total behaviour including receptors, effectors, nervous systems and related psychological processes is affected. Emotions are prolonged feelings which generally have both physiological and cognitive elements.

Table 5.2: Components of Emotion
(Physical and psychological changes associated with emotion)

Type of Change	Description	Example
1. Physiological arousal	Neural, hormonal, visceral and muscular changes	Increased heart rate, blushing
2. Feelings	Subjective interpretation of affective state	Anger, sadness and happiness
3. Cognitive processes	Interpretations, memories beliefs, expectations	Blaming somebody, looking forward to something, etc.
4. Behavioural reactions	Expressing emotion, taking action	Smiling, crying, screaming for help
5. Significance	Conscious or unconscious perception	Judgement that one is in love; realising that an event is an emergency

Feeling and Emotion

Emotion is a very complex and intricate psychological process. Still, without emotions, life would have been dull and colourless. Emotions make life pleasurable as well as miserable. This process has been a matter of discussion by physiologists and psychologists for the last hundred years or more.

When psychology was growing steadily towards a scientific status, Wilhelm Wundt proposed his famous tridimensional theory of feeling. Subsequently, this was studied by E.B. Titchener and William James.

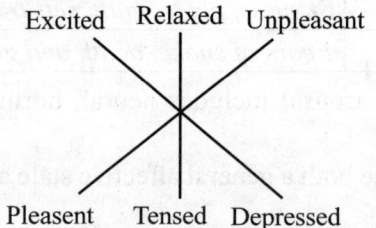

Fig. 5.1: Dimensions of Feeling

Wundt classified feeling into different dimensions: (i) Excited vs Depressed (b) Tensed vs Relaxed and (c) Pleasant vs Unpleasant.

According to his tridimensional theory, feeling can either be of excitation or depression, tensed or relaxed, pleasant or unpleasant. Before the declaration of results, a student remains in a tense state. After the declaration, he or she feels relaxed because the burden is over. In uncertainty, there is tension and in certainty, there is relaxation.

Feeling is an internal experience. It involves the entire body. It is the mild state of the organism. Feelings are various kinds of experiences, such as feelings of pleasure, familiarity, excitement, happiness, worry, tension, depression, etc.

Three Dimensions of Feeling
(a) Excited–Depressed
(b) Relaxed–Tensed
(c) Pleasant–Unpleasant
—*Wundt*

Feeling is:
(i) An internal experience
(ii) The mild state of the organism
(iii) Used for various kinds of experiences

According to Wundt, feelings have three distinguishable characteristics :

(a) Each feeling, whether pleasure, depression or excitement, can be said to have certain pleasant or unpleasant result. Thus feelings carry either pleasant or unpleasant experiences.

(b) All feelings have a tone of excitement or numbness. Pleasant feelings lead to excitement and sadness has a tone of numbness.

(c) Feeling can either be of tenseness or relaxation. Feeling of expectancy leads to tenseness. When there is no expectancy, it leads to relief.

Differences between Feeling and Emotion

(a) Feeling is always mild and dull, whereas emotion is acute and strong.
(b) During emotion, the entire organ is completely disturbed and disorganised; but feeling has only a mild disturbance.
(c) There are no bodily changes and overt expressions in feelings. But these are very pertinent in emotional reactions.
(d) Emotion continues for a brief time, whereas feeling has a longer continuation.
(e) Emotions are more disturbing than feeling.

From the above discussion, it is clear that emotion is a very complex and intricate psychological process. It is an acute or strong disturbance of the body which has a psychological origin. The disturbed state produced by an emotional experience creates bodily changes which are physiological in nature. Emotion is a conscious experience.

Basic Human Emotions

Though emotional experience is very complex, some experts believe that there is a set of basic emotions that is biologically and experientially distinct. Two models explaining this basic set of emotions are proposed by Robert Plutchik and by Caroll Izard.

(i) **Plutchik's Emotion Wheel:** In 1984, Robert Plutchik developed an emotional wheel which proposes an innate continuum of human emotions. The model depicts eight basic emotions. These eight basic emotions are made up of four pairs of opposites: joy–sadness, fear–anger, surprise–anticipation and acceptance–disgust.

All other emotions are said to be variations or blends of these basic eight emotions. Complex emotions, which are shown on the outside of the emotion wheel are the results of combinations of two adjacent primary emotions. For example, love is a combination of joy and acceptance.

According to Plutchik, emotions are best separated from each other when they are at high intensities. He also said that each primary emotion is associated with an adaptive evolutionary response.

Basic Human Emotions

(i) Plutchik's Emotion Wheel

i) Joy–Sadness
ii) Fear–Anger
iii) Surprise–Anticipation
iv) Acceptance–Disgust

(ii) Izard's Developmental Model

- Joy
- Surprise
- Anger
- Disgust
- Contempt
- Fear
- Shame
- Guilt
- Interest
- Excitement

(ii) Izard's Developmental Model: In 1977 Carrol Izard had proposed a slightly different set of basic emotions. His model projects ten emotions. These are joy, surprise, anger, disgust, contempt, fear, shame, guilt, interest and excitement. Other emotions are combinations of these emotions. For example, the emotional blend "love" is the combination of joy and interest.

As we know, a child's ability to think and to use language follows a timetable of development. The same principle is also applicable for emotional development. Physiologists confirmed that some developments in emotional response are linked to specific anatomical changes in the brain.

According to Izard, a neonate is capable of feeling only a generalised positive state, a generalised negative state and the emotions of interest and sadness. After a few months, joy and anger develop and by the age of nine months, shame and fear appear. Throughout life, emotional responses change, reflecting both physiological and cognitive changes.

Functions of Emotions

What functions do emotions serve for us? Different theorists talk of different functions. But we can consider the role of emotions in these psychological experiences:

(i) Emotions serve a motivational function by arousing us to move and to take action with regard to some experienced or imagined event.

(ii) Emotions direct and sustain our actions towards specific goals.

Nine Functions of Emotion

- Arousing function
- Directing and sustaining our actions
- Intensifying certain life experiences
- Organising our experiences
- Having self-relevance
- Awareness of inner conflicts
- Regulating social interactions
- Stimulating pro-social behaviour
- Communication function

(iii) Emotions intensify certain life experiences.

(iv) Emotions help to organise our experiences.

(v) Emotions signify that a response is especially significant or that an event has self-relevance.

(vi) Emotions can give us an awareness of inner conflicts.

(vii) In a social situation, emotions regulate relationships with others and social interactions.

(viii) Emotions help to stimulate our pro-social behaviour.

(ix) Lastly, the communication function of emotion reveals our attempts to conceal from others what we are feeling and intending. They are also a part of our nonverbal communication system.

Organic (Physiological) Changes During Emotion

A variety of body changes are associated with our emotional experience. Some of them are overt and some our covert. Overt or external body changes are observable, but the covert changes are detected only through special procedures or by modern recording devices.

- The following overt and covert changes occur in the body at the time of emotion:
- Eyes are protruded
- Face becomes red with excitement or anger
- The pupils of the eyes are dilated
- Respiration becomes more rapid
- The electrical resistance of the skin decreases
- Blood sugar level increases to make the organism energetic
- Gastrointestinal activities decrease or even stop totally.
- The hair stand on their roots.

All body changes during emotion are the result of a number of complex underlying processes originating in and integrated by autonomic nervous system (ANS), endocrine glands and cerebrospinal system. These internal changes are complex and difficult to measure.

The external body changes include changes in facial expressions, vocal expression, sweating and accelerated motor activities. The internal physiological changes include changes in the electrical activities of the skin, respiratory activities, blood pressure, pulse rate, sweat glands, reactions of the endocrine glands and the chemical activities in blood.

Physical Changes

(i) *Facial Expression*: People all over the world, regardless of cultural differences, race, sex and education, express basic emotions in the same way and are able to identify the emotions others are experiencing by reading their facial expression. Paul Ekman (1984) is a researcher in this area who holds that all people speak and understand the same "facial language".

Psychologists have recognised that facial expressions provide reliable cues to how people feel. This behavioural measure is easily observed, captured and interpreted by others. Researchers have shown that facial expression can be an accurate index of a person's emotional state.

No doubt, the face is the most expressive organ of the body. It is the barometer of emotion. Facial expressions vary from emotion to emotion Except for basic emotions, they may vary for other emotions from person to person.

Accurate judgement of emotion is, often, difficult from the facial expression of adults. There are some people who do not show any definite pattern of facial expressions for a particular emotion.

Instruments used for measuring organ changes during emotion
(i) Polygraph
(ii) Multichannel Amplifier
(iii) Optical Oscillographs
(iv) Pneumograph
(v) Sphygmomanometer
(vi) Psychogalvanometer
(vii) Electroencephalogram

All people speak and understand the same facial language.
—Ekman (1984)

Face is the barometer of emotion. It is the most expressive organ of the body.

James and Lange talked of gestures as expression of emotion in their theory for the first time.

Voice indicates different types of emotional experiences. From the verbal expression of a person, his or her emotional state may be easily detected.

External or overt bodily changes during emotion
(i) Facial Expression
(ii) Postural Reaction
(iii) Vocal Expression
(iv) Destruction
(v) Approach
(vi) Retreat or flight
(vii) Stopping of response

Internal or covert bodily changes of emotion
(i) Glandular response
(ii) Galvanic skin response
(iii) Gastro-intestinal functions

(ii) *Postural Reaction*: The significance of postural reaction in emotional experience was first discussed by James and Lange in their theory. They held that stimulations produced by assuming different postures contribute to the feeling aspect of emotion. For example, if someone puts their hands on their cheek and sit with a lowered face, they are supposed to be worried.

Different emotions arouse different postures. For instance, fear involves flight, whereas violent anger produces aggressive movements. We learn forward when we are anxious and expect to receive something. In sorrow, there is a general slumping posture, but in joy, the head is held high and there is a movement of hands. Whether the gestures are influenced by culture or not is a big question. Research has not produced definitive answer.

(iii) *Vocal Expression*: An individual's voice indicates his or her emotional state. The modulation of voice and changes in loudness and pitch represent the emotion of the person. A loud sound indicates excitement, loud laughter indicates joy and happiness, a slow monotonous voice expresses defeat and dejection, higher pitch indicates anger.

From the vocal expression, besides the facial expression, postural and other reactions of a person, his or her emotional condition can be easily deduced.

(iv) *Destruction*: Destruction is generally found in anger reaction. The most typical physical reaction during anger is overt reaction or attack. This type of attack varies from culture to culture. In case of sophisticated people, the attack is symbolic. But in case of uncivilised people, the attack can be "biting, hitting, shooting and piercing with a knife. For civilised people, attack is made through language, sarcastic remarks, abuses or taunting words."

(v) *Approach*: Approach reaction is obvious in happiness, joy, delight, pleasure and love. It leads to further stimulation. Elation comes out of success. This is also an approach reaction. Anticipation of success brings pleasant emotions. Sometimes approach behaviours are manifested as peace, satisfaction and contentment.

(vi) *Retreat or Flight Responses*: Due to fear, individuals may take flight and go away from the goal-object. An individual can save himself or herself by withdrawing from the fearful or dangerous situation. So flight is said to be the best medium of adjustment in a dangerous situation.

Direct Flight
- Running away from a biting dog.

Indirect Flight
- Psychological retreat: shifting of jobs, day-dream, childish behaviour and withdrawal responses.

The flight may be direct or indirect. If a boy runs away from a place out of fear of a biting dog, then this is an example of a direct flight. When direct flight is not possible, then psychological retreat is the only alternative. For cultured people, the retreat may be through symbols and withdrawal reactions like day-dreaming. According to Ruch, in civilised life, we often retreat symbolically through words, apologies, compromises, discussions and through various psychological mechanisms of withdrawal.

Some individuals frequently change their jobs or even marital partners. Sophisticated individuals demonstrate their flight through apology, excuses, reconciliatory approach and similar withdrawal responses. Besides day-dreaming, childish behaviour and regression are some of the examples of retreat responses.

(vii) *Stopping of Responses*: Sometimes an individual is confronted with situation where he or she stops all kinds of responses and remains inactive. Here the person remains in a state of complete inactivity due to excessive disappointment and sorrow. Due to extreme emotional shock, he or she ceases to work, talk and to take food. The person experiences a state of depression and loses pleasure. To some extent, stopping of response helps in adapting with the environment. It points out the person's limitations as well as deficiencies.

Physiological Changes

(viii) *Glandular Responses*: Our glands play important roles during emotion. Adrenaline is responsible for many characteristics of strong emotional responses. During the emotional state of anger, the medulla of the adrenal gland secrets excessive amount of adrenaline. The sugar level in blood rises due to excessive secretion of this hormone.

As a result, heartbeat increases and blood pressure increases due to release of glycogen from liver. There is every chance that pulse rate may rise and blood clots more quickly, more air enters into the lungs, pupils enlarge and profuse sweating may cause danger to the skin. The skin temperature also rises. Evidence indicates that non-adrenaline constricts the blood vessels at the surface of the body. As a result, more blood is sent to other parts of the body. Experimental evidence also indicates that thyroid and pituitary glands play major roles in emotion.

(ix) *Galvanic Skin Response*: The best measure of autonomic activities associated with the emotional state is the galvanic skin response (GSR). This also bears several names, such as psychogalvanic reflex, skin resistance, Palmer resistance, palmer conductance, electrodermal response and skin potential. GSR is measured by an apparatus known as "psychogalvanometer". The changes in GSR are called electrodermal changes. GSR is associated with blood pressure and respiration. During emotion, it is activated by sympathetic nervous system and decreases during emotional stimulations.

(x) *Gastrointestinal Activities*: Studies have shown some changes in gastrointestinal functions during emotion. These functions are generally measured by the help of balloons inserted into the stomach or intestines. In 1929, Cannon also demonstrated that emotions of fear or anger inhibit activities in the gastrointestinal tract.

(xi) *Pupillometrics*: As a diagnostic tool, pupillometrics is very useful in psychotherapy. Pupillometrics is a technique of measuring physiological changes during emotion. The parasympathetic and sympathetic divisions of autonomic nervous system never act together. Either of the two becomes active at one time depending on the situation. In other words, the two divisions are in active opposition to each other while in action. During emotion, pupils dilate through the sympathetic system and constriction of the pupil occurs by the parasympathetic system. Pupillary responses to pain and emotion-provoking stimuli have been studied extensively by Bender (1929). During lie detection, pupillometrics can also be used.

Theories of Emotion

Different theories have been developed to explain how emotional experience is generated. These theories also attempt to explain:

(i) What causes emotions

(ii) What are the necessary conditions for emotion

(iii) What sequence best captures the way emotions are built up from the complex interaction of the factors discussed earlier.

James–Lange Theory of Bodily Reactions

William James was the founder of the functional school of psychology. In his popular book *Principles of Psychology*, James said that profound bodily changes occur during emotional excitement.

James said that we feel after our body reacts. As he puts it, "We feel sorry because we cry, angry because we strike, afraid because we tremble." (James, 1950). But common sense says we are sorry because we lose our fortune and when we see a snake we get frightened and run. This sequence was rejected by James.

By developing this theory, James tried to explain how emotional experience is caused. First, emotion-provoking stimulus from the environment excites the receptors. Impulses aroused by the emotion-provoking situation follow classical pathways through the receptors to the sensory receiving areas of the cerebral cortex, where stimulus is perceived (path 1). Then somatic and autonomic impulses initiated in the cortex excite skeletal muscles and visceral organs (path 2).

This initiates changes in the physiological functions. These changes, in turn, excite further impulse which returns to cortex via paths 3 and 4. Then the perception of these impulses add emotional quality. Therefore, after some bodily changes, we feel emotional. We are afraid because we run, but do not run because we are afraid. So respective emotional situations have got corresponding bodily reactions.

Carl Lange (1885) independently proposed a peripheral origin theory of emotion quite similar to James theory. According to this theory, people experience physiological changes and then interpret them as emotional states.

Simply stated, the James–Lange theory says that people do not experience an emotion until after their bodies become aroused and respond with physiological changes. So feedback from the body produces the feeling or emotions (W. James, 1884; Lange, 1885, 1922).

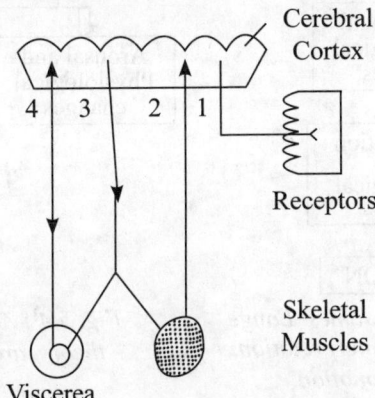

Fig. 5.2: A schematic representation of James–Lange Theory of Emotion

Most of the criticisms of the James–Lange theory have come from Walter Cannon (1871–1945). Cannon and his co-workers operated on some cats and had objections against the views of James and Lange.

(i) According to Cannon, total separation of the viscera from the central nervous system (CNS) does not change emotional behaviour. Later, Sherrington's experiments with dogs also confirmed this.

(ii) Artificial induction of visceral changes did not produce any emotion.

(iii) Visceral changes are too slow to be a source of emotional feelings.

(iv) Practical evidence indicated that emotional experiences might occur in less than a second. But viscera responds slowly. This evidence proves that emotional experiences precede visceral changes, but does not follow as James–Lange theory revealed.

Cannon–Bard Theory of Central Neural Processes

Physiologist Walter Cannon (1871–1945) and Philip Bard (1898–1977), a doctoral student of Cannon, together developed a model of emotion called the Cannon–Bard Theory. This theory rejected James–Lange theory in favour of a focus on the action of the central nervous system (CNS). With experimental evidences and logical analysis, they had four major objections to the James–Lange theory.

(i) Visceral activity was irrelevant for emotional experience.

(ii) Visceral reactions are similar across different arousal situations.

(iii) Many emotions cannot be distinguished from one another simply by their physiological components.

(iv) Autonomic nervous system responses are typically too slow to be the source of emotions.

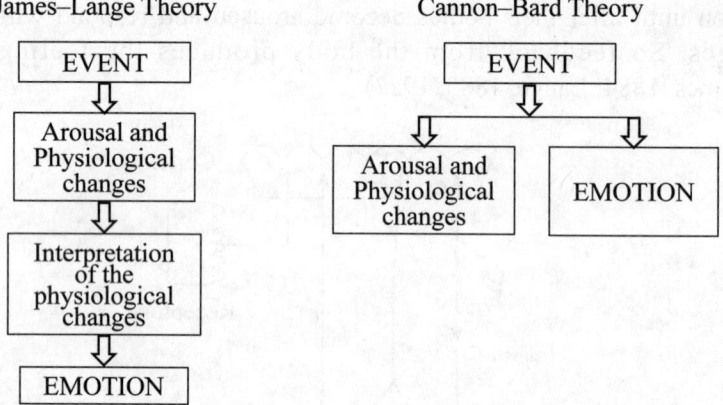

Fig. 5.3: According to the James–Lange theory, arousal precedes interpretation, which precedes the emotion.

Fig. 5.4 : According to Cannon–Bard theory, arousal and emotion occur simultaneously.

Cannon–Bard stated that the physiological changes in many emotional states were identical. When an individual is emotional, two areas of the brain – the thalamus and cerebral cortex – are stimulated simultaneously. Stimulation of cortex produces the emotional component of the experience, whereas stimulation of thalamus produces physiological changes in the sympathetic nervous system. They said that emotional feelings accompany physiological changes.

Cannon–Bard's theory is popularly known as the "Thalamic or Emergency Theory of Emotion". It was for the first time that an integrated physiological picture of emotion was developed. James and Lange suppose that emotional experience is an awareness of bodily changes. But Cannon and Bard suppose emotional behaviour and emotional experience are almost simultaneously aroused by a discharge of impulses from the hypothalamus.

According to Cannon-Bard, an external emotion provoking stimulus excites receptors and sends impulses towards the thalamus in path 1 (Fig. 5.5). These impulses then discharge via hypothalamus, viscera motor centres in path 2 and sends impulses that mediate an appreciation of his response to the cortex via path 4. Sensory impulses cannot directly disinhibit the thalamic mechanisms but travel on to cortex via path 1. They may invoke conditional responses which release cortical inhibition of the thalamus via path 3 and give rise to thalamic discharge via paths 2 and 4.

Cannon–Bard held that sensory impulses go directly to the cerebral cortex via hypothalamus. These discharges from the hypothalamus go simultaneously to the cortex, viscera and skeletal muscles, so that one feels emotional and acts emotionally at the same time.

Cannon–Bard mainly concerned themselves with bodily changes of emotion having biological value. Their theory was criticised on many grounds. They ignored the conscious experience of emotion. Actually, cerebral cortex perceives and understands a situation and reacts to it accordingly. The role of cerebral cortex in the theory was totally neglected. Some experts said that hypothalamus is not the only area responsible for emotion as Cannon-Bard said.

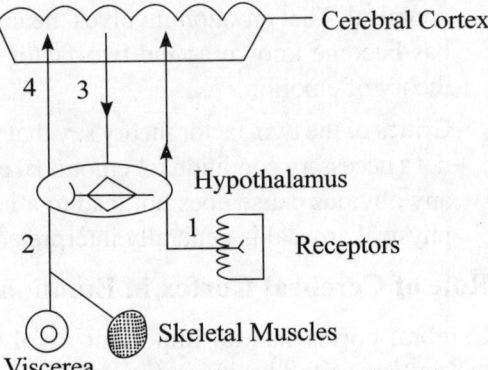

Fig. 5.5: Schematic representation of Cannon–Bard Theory of Emotion

Activation Theory of Emotion

Some psychologists made vigorous attempts to develop a more comprehensive theory of emotion. This is popularly known as the Activation Theory of Emotion. This theory includes both bodily changes and emotional experiences.

In 1951, Lindsey proposed this activation theory. To "activate" means to "arouse" or to "make active". This theory has connection with motivation. It grew from the findings of EEG and PGR. It is based on the integration of cerebral cortex and the sub-cortical structure. The activation theory holds that the cerebral cortex is activated by the discharge of the hypothalamus.

According to this theory, when the organism (O) becomes emotional, the level of activity rises high and there is more autonomic activity. As a result, the hypothalamus sends more impulse to the cortex and the behaviour becomes violent.

The experimental evidences of Berger, Magoun (1949), Lindsey and Bowden supported the activation theory. It was found that animals with decorticated hypothalamus and clinical patients show little evidence of emotion. It was also found that when the cerebral cortex was removed, the organism shows very strong or mild emotions, sometimes even no emotional responses. The cerebral cortex brings a balance between the violent and weak emotions.

But this theory leaves the intermediate and mixed states of emotion untouched and unexplained. It also does not answer why and how emotions take place.

Lazarus–Schachter Theory of Cognitive Arousal

Some theories suggest that cognitive processes direct most adaptive emotional responses (Lazarus, 1991; Leventhal, 1980). According to such theories, sensory experiences lead to emotion only when the stimuli are cognitively appraised as having personal significance. A particular emotion depends on the way a situation is interpreted and the meaning attributed to it by the individual.

Richard Lazarus (1984) said that emotional experience grows out of ongoing transactions with the environment that are evaluated. Stanley Schachter (1971) held that the experience of emotion is the joint effect of physiological arousal and cognitive appraisal. That emotion involves the cognitive interpretation of physiological arousal has become known as the two-factor theory of emotion or the Lazarus–Schachter theory of emotion.

Critics of the two-factor theory say that the awareness of one's physiological arousal is not a necessary condition for emotional experience. Experiencing strong arousal without any obvious cause does not lead to a neutral and undifferentiated state. Unexplained physical arousal is generally interpreted as negative.

Role of Cerebral Cortex in Emotion

Cerebral cortex has an important involvement in emotional behaviour. Changes in the pattern of the brain potentials during emotion had clear-cut indication about this fact. The cognitive factors play an important role in defining and directing emotional response. These cognitive factors depend upon the cortical functioning. The famous psychologist Ruch has stated the distinct ways in which the cortical functioning affects emotional response.

(i) Involvement of cerebral cortex was found in relating current events to past experience. It is a process which helps to interpret the situation and determines whether or not it arouses emotion.

(ii) Studies indicated that the cerebral cortex has some power to execute visceral activity which is commonly associated with emotional responses.

(iii) Experimental evidences shows that the cerebral cortex serves as a check on unrestricted response. For example, when certain parts of cerebral cortex are destroyed or affected by alcohol, the individual makes wrong or excessive emotional responses.

Experiments of Bart (1934) indicated that dogs and cats without cerebral cortex have shown no gradations in intensity of emotion, inhibiting only the most primitive emotional responses of pain, rage, fear and basic sexual responses.

Further studies indicated that prefrontal areas are also concerned with the inhibition of certain kinds of emotions and the expression of others. If these areas are destroyed, the kind and strength of emotions and their intensity are also affected. After damage, the animals or organisms become lazy and untidy in their personal appearance.

However, most of the complex functions of the cerebral cortex are still not known or understood. Systematic and meticulous studies can unravel the truth behind these critical functions.

Role of Hypothalamus in Emotion

According to many theorists, the hypothalamus plays a significant role in emotional behaviour of organisms. This fact is substantiated by numerous experimental studies on animals. Studies also show that removal of hypothalamus in cats and dogs has no effect on emotions. When hypothalamus is seriously impaired by accident, apathy occurs. Drugs like sodium amytal and metrozol have specific effect upon the hypothalamus, producing significant changes in emotional behaviour of animals as well as human beings.

Experimental evidence indicated that hypothalamus was responsible for executing primitive emotions of rage, fear and sex. Studies also show that the front portion of hypothalamus helps in suppressing primitive emotional reactions. When the septal area of hypothalamus is destroyed, it was found that the rats overact emotionally (Bray and Nauta, 1953).

Hypothalamus is somehow responsible for emotional behaviour of the organism. But it is not solely responsible for emotional behaviour. Although it is clear that hypothalamus plays a significant role in the motor expressions of emotions, its role in relation to feeling aspects is controversial.

Hypothalamus weighs about less than one per cent of the brain's entire weight. It is very vital to both emotions and motivation. So it is called the "brain within the brain". The "fight" or "flight" emergency responses are the preparatory processes of the body for appropriate kind of action and they are regulated by the autonomic nervous system under the direct control of the hypothalamus.

Aggressive behaviour can be elicited in animals by mild electrical stimulation of a particular part of the hypothalamus. Injected neurochemical stimulation of a hypothalamic region results in violent attack responses (Smith, King & Hoebel, 1970).

Role of Limbic System in Emotion

The limbic system is not a single structure. It is a group of structures of the brain lying in an area below the corpus callosum. The particular structures, which are grouped as limbic system, are: the hippocampus, anterior thalamus, amygdala, septum or septal area, hypothalamus and their interconnecting fibres. There are specific structures in the limbic system, which are involved in emotional and motivational reactions.

Studies showed that when there is a lesion in a particular part of the limbic system in human patients, they fail to carry out sequential activities. Monkeys having lesions on some regions of the limbic system express anger at minor provocations. But lesions on some other regions of the limbic system convert the monkeys into docile and calm animals and they do not show any hostility or anger when provoked.

Studies also showed that tumours and lesions in the limbic system lead to reduction of sexual drive (Blumer & Walker, 1967). Studies also show that stimulating limbic area may result in sexual arousal. In 1964, Heath conducted an interesting experiment. He took three males and a female as subjects. He found that the three males experienced sexual arousal due to electrical stimulation of the limbic system and the female also experienced orgasm. Many other researchers also confirmed the fact that the limbic system has a significant role in emotion.

❑ Key Terms

1. Activation theory
2. Amygdala
3. Arousal
4. Cannon–Bard theory
5. Electrocardiogram (ECG)
6. Electroencephalogram (EEG)
7. Emotion
8. Emovere
9. Facial Expression
10. Feeling
11. Gastrointestinal activities
12. James–Lange theory
13. Lie detector
14. Limbic system
15. Metabolism
16. Parasympathetic division (NS)
17. Pneumograph
18. Polygraph
19. Psychogalvanometer
20. Pupilliary response
21. Pupillometrics
22. Retreat and flight
23. Sphygmomanometer
24. Sympathetic division (NS)
25. Viscera

❑ Chapter Summary and Review

1. Emotion is an acute disturbance of the organism. As a whole, it is psychological in origin, involving behaviour, conscious experience and visceral functioning.
2. Both physiological and psychological activities are involved in emotion. It gives motion to the organism either to move towards the goal or move away from the goal.
3. Emotion is behaviour-arousal. It prepares a person to be active for a longer span of time. Also it activates the organisms to use their maximum potential at the time of life-threatening dangers.
4. Emotion can be expressed through destructive responses, approach responses, retreat or flight responses and stopping of responses.
5. There are internal (covert) and external (overt) bodily changes during emotion. These include electrical activities of the skin, respiratory activities, blood pressure, pulse rate, functioning of sweat glands, reactions of endocrine glands, changes in the chemical substances in the blood, skin temperature, pupilliary response, gastrointestinal activities, eye-blinking, muscle tension, tremor, etc.
6. Autonomic Nervous System (ANS) plays a significant role in emotion. It has two divisions – Parasympathetic and Sympathetic. The sympathetic division acts during excitement, fear, anger and delight. But parasympathetic division is involved with maintenance of life. Only one division of ANS acts at a time, the other division becomes dull at that moment.
7. Prolonged sympathetic over-activity due to emotion may lead to psychosomatic diseases like peptic ulcers, asthma, migraine, headache, etc.
8. Different studies show that the hypothalamus and limbic system play vital roles in regulating emotional behaviour.
9. James–Lange theory of emotion states that the internal state of emotion is experienced because of physiological changes occurring in response to the emotion-provoking stimuli. The Cannon–Bard theory states that the emotion-provoking stimuli simultaneously elicit physiological arousal and the internal cognitive state of emotion.
10. Lazarus–Schachter model says that, when aroused, the organism searches for a cognitive label or interpretation.

QUESTIONS

1. What is emotion? What role does emotion play in the life of an individual?
2. Define emotion. Discuss the nature of emotion.
3. Discuss the physiological changes that occur during emotion.
4. Discuss different organic changes which occur during emotion.
5. What is emotion? Discuss the role of hypothalamus and cerebral cortex during emotion with suitable experimental evidence.
6. Discuss different theories of emotion.
7. Critically examine the theories of emotion. Which one is the most acceptable theory to explain the origin of emotion?
8. Differentiate between feeling and emotion. Explain Wundt's tri-dimensional theory of emotion.
9. Explain the characteristics of emotion with reference to P.T. Young's definition.
10. Write short notes on the following:
    (a) Watson's experiment on Fear Conditioning
    (b) Activation Theory of Emotion
    (c) Role of hypothalamus in emotion
    (d) Pupillometrics
    (e) Lie-detector
    (f) Galvanic Skin Response (GSR)

UNIT III
EMPOWERED PRACTICES

CHAPTER - 6

SOCIAL THOUGHT AND SOCIAL BEHAVIOUR

❏ *Empathy and Social Cognition*

Empathy is the ability to put oneself in another person's place and feel what the other person feels. Social cognition is the cognitive ability to understand that other people have mental states and to gauge their feelings and intentions. Empathy depends on social cognition. Piaget believes that egocentrism delays the development of this ability, until the concrete operational stage. Some other experts feel that social cognition begins so early that it may be "an innate potential, like the ability to learn language". One-year-olds pick up emotional cues from television performers and 18-month-olds seem to impute mental states to others.

—*Meltozoff (1995)*

❏ *This chapter covers:*
- Social thought and social behaviour
- Aspects of social thought
- Attribution biases
- Social cognition
- Impression formation
- Attitude, social cognition and attitude change
- Information-processing routes to persuasion
- Key Terms, Summary and Questions

Social Thought and Social Behaviour

❑ **By the end of this chapter, you will be able to:**
- Know what social behaviour and social thought are
- Define social thought
- Know the meaning of attribution
- Learn about different biases of attribution
- Familiarise yourself with social cognition and attitude
- Gain preliminary knowledge about information-processing and cognitive dissonance
- Learn about impression formation

Cognitive Dissonance: When Attitudes and Behaviour Clash

- *Cognitive dissonance is the sense of discomfort or distress that occurs when a person's behaviour does not correspond to that person's attitudes.*

- *When people find themselves doing things or saying things that do not match their idea of themselves as smart, nice or moral, for example, they experience an emotional discomfort known as cognitive dissonance (Aronson, 1997; Festinger, 1957)*

- *Dissonance is a term referring to an inconsistency or lack of agreement. Dissonance is the conflict that occurs when a person holds two attitudes or thoughts (referred to as cognitions) that contradict each other.*

- *Dissonance explains a number of everyday occurrences involving attitudes and behaviour. Attitudes influence behaviour. The strength of the link between a particular attitude and behaviour varies, of course, but generally people strive for consistency between their attitudes and their behaviour. Not only do our attitudes influence our behaviour, but sometimes our behaviour shapes our attitudes.*

Introduction

For a long span of time, social psychologists have tried to study all aspects of social thought and social behaviour. In this chapter, we will discuss many of their findings. We will begin with the consideration of several aspects of social thought, i.e., how and what, we think about other individuals. Under the topic "Social Thought", we will discuss three important topics:

(a) *Attribution*: This is about our efforts to understand the causes behind other people's behaviour. The attribution theory depicts the theory of personality which seeks to explain how we decide, on the basis of samples of an individual's behaviour, what the specific cause of that person's behaviour are. We will also find the reasons why people act as they do.

(b) *Social Cognition*: This is about the manner in which we interpret, analyse, remember and use information about the social world. Social cognition is a very important area of research in social psychology. It has become a guiding framework for all research in the field.

(c) *Attitudes*: Attitudes are our evaluation of the various features of the social world. Attitudes are learned predispositions to respond in a favourable or unfavourable manner to a particular person, behaviour, belief or thing (Chaiken, 1995).

Attribution

As we have discussed earlier, attribution is the understanding the causes of others' behaviour or why people act as they do. We think about other people many times a day. But we do not count. Anytime we try to figure out why other people have acted in a particular way or attempt to make judgements about them, we are engaging in social thought. Why others act as they do is one question we face every day in many different contexts. The process through which we attempt to answer this question to determine the causes behind others' behaviour, is known as attribution.

Attribution is a fairly orderly process. First, we examine the behaviour of others for clues and try to find out causes behind what they say and do. Then we reach a conclusion.

But what kind of information do we consider? This depends on the specific question we want to answer. For example, one basic issue is: Did another individual's actions stem from internal causes (such as their own motives, traits or intentions) or from external causes (such as luck or factors beyond their control in a given situation)?

To answer this question, we have to focus on three informations: (i) Consensus, (ii) Consistency and (iii) Distinctiveness.

Consensus means whether other people behave in the same way as the person we are considering.

Consistency depends whether this individual behaves in the same manner over time.

Distinctiveness means whether this person behaves in the same way in different situations.

Suppose only a few people act like this particular individual. Then we can conclude that "consensus is low". If this person behaves in the same way over time, then "consistency is high". Further, if this person behaves in the same manner in many situations, then "distinctiveness is low". Here, the conclusion is that the behaviour stems from internal causes.

The general process we use to determine the causes of behaviour and other social occurrences proceeds in several steps, illustrated in Fig. 6.1.

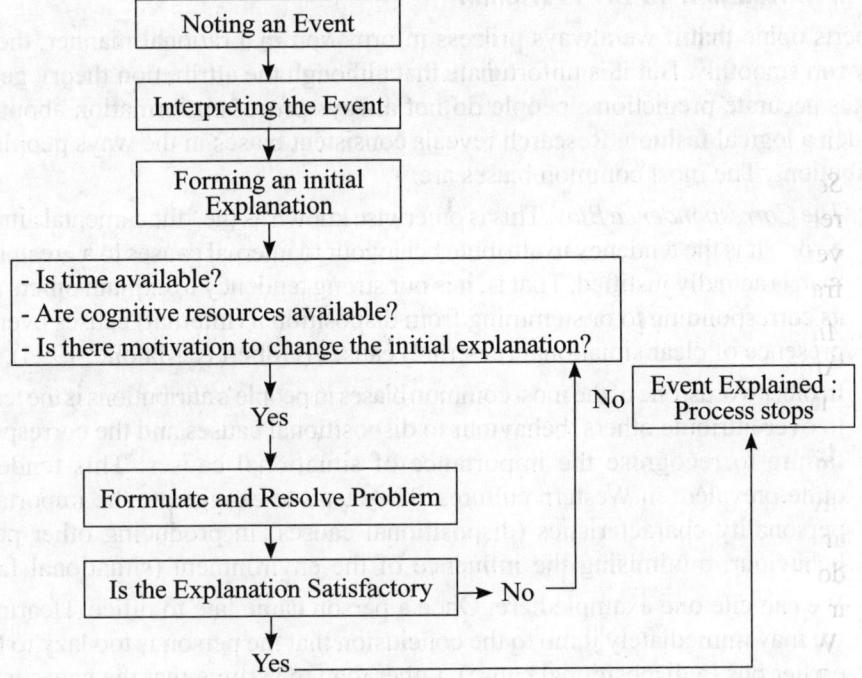

Fig. 6.1: The general process we use to determine the cause of others' behaviour (Anderson, 1997)

From Fig. 6.1 it is evident that after first noticing that a behavioural event has occurred, we must interpret the meaning of the event. This leads to formulation of an initial explanation. Whether we have to accept or modify the explanation depends on the time on hand, motivation and cognitive resources. If we have time, cognitive resources and motivation, the event becomes the trigger for deliberate problem solving as we seek a fuller explanation. We might try out several possibilities during the problem formulation and resolution stage before determining that we have reached a solution (Krull and Anderson, 1997).

One pivotal question we must answer is whether the cause is situational or dispositional when we seek an explanation for behaviour (Heider, 1958).

Situational causes are the elements of the environment. When an individual cleans up the milk from the floor, he or she does it because the situation requires it, not that he or she is a very neat person.

Dispositional causes are prompted by the person's disposition (i.e., his or her internal traits or personality characteristics). For example, if a householder spends hours shining the kitchen floor, probably he or she is doing so because they are a neat person.

Attribution usually involves the logical kind of reasoning. But that is not always true. In fact, the attribution process is subject to several kinds of errors which may lead to false conclusion about other persons. In the following section, we will discuss some biases in attribution.

Biases in Attribution: To Err Is Human

Experts opine that if we always process information in a rational manner, the world may run smoothly. But it is unfortunate that although the attribution theory generally makes accurate predictions, people do not always process information about others in such a logical fashion. Research reveals consistent biases in the ways people make attributions. The most common biases are:

(i) *The Correspondence Bias*: This is otherwise known as the "fundamental attribution error". It is the tendency to attribute behaviour to internal causes to a greater extent than is actually justified. That is, it is our strong tendency to explain others actions as corresponding to or stemming from dispositional (internal) causes even in the presence of clear situational (external) causes (Gilbert & Malone, 1995).

In other words, one of the most common biases in people's attributions is the tendency to over-attribute others' behaviour to dispositional causes and the corresponding failure to recognise the importance of situational causes. This tendency is quite prevalent in Western cultures. They tend to exaggerate the importance of personality characteristics (dispositional causes) in producing other person's behaviour, minimising the influence of the environment (situational factors).

We can cite one example here. Once a person came late to office. Hearing this, we may immediately jump to the conclusion that the person is too lazy to take an earlier bus (a dispositional cause), rather than to assume that the cause is due to situational factors such as the bus running late due to traffic jam or a breakdown.

- *Attribution:* The process through which we seek to determine the causes behind others behaviour. Attribution theory of personality seeks to explain how we decide, on the basis of samples of an individual's behaviour, and what the specific causes of that person's behaviour are.
- *Consensus:* Information regarding the extent to which behaviour by one person is shown by others as well.
- *Consistency:* Information regarding the extent to which a specific person shows similar behaviour to a given stimulus across time.
- *Distinctiveness:* Information regarding the extent to which a given person reacts in the same manner to different stimuli or situations.
- *Social Influence:* The process by which the actions of an individual or group affect the behaviour of others.

So the questions arise (i) Why do we show this type of tendency? (ii) What are the basic causes of fundamental attribution error? and (iii) Why should the fundamental attribution error be so common?

Many social psychologists accept the following explanation: When we focus on others' behaviour, we tend to begin by assuming that their actions reflect their underlying characteristics. In other words, when we view the behaviour of another person in a particular setting, the information that is most conspicuous is the person's behaviour itself. Because the individual's immediate surroundings are relatively unchanging, the person whose behaviour we are considering is the centre of our attention; the person's environment is less attention-grabbing. As a result, we are more likely to make attributions based on personal dispositional factors and less likely to make attributions relating to the situation (Ross, Nisbett, Gilbert, 1995). In the above example, we do not make enough allowance for the impact of external factors and we do not give enough weight to the possibility of a traffic jam (Cornielle, 1996).

The next question is: Is this tendency to emphasise dispositional causes universal or is it influenced by cultural factors? Research findings indicate that culture does play a role. Specifically, the fundamental attribution error appears to be more common or stronger in cultures which emphasise individual freedom. These are mostly found in individualistic cultures such as those in Western Europe or North America. But it is found less frequently in collective cultures, which emphasise group membership, conformity and interdependence, like India (Nisbett, 1998).

(ii) *The Self-Serving Bias*: This is our tendency to attribute positive outcomes to our own traits or characteristics (internal causes), but negative outcomes to factors beyond our control (external causes). This means, "I can do no wrong; but you can do no right."

For example, suppose a student, Leny, writes a term paper for her examination. After examining it, her professor gives her an A grade. To what she would attribute her success? If she is like most people, she may probably explain it in terms of internal causes – her own talent or hard work.

Attributions in a Cultural Context: How fundamental is the Fundamental Attribution Error
- *Studies indicate that not everyone is susceptible to attribution biases in the same way. Culture plays a vital role in the attributions we make about others' behaviour. The tendency to overestimate the importance of personal, dispositional factors and under-attribute situational causes when determining the cause of others behaviour is pervasive in Western cultures, but not in Asian societies. In 1964, social psychologist Joan Miller found that adult experimental participants in India were more likely to use situational attributions than dispositional ones in explaining events. These findings are the opposite of those based on experimental participants in the United States and they contradict the fundamental attribution error.*

Now let us suppose her professor gives her a D grade. How would she explain this outcome? She would focus mainly on external causes, i.e., she was unable to give sufficient time for the project or the professor has unrealistically high standards. In this situation, Leny is showing the attributional error self-serving bias (Brown and Rogers, 1991).

Why does this occur? One possible answer is due to cognitive factors. This suggests that self-serving bias stems mainly from certain tendencies in the way we process social information. This view states that we expect to succeed and have a tendency to attribute expected successful outcomes to internal causes more than to external causes (Ross, 1977).

Another explanation emphasises the role of motivation. This explanation suggests that the self-serving bias stems from our need to protect and enhance our self-esteem or the related desire to look good to others (Solomon, 1963).

While both cognitive and motivational factors may well play a role in this kind of attributional error, research evidence seems to offer more support for the motivational view (Brown and Rogers, 1991).

Self-serving bias has a negative impact in a joint task. It can be the cause of much interpersonal fiction. When individuals work with others, they believe that they, not the partners, have made the major contributions. They want to take the credit themselves. It is seen that when students work in a joint project, most students take more credit for themselves, if the project has gone well, but tend to blame their partners if it has not.

Is the self-serving bias a universal human tendency, occurring in all cultures? While it has been observed all over the world, evidence suggests that this bias is more common in individualistic societies (i.e., many Western countries), than in societies which emphasise group outcomes and harmony (Seligman, 1990).

(iii) *The Halo Effect*: Halo effect is the tendency to form a favourable or unfavourable impression of someone at the first meeting, so that all of that person's comments and behaviour after that first impression will be interpreted to agree with the impression – positively or negatively. It is a phenomenon in which an initial understanding that a person has positive traits is used to infer other uniformly positive characteristics. The opposite would also be true.

For example, suppose Leny is intelligent, kind and loving. Is she also conscientious? If you have to guess, your response probably would be "yes". Here, your guess reflects the halo effect. Learning that Leny is unsociable and argumentative would probably lead you to assume she is lazy as well. However, few people have uniformly positive or uniformly negative traits. So the halo effect leads to misconceptions about others (Larose & Standing, 1998).

The halo effect can occur in any social situation, including interviews between a professional psychologist and a client. First impressions really do count and people who make a good first impression because of clothing, personal appearance or some other superficial characteristic will seem to have a halo hanging over their heads – they can do no wrong after that (Lance, 1994). The negative impression is called the "horn effect".

(iv) *Assumed-Similarity Bias*: How are your friends and acquaintances similar to you in terms of attitudes, opinions and likes and dislikes?

Most of us believe that our friends and acquaintances are fairly similar to ourselves. But this feeling goes beyond just the people we know. There is a general tendency, known as the "assumed-similarity bias" to think of people as being similar to ourselves, even when meeting them for the first time. This means we are often wrong (Marks and Miller, 1987).

Social Cognition: Understanding Others

Social cognition are the processes which underlie our understanding of the social world. One of the dominant areas of study in social psychology during the last few years has focused on learning how we come to understand what others are like and how we explain the reasons underlying others behaviour (Taylor & Kunda, 1999). Social cognition is the process through which we notice, store, remember and later use social information.

We are exposed to enormous amount of information about other people every moment. But how are we able to decide what is important and what is not and to make judgements about the characteristics of others? This is due to social cognition – the processes that are the basis of our understanding of the social world.

Social cognition is a very important area of research in social psychology. One fascinating aspect of social thought is "schema" – mental frameworks for organising and using social information. In other words, schemas are mental frameworks centring around a specific theme that help us to organise "social information" in an efficient manner. Once schemas are formed, they exert powerful effects on several aspects of social cognition and therefore on our social behaviour.

We typically hold schemas for particular types of people. Our schema for a teacher is different from a mother. Schema for a mother might include the characteristics of a warm, nurturing and caring person. Schemas for teacher may consist of recognition that he or she has knowledge of the subject-matter, the desire to impart knowledge, etc. Regardless of their accuracy, schemas are important because they organise the ways in which we recall, recognise and categorise information about others.

Another component of social thought is "heuristics". These are shortcuts or strategies we use in our efforts to make sense out of the social world. Heuristics are simple rules for making complex decisions or drawing inferences in a rapid and seemingly effortless manner.

Our schemas are also susceptible to error. For example, our mood affects how we perceive others. People who are happy form more favourable impressions and make more positive judgements than people who are in a bad mood (Kenny, 1994). Even when schemas are not entirely accurate, they serve an important function – they allow us to develop expectations about how others will behave. These expectations permit us to plan our interactions with others more easily and they simplify a complex social world.

Impression Formation

The earliest work on social cognition was designed to examine "impression formation". Impression formation is a process by which an individual organises information about another person to form an overall impression of that person. We can cite a classic study done by Kelley (1950) here.

The students were told that they were about to hear a guest lecturer. One group of students were told that the lecturer was a "warm" person, industrious, critical, practical and determined. A second group was told that he was a rather "cold" person, industrious, critical, practical and determined. The only difference was that one group of students was told that the lecturer was a warm person and another group was told that he was a cold person. Other personality characteristics informed to both the groups were the same. Kelley discovered that the attribution of a central quality such as warmth significantly influenced subjects' total impression of the person. For example, he found that students who were told that the lecturer was warm consistently gave him more favourable ratings on several personal attributes than did subjects who were told that he was cold.

The findings of the experiment led to additional research on impression formation which focused on how people pay particular attention to certain unusually important traits called "central traits". These central traits help people to form overall an impression of others. The presence of a central trait, very often, changes the meaning of other traits. In the above example, the central trait was "warm" and "cold"'(Asch, Ley, 1988).

Some researches on impression formation have used information-processing approaches to develop mathematically oriented models of how individual personality traits are combined to create an overall impression. Findings of these research suggest that in forming an overall judgement of a person, we use a psychological "average" of the individual traits we see, in a manner that is analogous to finding the mathematical average of several numbers (Anderson, 1996).

As we gain more experience with people and observe them in a variety of situations, our impressions of them gradually becomes more complex. But, because usually there are gaps in our knowledge of others, we still tend to fit them into personality schemas which represent particular type of people.

- *Schemas: The notion that memory is based on constructive processes was first put forward by Sor Frederic Bertlett, a British psychologist. He suggested that people tend to remember information in terms of schemas or organised bodies of information stored in memory that bias the way new information is interpreted, stored and recalled (Bertlett, 1932). Our reliance on schemas means that memory often consists of general reconstruction of previous experience. Bertlett said that schemas are based not only on the specific material to which people are exposed, but also on their understanding of the situation, their expectations about the situation and their awareness of the motivations underlying the behaviour of others.*

Take the example of a "gregarious person" (a trait is gregariousness). It includes the traits of friendliness, aggressiveness and openness. The presence of just one or two of the associated traits might be sufficient to make us assign a person to a particular schema (Klein, 1994). As we discussed earlier in this chapter, these schemas are also susceptible to error. They often depend on the moods of individuals.

Attitudes and Social Cognition

Attitudes are learned predispositions to respond in a favourable or unfavourable manner to a particular person, behaviour, belief or thing (Eagly & Chaiken, 1995). Persuasion is a process of changing attitudes.

Attitude Change

Attitude change depends on many factors – (i) Message source (ii) Characteristics of the message and (iii) Characteristics of the target.

(i) *Message Source*: The characteristics of a person who delivers a particular message (known as the attitude communicator), have a major impact on the effectiveness of the message. Different observations show that communicators who are physically and socially attractive produce greater attitude change than those who are less attractive. However, the expertise and trustworthiness of a communicator are related to the impact of the message.

(ii) *Characteristics of the Message*: Sometimes it is not important "who" delivers a message, but "what" the message is that affects attitude and behaviour change. Often, a one-sided argument from the communicator's side is helpful. But if the target receives a message presenting an unpopular viewpoint, two-sided viewpoints are effective. Further, fear-producing messages are effective, although not always. Consider the following examples:

If you do not practice safer sex, you will get AIDS (fear producing message).

If you smoke, you will suffer from cancer (fear producing message).

Again, if the fear aroused is too strong, such messages can arouse people's defence mechanisms and can be ignored (Keerlins and Abelson, 1979; L.H. Rosenthal, 1997).

(iii) *Characteristics of the Target:* Studies also indicated that once a message has been communicated, characteristics of the target of the message can determine whether the message will be accepted or not. For example, intelligent people are more resistant to persuasion than those who are less intelligent.

Some findings indicate that there are gender differences in persuasibility. Women are somewhat more easily persuaded than men, particularly when they have less knowledge of the message topic. But some studies state that the magnitude of the difference between men and women is not large (Wood & Stronger, 1994).

Information-Processing Routes to Persuasion

The recipients may or may not be receptive to persuasive messages. It depends on the type of information processing they use. Experts and social psychologists discovered two primary information-processing routes to persuasion: (i) Central-route Processing and (ii) Peripheral-route Processing.

Central-route processing occurs when the recipient thoughtfully considers the issues and arguments involved in persuasion. In contrast, peripheral-route processing occurs when people are persuaded on the basis of factors unrelated to the nature or quality of the content of a persuasive message. Instead, they are influenced by factors that are irrelevant or extraneous to the topic or issue, such as who is providing the message or how long the arguments are (Petty, 1994).

Central-route processing occurs when targets are highly involved and motivated to comprehend the message. If central-route processing is not employed because the target is uninvolved, unmotivated, bored or distracted, then the nature of the message becomes less important and peripheral factors more critical (Fig. 6.2). Psychologists say that although both central-route and peripheral-route processing lead to attitude change, central-route processing generally leads to stronger, more lasting attitude change.

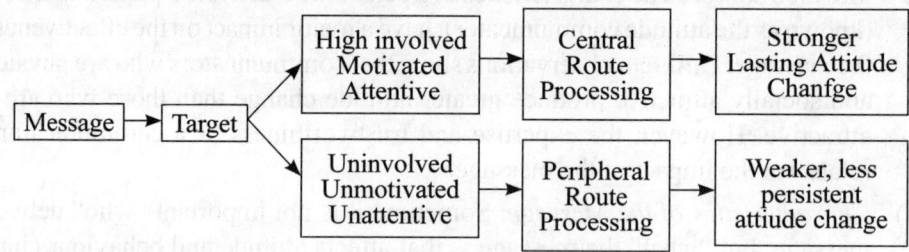

Fig. 6.2: Routes to persuasion

Are some people more likely than others to use central-route processing rather than peripheral-route processing?

The answer is yes. People who are high in "the need for cognition" (a person's habitual level of thoughtfulness and cognitive activity) are more likely to employ central-route processing. Consider the statements shown in Table 6.1. People who agree with the first two statements and disagree with the rest, have a relatively high need for cognition (Cacioppo, 1996).

Table 6.1: The Need for Cognition

Which of the following statements apply to you?
1. I really enjoy a task that involves coming up with new solutions to problems.
2. I would prefer a task that is intellectual, difficult and important compared to one that is somewhat important but does not require much thought.
3. Learning new ways to think doesn't excite me very much.
4. The idea to rely on thought to make my way to the top does not appeal to me.
5. I think only as hard as I have to.
6. I like tasks that require little thought once I've learned them.
7. I prefer to think about small, daily projects rather than long-term ones.
8. I would rather do something that requires little thought than something that is sure to challenge my thinking abilities.
9. I find little satisfaction in deliberating hard and for long hours.
10. I don't like to be responsible for a situation that requires a lot of thinking.
Scoring: The more you agree with statements 1 and 2 and disagree with the rest, the greater the likelihood that you have a high need for cognition.

Source: Adapted from Cacioppo (1996)

It is found that individuals who are high in the need for cognition enjoy thinking, philosophising and pondering about the world. As a result, they tend to reflect more on persuasive messages using central-route processing and they are likely to be persuaded by complex, logical and detailed messages. On the contrary, those who are low in the need for cognition become impatient when forced to spend too much time thinking about an issue. Consequently, they are more likely to use peripheral-route processing and to be more persuaded by factors other than the quality and detail of the messages (Petty & Cacioppo, 1992).

The Link between Attitudes and Behaviour

Attitudes influence behaviour. The strength of the links between particular attitudes and behaviours vary. Generally, people strive for consistency between their attitudes and their behaviour and are fairly consistent in their attitudes. Not only do our attitudes influence our behaviour, but sometimes our behaviour shapes our attitudes. According to Leon Festinger (1957), cognitive dissonance occurs when an individual holds two attitudes or thoughts (referred to as cognitions) that contradict each other. His theory of cognitive dissonance predicts that participants will reduce dissonance by adopting more positive attitudes towards the task (Kelly, 1995).

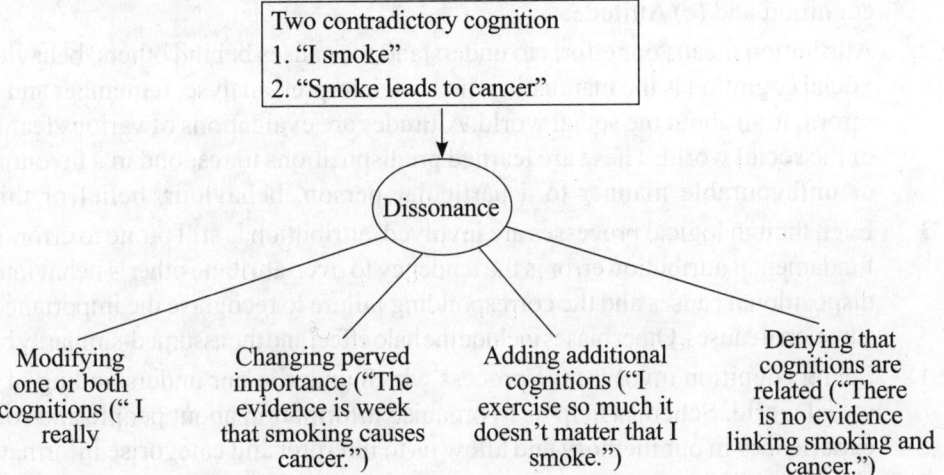

Fig. 6.3: *The simultaneous presence of two contradictory cognitions (I smoke and smoking leads to cancer) produces cognitive dissonance, which can be reduced through several methods.*

Dissonance explains a number of everyday occurrences involving attitudes and behaviour. For example, a smoker who knows that smoking leads to lung cancer holds contradictory cognitions (i) I smoke (ii) Smoking leads to lung cancer. The theory predicts that these two thoughts will lead to a state of cognitive dissonance (Fig. 6.3). Whatever technique is used, the result is a reduction in dissonance..

Key Terms

1. Assumed-similarity bias
2. Attitude
3. Attitude change
4. Attribution
5. Central-route processing
6. Cognitive dissonance
7. Consensus
8. Consistency
9. Correspondence bias
10. Distinctiveness
11. Halo effect
12. Impression formation
13. Information-processing
14. Message source
15. Peripheral-route processing
16. Persuasion
17. Self-serving bias
18. Social behaviour
19. Social cognition
20. Social thought

Chapter Summary and Review

1. Social thought denotes how and what we think about other individuals. Three important aspects come under "social thought" are (a) Attribution (b) Social cognition and (c) Attitude.

2. Attribution means our efforts to understand the causes behind others' behaviour. Social cognition is the manner in which we interpret, analyse, remember and use information about the social world. Attitudes are evaluations of various features of the social world. These are learned predispositions to respond in a favourable or unfavourable manner to a particular person, behaviour, belief or thing.

3. Even though logical processes are involved, attribution is still prone to error. The fundamental attribution error is the tendency to over-attribute other's behaviour to dispositional causes and the corresponding failure to recognise the importance of situational causes. Other biases include the halo effect and the assumed-similarity bias.

4. Social cognition involves the process which underlie our understanding of the social world. Schemas help us to organise information about people and social experiences in our memory and allow us to interpret and categorise information about others.

5. Individuals form impressions of others in part through the use of central traits or personality characteristics that are given unusually heavy weight when an impression is formed.

6. Information-processing approaches have found that we tend to average sets of traits to form an overall impression. Attribution theory tries to explain how we understand the causes of behaviour, particularly with respect to situational or dispositional factors.

7. Cognitive dissonance occurs when two cognition attitudes and thoughts which contradict each other are held simultaneously by an individual. To resolve the contradiction, the person might modify the cognition, change its importance or deny a link, thereby bringing about a reduction in dissonance.

QUESTIONS

1. What is social cognition? How do we form impressions of what others are like and of the causes of their behaviour?
2. What biases influence how we view others' behaviour?
3. What is cognitive dissonance? How does it occur? How can dissonance be reduced?
4. Describe the relationship between attitude and cognition.
5. What do you mean by "persuasion"? Point out the differences between "Central-route Processing" and Peripheral-route Processing".
6. Discuss how attitudes and behaviour are linked.
7. What is impression formation? How are central traits responsible for forming impressions of others?
8. How is attribution process helpful in understanding the causes of behaviour?
9. Discuss different biases in attribution, with examples.
10. Write short notes on:
    (a) Cognitive dissonance
    (b) Halo effect
    (c) Persuasion
    (d) Fundamental attribution error
    (e) Impression formation

CHAPTER - 7

POSITIVE PSYCHOLOGY

❑ *Positive Psychology has a long history and a short past. The positive side of human nature has been of long-standing interest to both philosophers and psychologists. According to many researchers in this area, it is only some time ago that the positive side of human nature has attracted serious and more widespread empirical study. This relatively new field addresses important questions about how we lead our lives, find happiness and satisfaction in life and deal with life challenges. Positive psychology may be used to increase individual happiness. It deals with self-improvement and personal growth. Positive psychology can be considered a dynamic new area with a promising future.*

❑ **This chapter covers:**
- Positive psychology: introduction
- Traditional psychology and negative focus
- Emergence of positive psychology
- Relationship of positive psychology with other branches of psychology
- Relation of positive psychology with social/personality psychology and psychology of religion
- Positive psychology: assumptions, goals and definitions
- Why we are interested to know about positive psychology
- Positive psychology and the status-quo
- Key Terms, Summary and Questions

❑ **By the end of this chapter, you will be able to:**
- Know what is positive psychology
- Define positive psychology
- Bring out the differences between positive psychology and traditional psychology
- Know about the relationships between positive psychology, developmental psychology, social/personality psychology, survey research and subjective well-being
- Understand the nature, scope and aim of positive psychology as a social-science discipline
- Familiarise yourself with various concepts like "Life Above Zero", "Good Life" and "Status-Quo"
- Know about "happiness"

Introduction

Positive psychology has a long history and a short past. The positive side of human nature has been of long-standing interest to both philosophers and psychologists. From some time now, this positive side of human behaviour has attracted serious and more widespread empirical study.

A professor once remarked that human nature is even worse than we had imagined. How bad is human nature, actually? Milgram's classic study suggests that ordinary people will go against their own judgement and moral values under minimal pressure from a legitimate authority.

A positive psychologist might ask: "Why aren't there equally dramatic studies showing the human capacity for goodness?"

It certainly is not so because goodness does not exist in the world. History provides a large number of examples. Who can forget the imagery of heroic fire-fighters, police officers and ordinary citizens following the 9/11 terrorist attacks?

A basic viewpoint of positive psychology is that the field of psychology is out of balance, with more focus on the negatives in human behaviour than on the positives. Positive psychology does not deny the negatives, nor does it suggest that all of psychology focuses on the negative. Positive psychology takes a more realistic and balanced view of human nature that includes human strengths and virtues, without denying human weakness and capacity for evil. Each of us has a share of sadness and trauma in our life, but we also experience our share of joy and happiness. But if we look at history, it seems we have had more to say about the downs than about the ups of human behaviour. A large number of students of psychology recall mostly the negatives of human behaviour such as mental illness rather than recalling the positive emotions.

Traditional Psychology and Negative Focus

Among the popular psychoanalysts, Sigmund Freud had emphasised on negatives in his theory. Freud believed that human behaviour is motivated primarily by self-serving drives that must be controlled and channelled in productive ways for society to function effectively. He did not necessarily believe that self-serving behaviours were bad. From his perspective, they simply expressed our biologically inherited needs and impulses.

Within psychology, the legacy of Freud's views has been to perpetuate a negative image of human nature. Behaviours and traits which are seemingly positive on the surface are sometimes rooted in negative motives. But positive psychology emphasises that this is not always the case. From a positive psychology perspective, positive qualities and motives are just as authentic as negative ones and they affirm the positive side of human nature.

Freud believed that negative motives lie beneath the surface of positive behaviours. Based on these facts, other science-inspired scepticism concerning the scientific legitimacy were developed which are studied in positive psychology. Many experts perceive these topics as reminiscent of popular psychology literature. From history and literature, it is obvious that psychologists have used pop-psychology and self-help books as examples of the folly of unscientific and empirically unsupported ideas about human behaviour. Experts and many psychologists view the success of the self-help industry as evidence of lay people's gullibility and the importance of a critical scientific attitude.

Some psychologists and experts say "positive psychology is pop-psychology with a scientific basis." This description is insightful because it acknowledges the connection between the subject matter of positive psychology and many, long-lasting mainstays of pop-psychology. Many studies in positive psychology include the study of happiness, love, hope, forgiveness, positive growth after trauma and the health-promoting benefits of a positive, optimistic attitude.

Thus, the reasons for psychology's greater focus on negative than positive phenomena are rooted in negative beliefs about the basic nature of humanity, of scepticism about the scientific basis of the subject matter of positive psychology.

Negatives Are More Important in Human Life

Generally, in human behaviour, the bad is stronger than the good (Baumister & Finkenaur, 2001). Research findings suggest that the greater weight and attention given to the negatives in human behaviour compared to the positives may reflect a universal tendency, that is, such a focus is inherent in human nature. Studies on impression formation suggest that information about negative traits and behaviours contributes more to how we think about others than does positive information.

Evidences also indicates that the presence of conflict and negative behaviour makes a greater contribution to relationship satisfaction (or lack thereof) than does the amount of positive behaviour (Reis & Gable, 2003). Many instances show that one negative comment can undo many acts of kindness and one bad trait can undermine a person's reputation.

Here, one reason is pertinent. We seem to assume that life is going to be good, or at least acceptable. This assumption may reflect our everyday experience in which good or neutral events are more frequent than bad ones. Consequently, negative events and information stand out in distinct contrast to our general expectations. Research supports this idea that because positive events are more common in our experience, negative ones violate our expectations and are consequently given more attention (Heidt, 2005).

Disease Model

This idea came from Martin Seligman (2003). He argues that the dominance of the disease model within psychology has focused psychologists on treating illness and defocused them from building strengths. The disease model has produced many successes in treating psychopathology. Based on the disease model, psychology has built an extensive library of case studies of mental illness and a language to describe the different pathologies which affect millions of people. Ryff and Singer (1998) said that psychology should be more than a "repair shop" for broken lives. However, we should acknowledge that the reason for the focus of psychology on the negative has been the well-intentioned desire to reduce human misery,

The disease model is of limited value when it comes to promoting health and preventing illness. Psychologists appear to know far less about mental health than about mental illness. Even now, we lack a comparable understanding or even a language for describing the characteristics of mentally healthy people. It is clear that mental health is not simply the absence of mental illness. Eliminating illness does not ensure a healthy, thriving and competent individual.

Emergence of Positive Psychology

Martin Seligman (1998) was the first contemporary psychologist to call this perspective as "positive psychology". Seligman was the president of the American Psychology Association at that time. He made a plea in his presidential address for a major shift in psychology's focus from studying and trying to correct the worst in human behaviour to studying and promoting the best in human behaviour. A particular question he asked to his audience was "Why should psychology not study things like joy and courage?" By highlighting the imbalance in psychology, he supported his call for positive psychology.

Earlier attention was given to weaknesses and human misery, but not on strengths and promotion of health. Seligman's hope was that positive psychology would help expand the scope of psychology beyond the disease model to promote the study and understanding of healthy human functioning.

New areas of psychology do not emerge in a vacuum. The perspectives and concerns of psychology were designed by Seligman. His ideas were scattered throughout the world. Terman's studies of gifted children and determinants of happiness in marriage are early examples of research emphasising positive characteristics and functioning. The origins of research of subjective well-being can be found in early research starting in the 1920s and reinforced by the polling techniques by George Gallup and others (Lucas & Diener, 2002).

The humanistic movement may have been one of the stronger voices for a more positive psychology. As a popular perspective in the 1960s, humanistics psychology also criticised the tendency of traditional psychology to focus on negative aspects of human functioning. For example, psychologists like Abraham Maslow and Carl Rogers viewed human nature as basically positive, insisting that every individual is born with positive inner potentials and that the driving force in life is to actualise these potentials. Humanistic psychologists believed that the goal of psychology should be to study and promote conditions that help people achieve productive and healthy lives.

Now the area of positive psychology has a large amount of research and theory it has generated and the scientific respectability it has achieved. Psychologists can study hope, forgiveness, or the physical and emotional benefits of positive emotions without feeling that they are leaving their scientific sensibilities behind and without being regarded as pop-psychologists. Often, students call the positive psychology class as "happiness course".

However, there is no official or universally accepted definition of positive psychology. It draws on research and theory from established areas of psychology. In part, positive psychology is a mosaic of research and theory from many different areas of psychology tied together by their focus on positive aspects of human behaviour.

In the following section, we will discuss about a brief sketch of research and theory from different areas of psychology which have contributed most to positive psychology. An overview of its relationship with the more established and familiar areas of psychology will clarify what positive psychology is about.

Relationship of Positive Psychology with Other Branches of Psychology

Positive psychology has borrowed some ideas from other branches of psychology. Here, we will discuss briefly the relationship of positive psychology with other established and familiar areas of psychology.

Relationship of Positive Psychology with Health Psychology

Positive psychology and health psychology share much in common (Taylor & Sherman, 2004). For a long time, health psychologists suspected that negative emotions can make us sick and positive emotions can be beneficial. But scientific and biological foundation for this was not developed for these long-standing assumptions till much later. Our understanding of the relationship between body and mind has advanced dramatically in the last few decades. Experts and health psychologists affirm the potential health-threatening effects of stress, anger, anxiety, resentment and worry (Cohen & Kewley, 2005).

The pathways and mechanisms involved are complex and are just beginning to be understood. They involve the brain, the nervous system, the endocrine system and immune system (Maier & Watkins, 1994). Research findings show that people going through long periods of extreme stress are more vulnerable to illness (Cohen and Glasher, 2004). The reason may be stress and negative emotions are bad for us and they seem to suppress the functioning of the immune system and reduce our body's ability to fight diseases.

Positive psychologists suggest that positive emotions may have effects equal to negative emotions, but in the opposite direction. While negative emotions compromise our health, positive emotions seem to help restore or preserve the health of our minds and bodies. In a way, positive emotions appear to set in motion a number of physical, psychological and social processes that enhance our physical well-being, emotional health, coping skills and intellectual functioning. Fredrickson's (2001) broaden-and-build theory states that "positive emotions like joy, contentment, interest, love and pride, all share the ability to broaden people's thought-action repertoires and build their enduring personal resources, ranging from physical and intellectual resources to social and psychological resources."

Our increasing knowledge of the physiological processes underlying emotions provides a biological foundation to positive psychology. Conclusion may be drawn that positive emotions have as much biological and evolutionary significance as the negative emotions which have attracted so much research attention in the past. Positive psychology becomes consistent with the goal of restoring balance to the field. Also it emphasises examination of the value of positive emotions in our daily life.

Living Longer through Positive Emotions: Focus on Research

Do people who experience an abundance of positive emotions in their lives – emotions like joy, cheerfulness and contentment live longer than those whose emotional lives are less positive?

Of course, it sounds reasonable. But how could we untangle all the complex factors which affect people's health to show that emotions made the difference? A classic study on nuns known as "The Nun Study" could give answer to this question. This study was conducted by Danner, Snowdon and Frieson (2001) in the University of Kentucky. Danner and her colleagues examined the relationship between positive emotions and longevity in a sample of 180 nuns. Nuns were taken as subject (Ss) because they were an ideal group of people for such a study as many of the factors affecting physical health were controlled or minimised. The main reason to take them as subjects was the "sameness" of their lives which eliminated many of the variables, so that the researchers would be able to understand which specific factors were responsible for longer life-span. Nuns don't smoke or drink. They live in similar circumstances without having family relations. Also, they are childless. Therefore, they have the same reproductive histories. They usually have same bland diet. Findings showed that positive emotions may lead to a longer life.

At this stage, another question comes to our minds: "What led the researchers to believe that an individual's emotional life might predict longevity?" Some reasons are as follows:

First, previous research supports the connection between emotions and health. Negative emotions always suppress the immune system and other aspects of physiological functioning and thereby increase the risk of disease. On the other hand, positive emotions seem to enhance these same processes and thus reduce the risk of disease.

Second, temperament has shown long-term stability over the life-span. In other words, emotional expressiveness, such as whether we have a positive and cheerful outlook or a negative and more guarded outlook, tends to be fairly consistent over a person's lifetime, from childhood through adulthood.

Third, a person's temperament is known to influence how well the individual copes with the stress and challenges of life. People with cheerful temperaments and positive outlooks fare better than those with less cheerful and more negative outlooks.

Finally, some studies have shown that writing about significant life events can capture a person's basic emotional outlook. When we write about things which are important to us, we express emotions that reflect aspects of our basic temperament. So autobiographies written early in life would capture basic aspects of emotional expressiveness. Then, differences in emotional expressiveness might predict health and longevity.

> ***Positive Emotions in Early Life and Longevity: Findings from the Nun Study***
> - *The Nun Study is a classic in positive psychology which brought about the features of the religious life of sisters of the Catholic church. It was conduced by Danner, Snowdon and Friesen (2001) at the University of Kentucky. Danner and her colleagues examined the relationship between positive emotions and longevity in a sample of 180 nuns. Nuns were taken as subjects (Ss) because they were an ideal group of people for such a study. They do not smoke, drink and they have no children. They live in similar life circumstances. Also they eat the same bland diet. Findings showed that positive emotions may lead to a longer life.*

In the study of Danner and her colleagues, the nuns had been asked to write a brief 2 to 3 page autobiographical sketch as a part of their religious vows. These sketches were written in the 1930s and 1940s when the sisters were about 22 years old and just beginning their careers with the church. Experts were able to retrieve the autobiographies from church archives. Then they coded each autobiography by counting the number of positive, negative and neutral emotion words and sentences. Researchers concentrated on only positive emotion words and positive emotion sentences.

Scores were taken from the coding system which provided numeric indices to describe their early emotional lives. These scores were then analysed in relation to mortality and survival date for the same group of women 60 years later. When this study was conducted in 2001, the surviving nuns were between 75 and 94 years of age. Near about 42 per cent of the sisters died by the time of the follow-up study.

However, the results of the study were amazing. Researchers found a strong relationship between longevity and the expression of positive emotion early in life. The most cheerful nuns lived a full decade longer than the least cheerful. By age 80, some 60 per cent of the least cheerful group had died. The probability of survival to an advanced age was strongly related to the early life expression of positive emotions. The probability of survival to age 85 was 80 per cent for the most cheerful nuns and 54 per cent for the least cheerful. By age 94, the survival odds were over half (54 per cent) for the most positive sisters and only 15 per cent for the least positive.

It was found that the phrase "don't worry and be happy" was an excellent advice throughout the study. Another advice was "you may live longer".

Relationship of Positive Psychology with Clinical Psychology

In recent past, application of psychology's knowledge about human behaviour has expanded beyond psychology itself. Several branches of applied psychology are there. Not only do they seek to acquire basic knowledge about human behaviour, they also attempt to put it to practical use. Clinical psychology is an applied branch of psychology. Clinical psychologists help individuals deal with emotional and psychological problems.

Clinical psychologists used to have disillusionment due to sole reliance on the disease model. This is another reason for the development of positive psychology. Mental health psychologists are beginning to view the work of reducing psychological misery as only part of their role. Clients need help at every moment. It is an important mission of psychologists to provide such help. Many clinicians have begun shifting from the single-minded purpose of treating psychopathology towards a perspective which includes prevention of illness and promotion of positive mental health.

This kind of shift has highlighted the need to develop models of positive mental health. Previously, mental health was defined mostly in terms of the absence of disease. Now the main goal of positive psychology is to establish criteria and a language defining the presence of mental health which parallels our current criteria and language for describing and diagnosing mental illness.

Relation of Positive Psychology with Developmental Psychology

Developmental psychology is the branch of psychology which focuses on the many ways we change throughout life. Development refers to systematic continuities and changes in the individual that occur between conception and death. If development represents the continuities and changes an individual experiences from "womb to tomb", the developmental sciences refer to the study of these phenomena and are a multidisciplinary enterprise.

Developmental psychologists study the conditions which threaten healthy development. It used to be assumed that most children grow up under conditions of adversity (i.e., poverty, abuse, parental alcoholism, mental illness). These children show deficits in social, cognitive and emotional development. During the 1970s, these assumptions were changed. Many psychiatrists and psychologists drew attention to the amazing resilience of certain children and adults subjected to potentially debilitating life challenges (Masten, 2001). Resilience in development is the capacity of some adolescents raised in harmful environments to somehow rise above these disadvantages and achieve healthy development.

Children can grow and flourish even in very harsh environments. Despite their exposure to truly devastating conditions, some children develop into competent, confident and healthy adults (Jessor, 1991). Such persons are described as showing resilience in development. Research findings suggest that they do so because of several protective factors. Some of these factors are:

First, resilience in development stems from protective factors within the individuals themselves. Studies suggest that they possess traits and temperament which elicit positive responses from many caregivers. They are active, affectionate, good-natured and easy to deal with. They have an "easy temperament". Such children are often highly intelligent and have good communication and problem-solving skills. They get along well with others and form friendships easily. These factors contribute to their resilience.

Second, such children also benefit from protective factors within their families. They even get emotional support from people outside the family. What is crucial is not the biological relationship between the adolescent and the adult or adults in question, but rather the fact that these adults serve as models and provide encouragement.

Third and last, resilient youngsters often benefit from protective factors relating to their community. Favourite teachers are often positive role models for them. Caring neighbours and youth workers can give children the boost they need to rise above instability that mark their lives (Fig. 7.1:gives a summary of these factors). When children benefit from these and perhaps other protective factors, they can beat the odds and develop into competent, confident, responsible and caring adults, good parents and role models for their own children (Werner, 1995).

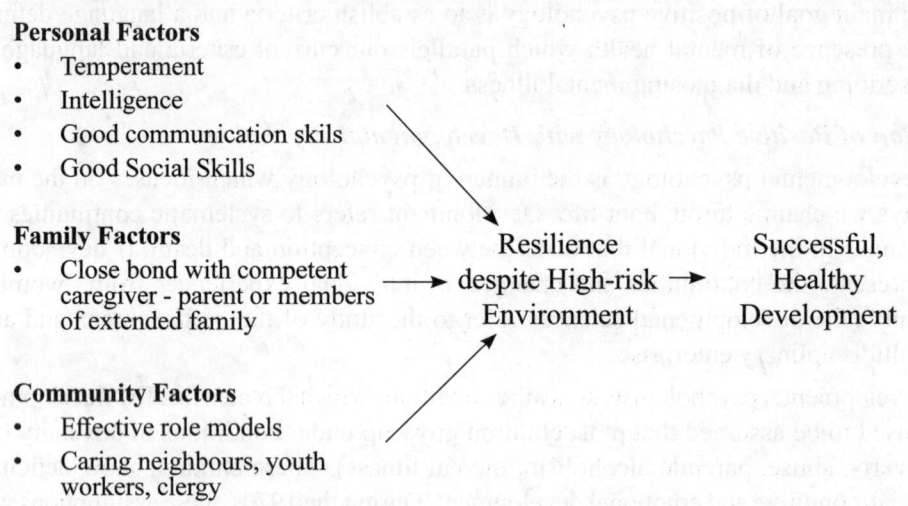

Fig. 7.1: Factors contributing to adolescent resilience
Source: Based on suggestions by Werner, 1995

The amazing resilience of ordinary people facing difficult life circumstances highlights a major theme of positive psychology, namely, human strengths. Another concept "post-traumatic growth" (PTG), which is a counter to "post-traumatic stress disorder" (PTSD) can be considered here. Experts and researchers found that positive growth can occur as a result of traumatic experiences like serious illness, loss of loved one or a major accident or disability. Many people report a greater appreciation of life, an increased sense of personal strength and more clarity about what is most important in life in the aftermath of such events.

Relation of Positive Psychology with "Survey Research" and "Subjective Well-Being"

Sociologists and social psychologists used public opinion polls for a long time. It was a major research tool for them. Later, survey research came to include quality of life measures. Ed Diener (2000) is a prominent researcher who studies happiness, defined as subjective well-being (SWB).

Measures of SWB assesses an individual's level of life satisfaction and the frequency of positive and negative emotional experiences. Research of happiness has established a reliable pattern of intriguing findings. The most noteworthy of these is that material success (i.e., money and wealth) bears only a weak relationship with happiness. Large income and possession of consumer goods beyond what is necessary to meet basic needs are not reliably related to increases in happiness.

The survey research raises an interesting question: "If money does not buy happiness, what does?"

This particular question is connected with positive psychology. Once basic needs are met, objective life circumstances (such as the amount of money you make or your age, race or gender) do not have much influence on your level of happiness. Therefore, the difference between happy and unhappy people involves more psychological and subjective factors.

Positive psychology follows the early survey research in examining the "traits" and "states" that help explain differences in the level of happiness. Research in positive psychology is focused on "traits" such as work situation, involvement in religion, number of friends, marital status and the quality of relationships. Taken together, these traits and states help explain one of the major questions of positive psychology: "Why are some people happier than others?"

Relation of Positive Psychology with Social/Personality Psychology and Psychology of Religion

Evidence from social psychology indicates the critical importance of satisfying social relationships and support from others for our health and happiness (Taylor & Seeman, 1997). Satisfaction in life is founded on satisfying relationships, such as happy marriage and good friends. Experts and researchers in social psychology have also sensitised us to the different cultural understandings of well-being and happiness. For instance, concepts of happiness in USA and Japan are quite different. Many researchers worked on a single problem "Why does money not buy happiness?"

Personality psychologists have identified positive traits and personal strengths which form the foundation of health and happiness. Their studies include investigations of the genetic basis of a happy temperament and personality traits related to individual well-being such as optimism, self-esteem, extraversion and how the pursuit of personally meaningful goals contributes to happiness.

The researchers in social and personality psychology have contributed to an understanding of the roles that religion and morality play in our lives. Religion has become an important topic in positive psychology because it is a significant foundation of well-being for most people. Another important topic is the study of virtue which has a prominent position because the meaning of a good life and a life well-lived is strongly connected to human virtues such as honesty, integrity, compassion and wisdom (Peterson & Seligman, 2004). Having human virtues contributes to individual well-being and the well-being of others. As we gain experience, acts of forgiveness and gratitude tend to increase life satisfaction for both givers and recipients.

Positive Psychology: Assumptions, Goals and Definitions

Positive psychology is both a general part of the discipline of psychology and a collection of research topics focused on positive aspects of human behaviour. Martin Seligman's call for positive psychology was aimed at refocusing the entire field of psychology, from physiological to clinical psychology. A major assumption of positive psychology is that the field of psychology has become unbalanced. The main aim of positive psychology is to restore balance within the discipline.

This goal is reflected in two areas of research and theory which need further development: (i) There is a need for improved understanding of positive human behaviours to balance the negative focus of much mainstream research and theory (King, 2001) and (ii) There is a need to develop an empirically-based conceptual understanding and language for describing healthy human functioning that parallels our classification and understanding of mental illness (Keyes, 2003).

Positive psychology attempts to define these new areas of psychology. Sheldon and King (2001) define positive psychology as "nothing more than the scientific study of ordinary human strengths and virtues". This definition reflects the emphasis on psychology's lack of attention to people's everyday lives, which are typically quite positive.

According to Gable and Haidt (2005), positive psychology is "the study of the conditions and processes that contribute to the flourishing or optional functioning of people, groups and institutions."

This definition has much in common with Seligman's (2003) description of the three pillars of positive psychology. Positive psychology is built on the study of (i) Positive subjective experiences (such as joy, happiness, contentment, optimism and hope), (ii) Positive individual characteristics (such as personal strengths and human virtues which promote mental health and (iii) Positive social institutions and communities which contribute to individual health and happiness. Seligman proposed that "happiness" is the central theme of positive psychology.

Seligman and his colleagues said that "happiness" as a central focus of positive psychology can be divided into three components: (i) The pleasant life (ii) The engaged life and (iii) The meaningful life (Seligman, Rashid & Parks, 2006). These three formulations of happiness capture two major themes in positive psychology, namely, that positive psychology is the scientific study of optimal mental functioning and happiness.

The pleasant life puts emphasis in positive psychology on understanding the determinants of happiness as a desired state. Some people call it "good life". It describes what life circumstances and personal qualities make people happy, contented and fulfilled.

The engaged life is another aspect of happiness focused on active involvement in activities (e.g., work and leisure) and relationship with others which express our talents and strengths and which give meaning and purpose to our lives.

> ***What Is Positive Psychology?***
>
> *Positive psychology is nothing more than the scientific study of ordinary human strengths and virtues.*
>
> —Sheldon & King (2001)
>
> *Positive psychology is the study of the conditions and processes that contribute to the flourishing or optimal functioning of people, groups and institutions.*
>
> —Gable and Haidt (2005)
>
> *Three pillars of positive psychology*
>
> Positive psychology is built on the study of:
> (i) Positive subjective experiences (joy, happiness, contentment)
> (ii) Positive individual characteristics (strength and virtues)
> (iii) Positive social institutions and communities which contribute to individual health and happiness.

But a meaningful life is another aspect of happiness which derives from going beyond our own self-interests and preoccupations. This is a deeper and more enduring aspect of happiness, according to Seligman and his colleagues, which stems from giving to and being involved in, something larger than yourself. Seligman and his colleagues call it "positive institutions".

Examples of Seligman's "positive institutions" might include a religious community, a personal philosophy of life, your family, a charitable community organisation or a political, environmental or social cause. The fact is that a life well-lived means being connected to something "larger than the self" (Seligman, 2006).

Life above Zero

Now, in conclusion, we can think of positive psychology as the study of what we might call life on the positive side of zero, where zero is the line that divides illness from health and unhappiness from happiness. Here it must be noted that traditional psychology has told us much about life at and below zero, but less about life above zero.

What takes us from just an absence of illness and unhappiness to a life that is meaningful, purposeful, satisfying and healthy? In short, how we can make our lives worth living?

On the whole, positive psychology is all about the personal qualities, life circumstances, individual choices, life activities, relationships with others, transcendent purposes and socio-cultural conditions which foster and define a good life. Taking all these factors into account and by combining these factors with the positive criteria psychologists have used to define a good life, the following definition is suggested:

Positive psychology is the scientific study of the personal qualities, life choices, life circumstances and socio-cultural conditions which promote a life well-lived, defined by the criteria of happiness, physical and mental health, meaningfulness and virtue.

Culture and the Meaning of a Good Life

Obviously, culture shapes the particular meanings of a good life and a life well-lived. Conceptions of a good life are part of every culture's ideals, values and philosophic/religious traditions (Ryff & Singer, 1998). Since the idea of positive psychology is a Western proposition, it is appropriate to ask whether the concepts of health and happiness reflect only a Western view and, therefore, do not apply to other cultures.

This is largely an empirical issue for positive psychologists. Experts and researchers in the emerging field of positive psychology do not want to impose a one-size-fits-all definition which suggests there is only one kind of good life. Instead, they want to bring out a universal definition which includes a flexible criteria that allows for individual and cultural differences. We will discuss culture and well-being and culture and the meaning of happiness later in this book.

Why Are We Interested to Know about Positive Psychology?

Why is positive psychology so attractive today? Psychologists have given a call for positive psychology earlier during the 19th and 20th century also. But why did intellectuals turn a deaf ear to them? Why were they heard only recently? New ideas emerge in part because they fit or capture some essential theme that is prominent at a particular point in time. Positive psychology came to the forefront in the 1990s and continued into the new millennium.

Our affluent societies have increased signs of subjective distress. Sikszentmihalyi (1999) has shown his concern in the title of his article, "If we are so rich, why are not we happy?" Most indicators of material affluence, from personal income and ownership of computers and motor vehicles to GDP, have gone up over the last several decades. As Myers (2000) has described it, many indicators of distress and unhappiness have also gone up. Further, the "misery index", which includes rates of divorce, child abuse, childhood poverty and adolescent suicide, has also gone up. Seligman remarked that we are twice as rich as we were 40 years ago, but we are also ten times more likely to get depressed. Depression is currently at an epidemic level everywhere. In every society, young people tell painful stories of their inner emptiness and unfulfilled as well as miserable lives.

In every culture, there is a saying "Money does not buy happiness". Personal satisfaction may be a source of healthy and satisfying life. Psychology has not offered ready answers to many of these questions. So there is a need of positive psychology. After the terrorist attack of 9/11 and Mumbai attack, our safety and security is under question. So the questions addressed by positive psychology are enduring and much of its subject matter is directly relevant to our daily activities.

Positive Psychology Is Not Opposed to Psychology

How is positive psychology different from psychology as a whole?

Positive psychologists frequently contrast this new area with "traditional psychology". There is an impression that positive psychology is somehow opposed to psychology.

But this is not true. Psychologists have developed an extensive understanding of human behaviour and the treatment of psychopathology. History of psychology shows a steady advance in knowledge and in effective treatments.

Positive psychologists are not so concerned about what has been studied in psychology. They are more concerned about what has not been studied. The fundamental message of positive psychology described by Sheldon and King (2001) was as follows:

Positive psychology is thus an attempt to urge psychologists to adopt a more open and appreciative perspective regarding human potentials, motives and capacities. On the whole, positive psychology aims to expand – not replace – psychology's understanding of human behaviour.

Positive Psychology and the Status Quo

Positive psychologists state that our attitude towards life makes a significant contribution to our happiness and health. But does it mean that life circumstances are not important? Do they have no contributions?

If an individual is poor and lives in a slum which is in a high-crime area, has no job or engagement, is his or her happiness dependent on their attitude and not the situation? The question is, if happiness is more a matter of attitude than money, do we need to worry much about the amount of poverty in our country? In other words, does positive psychology serve the status quo by helping to justify the unequal distribution of resources and power in our society? If our happiness is more a product of subjective personal factors than it is of material factors, why should we be concerned about who gets what share of resources?

Let us discuss the reasons why positive psychology should not be seen as justifying the status quo.

First, the external situation of an individual is important to the quality of his or her life. There are limits to people's ability to maintain a positive attitude in the face of challenging life experiences. Poor people are less happy than those who are not poor. Further, certain traumas, like death of a spouse, do not have lasting effects on personal happiness (Dinner, 2000).

Second, research on subjective well-being reveals that economically sound people live relatively comfortable lives. For these people, life satisfaction is more dependent on psychological and social factors, because their basic needs have been met. Most of the Americans seem to be happy because they reflect optimism and satisfaction that results from having the freedom to make personal choices and pursue satisfying endeavours. Both are made possible due to the economic comfort they enjoy. Knowing that someone is economically well-off does not tell us whether he or she is happy or satisfied with life. Positive psychology gives the message: "A shortage of money can make you miserable, but an abundance of money does not necessarily make you happy."

Finally, the following questions arise: "What makes us happy? What is just and fair in the distribution of resources and how people are treated?" Even if positive psychologists discover the "sources of happiness", issues of justice and fairness, will remain. However, the reasons for promoting equality, equal opportunity and equal treatment have to do with the fundamental values of every society. Policies to remove discriminatory barriers or to improve the equitable distribution of resources do not require misery or unhappiness of anyone as justification. Inequality and discrimination may create misery. But being treated fairly and having equal opportunity are the rights of every citizen of a country. Not a single individual should have to show that he or she is miserable and unhappy to justify equal opportunity and fair treatment.

❑ **Key Terms**

1. Bad is stronger than the good
2. Clinical psychology
3. Developmental psychology
4. Disease model
5. Health psychology
6. Life above zero
7. Meaningful life
8. Negative emotions
9. Negative focus
10. Personality psychology
11. Pleasant life
12. Positive emotions
13. Positive psychology
14. Post Traumatic Growth (PTG)
15. Post Traumatic Stress Disorder (PTSD)
16. Social psychology
17. Subjective well-being
18. Survey research
19. Traditional psychology
20. Pop-psychology

❑ Chapter Summary and Review

1. Positive psychology is not opposed to traditional psychology. Rather, it is an expansion of traditional psychology. It has a short past, but a long history. Philosophers and psychologists have known about positive side of human nature. But they were attracted towards this concept only some time ago. Before that, they were studying the negative side of the human nature.

2. Now, positive psychology is considered a dynamic new area with a promising future. It deals with questions of how we lead our lives, find happiness and satisfaction in life and deal with life challenges. It is also used to increase individual happiness.

3. Positive psychology also deals with self-improvement and personal growth. In the last part of the 20th century, Freud believed that negative motives lie beneath the surface of positive behaviours. Many psychologists described positive psychology as pop-psychology with a scientific basis. But this is incorrect. Current topics in positive psychology include the study of happiness, love, hope, forgiveness, positive growth after trauma and the health promoting benefits of a positive, optimistic attitude.

4. In human behaviour, the bad is stronger than the good. Negatives are more important in human life. Research on impression formation suggests that information about negative traits and behaviours contributes more to how we think about others than does positive information.

5. Some experts feel that psychology should be more than a "repair shop" for broken lives. Disease model is of limited value when it comes to promoting health and preventing illness. Psychologists know far less about mental health than about mental illness. It should be remembered that mental health is not simply the absence of mental illness. Eliminating illness does not ensure a healthy, thriving and competent individual.

6. The idea concerning positive psychology was first initiated by Martin Seligman (1998). His question was why psychology studied the worst in human behaviour. Why should psychology not study things like joy and courage? Then he gave a call for positive psychology.

7. Positive psychology and health psychology share much in common. Health psychologists have suspected that negative emotions can make us sick and positive emotions can be beneficial. They get a scientific and biological foundation through positive psychology. Experts in positive psychology believe that positive emotions may have effects similar to negative emotions, but in opposite directions. In recent years, our increasing knowledge of the physiological processes underlying emotions provides a biological foundation to positive psychology.

8. Results of the Nun Study (a classic study by Danner) have shown amazing results. Researchers found a strong relationship between longevity and the

expression of positive emotions early in life. The excellent advice throughout the study was (i) "Do not worry and be happy" and (ii) "you may live longer".

9. Survey research raises a particular question: "If money does not buy happiness, what does?" This question is connected with positive psychology. Positive psychology follows the early survey research in examining the "traits" and "states" which help explain the differences in the level of happiness. Researches of positive psychology are focused on traits like work situation, involvement in religion, marital status and the quality of relationships. States and traits help explain one of the major questions of positive psychology: "Why are some people happier than others?"

10. Concepts of happiness in USA and Japan are quite different. Experts work on the problem: "Why does money not buy happiness?"

11. Sheldon and King (2001) define positive psychology as "nothing more than the scientific study of ordinary human strengths and virtues". Seligman proposed that "happiness" is the central theme of positive psychology.

12. Three pillars of positive psychology are: (i) Positive subjective experiences (ii) Positive individual characteristics and (iii) Positive social institutions and communities which contribute to individual health and happiness.

13. According to Seligman and his colleagues, "happiness" as a central focus of positive psychology can be divided into three components: (i) The pleasant life (ii) The engaged life and (iii) The meaningful life.

14. We can think of positive psychology as the study of life on the positive side of zero, where zero is the line that divides illness from health and unhappiness from happiness. Traditional psychology has told us much about life at and below zero, but less about above zero.

15. Culture shapes the particular meanings of a good life and a life well-lived. Conceptions of a good life are a part of every culture's ideals, values and philosophic/religious traditions. Positive psychology came to the forefront in the 1990s and continued into the new millennium.

16. Money does not buy happiness. Personal satisfaction may be a source of healthy and satisfying life. Positive psychologists are not so much concerned about what has been studied in psychology. But they are concerned about what has not been studied. In their opinion, our attitude towards life makes a significant contribution to our happiness and health. Situation and environment also play significant roles.

QUESTIONS

1. What is positive psychology? Why is positive psychology necessary? How is positive psychology is related to humanistic psychology?
2. How does the disease model promote a focus on negatives?
3. Define positive psychology. Discuss the scope and goals of positive psychology.
4. Why are negative behaviours given more weight than positive behaviours?
5. Why are negative aspects of human behaviour perceived as more authentic and real than positive aspects?
6. What does recent evidence from health psychology suggest about the differing effects of positive and negative emotions in our physical health?
7. How does developmental psychologists' studies of resilience and post traumatic growth contribute to positive psychology?
8. What does survey research suggest about the importance of money to individual happiness?
9. How have social and personality psychology contributed to positive psychology?
10. Describe the components of Seligman's three-part definition of happiness (i.e., pleasant, engaged and meaningful life).
11. How may positive psychology be thought of as the study of life above zero?
12. What cultural changes and paradoxes have contributed to the development of positive psychology?
13. How does positive psychology complement rather than oppose traditional psychology?
14. Discuss the issue of positive psychology's relationship with the status quo.
15. Write short notes on the following:
    (a) Disease Model (b) Post traumatic growth
    (c) Subjective well-being (d) Meaningful life
    (e) Survey research (f) Negative focus
    (g) Pop-psychology
16. Point out the differences between:
    (a) Positive psychology and traditional psychology
    (b) Positive emotions and negative emotions
    (c) Pleasant life and engaged life
    (d) Post traumatic growth and post traumatic stress
    (e) Social psychology and personality psychology

CHAPTER - 8
THE PSYCHOLOGY OF HAPPINESS

❏ *It is sometimes said that the very concept of "happiness" is obscure and mysterious. We cannot or should not pursue "happiness", that it is the by-product of hard work or some other aspects of a good life. It is clear that most people know very well what it is. Surveys have asked people what they mean by it and they say either that it is often being in a state of joy or other positive emotion or it is being satisfied with one's life. Psychologists are quite successful in relieving depression in other people and the aim is to make them happier. Happiness seems to be an important part of how people define a good life.*

❏ **This chapter covers:**
- What is happiness?
- Two Traditions: Hedonic happiness and Eudaimonic happiness
- Positive effect and meaningful life
- Subjective well-being: the Hedonic basis of happiness
- Measuring subjective well-being (SWB) or happiness
- Life satisfaction
- Positive effect, Negative effect and happiness
- Self-realisation: the eudaimonic basis of happiness
- (i) Psychological well-being and positive functioning
- (ii) Need fulfilment and self-determination theory
- (iii) What makes a good day?
- Comparing Hedonic and Eudaimonic views of happiness
- Definition and causes of happiness and well-being
- Complementarity and interrelationship
- Subjective well-being and personal growth
- Key Terms, Summary and Questions

❏ **By the end of this chapter, you will be able to:**
- Know what is "happiness"
- Define Hedonic and Eudaimonic happiness
- Bring out the differences between positive effect and meaningful life
- Know about subjective well-being (SWB)
- Measure SWB or happiness
- Define life satisfaction
- Understand the terms self-realisation and self-actualisation
- Compare Hedonic and Eudaimonic views of happiness
- Learn about the relation between complementarity and interrelationship
- Familiarise yourself with the relationship between SWB and personal growth

Introduction

In this chapter, we will try to explore the answers to some ancient questions. Can "psychology" give these answers? The first question is "What is a good life?" Then, "What is a life worth living?" "What is the basis for happiness that endures beyond short-term pleasure?" The ancient Greeks contemplated the answers to these questions: "Is a good life built on maximising pleasures and minimising pain?"

There is a question, we are asked every day "How are you doing?" Our answers reflect some assessments of our well-being, even if it is only the temporary assessment of our feelings at the given moment. Much depends upon on how we describe and define happiness and the "good life". Each of us has some notion of the life we hope to lead and the goals and ambitions we want to pursue. Most of us hope for a happy and satisfying life. Now, what makes a happy and satisfying life is the question.

Positive psychology has addressed these questions from a psychological point of view. Priority is given to people's own judgements of well-being based on their own criteria for evaluating the quality of life. In the following section, we will discuss why a subjective and psychological perspective is important.

Two Traditions

Some people believe that we cannot or should not pursue happiness, that it is the by-product of hard-work or some other aspect of a good life. On the other hand, psychologists are quite successful in relieving depression in people and the aim is to make them happier. We shall discuss later the possible ways of enhancing the happiness both of others and oneself and, indeed, of the whole community.

Some people also think that every concept of happiness is obscure and mysterious. But it is clear that most people know well what it is. Surveys have asked people what they mean by happiness and they say either that it is often being in a state of joy or other positive emotion or it is being satisfied with one's life. These two components – positive emotions and satisfaction – are often measured and we shall see that they have somewhat different causes. Often, a third component is included – the absence of depression, anxiety or other negative emotions.

Often, happiness has been measured by the answer to a single question in big surveys, but this has led to some improbable results, especially on international comparisons. Of course, larger sample sizes are better. However, we will discuss about the measurement of happiness in a separate section.

There is a great imbalance between the number of psychology books and papers on depression and on happiness. Positive emotions were neglected in many surveys. The situation has been changed some time ago. There are now many studies conducted on the concept of what has come to be called "subjective well-being" (SWB). SWB means exactly the same thing, an alternative to "happiness". "Well-being" is different, since it usually includes objective variables such as income and health.

Happiness can take different forms. There is a high arousal kind of happiness of those who enjoy noisy and exciting social events and the quieter happiness of those who enjoy quieter and solitary activities. This becomes a problem when comparing the happiness level in different cultures. We will discuss how happiness can be best measured in a later section.

Many questions create confusing circles around us: What is a good life? What is happiness? What defines a satisfying life or life well-lived? What kind of life do you wish to lead? And in the end, How do you want people to remember you?

Hedonic Happiness

Many of us hope for a long life. However, suicide is a reminder that the quality of life is more important to many people than the quantity or duration of life. As for quality of life, happiness might be number one on our list. Most people would hope for a happy and satisfying life in which good things and pleasant experiences outnumber bad ones. In many Western cultures, happiness seems to be an important part of how people define a good life.

Defining the good life in terms of personal happiness is the general thrust of the hedonic view of well-being (Ryan & Deci, 2001; Waterman, 1993). Hedonic psychology parallels aspects of the philosophy of hedonism. There are many varieties of philosophical hedonism dating back to ancient Greeks. A general version of hedonism holds that the chief goal of life is the pursuit of happiness and pleasure. Within psychology, this view of well-being is expressed in the study of subjective well-being (SWB) (Diener, 1999).

SWB takes a broad view of happiness. SWB is defined as life satisfaction, the presence of "positive affect" and a relative absence of "negative affect". Together, these three components are often referred to as happiness. During last few years, researches were based primarily on the SWB model. Findings have highlighted a variety of personality characteristics and life experiences which help to answer questions about who is happy and what makes people happy. We will discuss and review the research and theory of SWB in a later section.

- *Satisfaction lies in the effort, not in the attainment. Full effort is full victory.*
    —*Mahatma Gandhi*
- *Subjective well-being (SWB) is defined as life satisfaction, the presence of positive effect and a relative absence of negative effect. Together, the three components are often referred to "happiness".*
- *Hedonic psychology parallels aspects of the philosophy of hedonism. While there are many varieties of philosophical hedonism dating back to the ancient Greeks, a general version of hedonism holds that the chief goal of life is the pursuit of happiness and pleasure. Within psychology, this view of well-being is expressed in the study of SWB.*

Eudaimonic Happiness

There are some more questions: "Is happiness enough for a good life? Would you be content and satisfied of you were happy and nothing else?"

Seligman (2002) cited a good example. If you are cheerful and happy for a longer period of time, you will experience only one of the many emotions. To have the same cheerful reaction to the diversity of life events and challenges, might actually impoverish the experience of life.

Often, negative emotions are helpful. For example, negative emotions like fear help us make choices that avoid threats to our well-being. Without fear and other negative emotions, we might make some very bad choices. We would be happy but we might not live very long. It should be remembered that disconnected from reality, pleasure does not affirm or express our identity as individuals. Beyond pleasure, there is deeper and more "authentic happiness".

Much of the classical Greek philosophy was concerned with these deeper meanings of happiness and the good life. Waterman (1993) describes two psychological views of happiness distilled from classical philosophy: (i) Hedonic conceptions and (ii) Eudaimonic conceptions.

We have already discussed hedonic conceptions which define happiness as the enjoyment of life and its pleasures. The hedonic view captures a major element of what we mean by happiness in everyday terms: We enjoy life, we are satisfied with how our lives are going and good events outnumber bad events.

Eudaimonic conceptions borrowed ideas from Aristotle. It defines happiness as self-realisation, meaning the expression and fulfilment of inner potential. From this perspective, the good life results from living in accordance with our "daimon" (in other words our true selves). Happiness results from striving towards self-actualisation, a process in which our talents, needs and deeply-held values direct the way we conduct our lives.

"Eudaimonia" (or happiness) results from realisation of our potentials. We become happy when we follow and achieve our goals and develop our unique potentials. Eudaimonic happiness has much in common with humanistic psychology's emphasis on the concepts of self-actualisation (Maslow, 1968) and the fully-functioning person (Rogers, 1961) as the criteria for optimal functioning and healthy development.

What kinds of experiences lead to eudaimonic happiness? Waterman (1993) said that eudaimonic happiness results from experiences of personal expressiveness. Such experiences generally occur when we are fully engaged in life activities that fit and express our deeply held values and our sense of who we are. We experience a feeling of fulfilment under these circumstances. According to Waterman (1993), there are many more activities that produce hedonic enjoyment than activities that provide eudaimonic happiness, based on personal experience. Eating chocolate or drinking alcohol can bring us pleasure, but there are many activities which engage significant aspects of our identity and give a deeper meaning to our lives.

Positive Affects and Meaningful Life

Waterman was one of the few researchers who examined the similarities and differences between hedonic and eudaimonic concepts of happiness. Laura King and her colleagues (2006) have revisited this issue by examining the relationship between positive affect and meaningfulness. According to them, "positive affect" is a summary term for pleasurable emotions such as joy, contentment, laughter and love. But "meaningfulness" refers to more personally expressive and engaging activities that may connect us to a broader and even transcendent view of life. In their findings, positive affect has been thought of as more central to hedonic than to eudaimonic concepts of well-being. Pleasure is seen as a shallow and unsatisfying substitute for deeper purpose in life. Their study suggests that the line between positive affect and meaning in life is not as clear as previously imagined. Positive affect may enhance people's ability to find meaning and purpose in their lives.

Their study also shows that experiencing life as meaningful consistently predicts health and happiness across the life-span. Finding meaning in life's difficulties contributes to positive coping and adaption. Meaning in life may stem from a person's goals, self-improvement efforts or religion that provides a larger sense of understanding.

Positive affects have contributions to meaning in life. King and her colleagues believe that positive emotions open up people's thinking to more imaginative and creative possibilities by placing current concerns in a broader context. These effects of positive emotions may enhance meaning if they also cause people to think of their lives in terms of a longer system. For example, a fun evening with friends may lead us to think of our place in nature's scheme of things. Again, positive emotions may also be makers of meaningful events or activities. Progressing towards important goals makes us feel good. Meaningful and expressive activities are typically accompanied by enjoyment. In a series of six studies, King and her colleagues found positive affect to be consistently related to meaning in life.

In a way, taking a long-term view, people who characteristically experience many positive emotions (i.e., the trait of positive affectivity) report greater meaningfulness in their lives than people who typically experience more frequent negative emotions (i.e., the trait of negative affectivity). In day-to-day life, the same relationship was found. A day judged as meaningful included more positive than negative emotional events.

The work of King and her colleagues suggests that meaningful activities and positive emotions may be interconnected. Meaningful activities and accomplishment bring enjoyment and satisfaction to life and positive emotions may bring an enhanced sense of meaning and purpose. Despite their apparent overlap, hedonic and eudaimonic concepts of happiness are the basis for two distinct lines of research on well-being (Ryan & Deci, 2001).

Subjective Well-being: The Hedonic Basis of Happiness

The term "happiness" is related to "subjective well-being". The word "subjective" means "from the point-of-view of the individual". That is, it refers to an individual's own assessment of his or her life, rather than assessment by an external observers or evaluator. The well-being might be inferred from more objective measures of factors such as physical health, job status or income.

According to Myers and Diener (1995), the final judge of happiness is "whoever lives inside the person's skin". In his book, Diener (2000) describes subjective well-being (SWB) as follows:

"SWB refers to people's evaluations of their lives – evaluations that are both affective and cognitive people experience an abundance of SWB when they feel many pleasant and few unpleasant emotions, when that are engaged in interesting activities, when they experience many pleasures and few pains, when they are satisfied with their lives."

An individual with high SWB has pervasive sense that life is "good". In our later discussions, we will use the terms subjective well-being (SWB) and happiness interchangeably.

Measuring Subjective Well-Being (SWB) or Happiness

People's sense of well-being was directly assessed by early survey researchers. In national surveys, people responded to questions asked for an overall global judgement about happiness, life satisfaction and feelings (Andrews & Withey, 1976). However, survey researchers asked questions like the following one:

Taking all things together, how would you say things are these days: would you say you are very happy, pretty happy or not too happy?

How satisfied are you with your life, as a whole? Are you very satisfied, satisfied, not very satisfied or not at all satisfied?

Some other researchers asked people to choose from a series of faces to indicate their degree of happiness (Andrew, 1976). The subjects were simply asked to indicate which face comes closest to expressing how they feel about their life as a whole.

SWB or happiness is widely considered to have three primary components which are assessed by multi-item scales or inventories in current research. These three components are life satisfaction, positive affect and negative affect.

Life satisfaction is a cognitive judgement concerning how satisfied an individual is with his or her life. The emotional components – positive and negative affect – refer to people's feelings about their lives. Positive affect refers to the frequency and intensity of pleasant emotions such as happiness and joy. Negative affect refers to the frequency and intensity of unpleasant emotions such as sadness and worry.

Large samples of people were given this three-part structure of SWB by researchers, who recorded a variety of measures of happiness, satisfaction and emotions (Bryant and Verhaff, 1982). By a statistical techniques and factor analysis, responses were analysed. The results produced two prominent findings:

First, statistical analyses reveal a single factor that underlies all the different measures, despite the diversity of SWB measures, thus all seem to tap a common dimension.

Second, studies also reveal three components of SWB: "a life situation factor", "a positive affect factor" and "a negative affect factor".

These three components (life satisfaction, positive affect and negative affect) correlate strongly with the common dimension, but only moderately with one another. That means each makes a relatively independent and distinct contribution. This finding (that measures of SWB reliably parcel themselves out into three related, but somewhat independent parts) serves as the basis for the three component view of SWB.

Here are some faces expressing various feelings. Which face comes closest to expressing how you feel about your life as a whole?

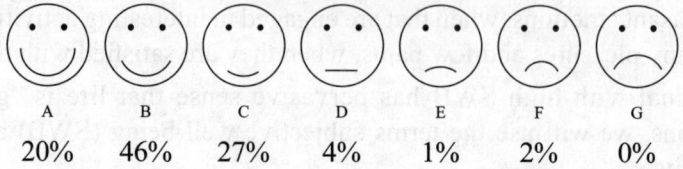

A	B	C	D	E	F	G
20%	46%	27%	4%	1%	2%	0%

Fig. 8.1: Faces and feelings (Andrews and Withey, 1976)

Table 8.1: The Revised Oxford Happiness Inventory

Below, there are groups of statements about personal happiness. Please read all four statements in each group and then pick out the one statement in each group that best describes the way you have been feeling in the past week, including today. Circle the letter (a, b, c or d) beside the statement you have picked.

01. a   I do not feel happy.
    b   I feel fairly happy.
    c   I am very happy.
    d   I am incredibly happy.
02. a   I am not particularly optimistic about the future.
    b   I feel optimistic about the future.
    c   I feel I have so much to look forward to.
    d   I feel that the future is overflowing with hope and promise.
03. a   I am not really satisfied with anything in my life.
    b   I am satisfied with some things in my life.
    c   I am satisfied with many things in my life.
    d   I am completely satisfied about everything in my life.
04. a   I feel that I am not especially in control of my life.
    b   I feel at least partially in control of my life.
    c   I feel that I am in control most of the time.
    d   I feel that I am in total control of all aspects of my life.
05. a   I don't feel that life is particularly rewarding.
    b   I feel that life is rewarding.
    c   I feel that life is very rewarding.
    d   I feel that life is overflowing with rewards.
06. a   I don't feel particularly pleased with the way I am.
    b   I am pleased with the way I am.
    c   I am very pleased with the way I am.
    d   I am delighted with the way I am.

07. a I never have a good influence on events.
     b I occasionally have a good influence on events.
     c I often have a good influence on events.
     d I always have a good influence on events.
08. a I get by in life.
     b Life is good.
     c Life is very good.
     d I love life.
09. a I am not really interested in other people.
     b I am moderately interested in other people.
     c I am very interested in other people.
     d I am intensely interested in other people.
10. a I do not find it easy to make decisions.
     b I find it fairly easy to make some decisions.
     c I find it easy to make most decisions.
     d I can make all decisions very easily.
11. a I find it difficult to get started to do things.
     b I find it moderately easy to start doing things.
     c I find it easy to do things.
     d I feel able to take anything on.
12. a I rarely wake up feeling rested.
     b I sometimes wake up feeling rested.
     c I usually wake up feeling rested.
     d I always wake up feeling rested.
13. a I don't feel at all energetic.
     b I feel fairly energetic.
     c I feel very energetic.
     d I feel I have boundless energy.
14. a I don't think things have a particular "sparkle".
     b I find beauty in some things.
     c I find beauty in most things.
     d The whole world looks beautiful to me
15. a I don't feel mentally alert.
     b I feel quite mentally alert.
     c I feel very mentally alert.
     d I feel fully mentally alert.
16. a I don't feel particularly healthy.
     b I feel moderately healthy.
     c I feel very healthy.
     d I feel on top to the world.
17. a I do not have particularly warm feelings towards others.
     b I have some warm feelings towards others.
     c I have very warm feelings towards others.
     d I love everybody.
18. a I do not have particularly happy memories of the past.
     b I have some happy memories of the past.
     c Most past events seem to have been happy.
     d All past events seem extremely happy.

19.   a   *I am never in a state of joy or elation.*
      b   *I sometimes experience joy and elation.*
      c   *I often experience joy and elation.*
      d   *I am constantly in a state of joy and elation.*
20.   a   *There is a gap between what I would like to do and what I have done.*
      b   *I have done some of the things I wanted.*
      c   *I have done many of the things I wanted.*
      d   *I have done everything I ever wanted.*
21.   a   *I can't organise my time very well.*
      b   *I organise my time fairly well.*
      c   *I organise my time very well.*
      d   *I can fit in everything I want to do.*
22.   a   *I do not have fun with other people.*
      b   *I sometimes have fun with other people.*
      c   *I often have fun with other people.*
      d   *I always have fun with other people.*
23.   a   *I do not have a cheerful effect on others.*
      b   *I sometimes have a cheerful effect on others.*
      c   *I often have a cheerful effect on others.*
      d   *I always have a cheerful effect on others.*
24.   a   *I do not have any particular sense of meaning and purpose in my life.*
      b   *I have a sense of meaning and purpose.*
      c   *I have a great sense of meaning and purpose.*
      d   *My life is totally meaningful and purposive.*
25.   a   *I do not have particular feelings of commitment and involvement.*
      b   *I sometimes become committed and involved.*
      c   *I often become committed and involved.*
      d   *I am always committed and involved.*
26.   a   *I do not think the world is a good place.*
      b   *I think the world is a fairly good place.*
      c   *I think the world is a very good place.*
      d   *I think the world is an excellent place.*
27.   a   *I rarely laugh.*
      b   *I laugh fairly often.*
      c   *I laugh a lot.*
      d   *I am always laughing.*
28.   a   *I don't think I look attractive.*
      b   *I think I look fairly attractive.*
      c   *I think I look attractive.*
      d   *I think I look extremely attractive.*
29.   a   *I do not find things amusing.*
      b   *I find some things amusing.*
      c   *I find most things amusing.*
      d   *I am amused by everything.*

However, the interrelationship of the three components is noteworthy because most researchers don't assess all three components (Diener, 2003). But Diener notes that this situation is not ideal. It would be better, from a scientific point-of-view, if studies assessed all three components. Adopting more detailed and widely shared measures of SWB is an important task for the development of positive psychology.

Life Satisfaction

The most widely-used measures of life satisfaction is the "Satisfaction-with-Life Scale" (Diener, Emmons & Griffen, 1985). This five-item scale asks the participant to make a global evaluation of his or her life.

You may be interested in completing the items yourself. To fill out the scale, simply indicate your degree of agreement or disagreement with each of the five statements using 1–7 ratings described below :

7.	*Strongly agree*
6.	*Agree*
5.	*Slightly agree*
4.	*Neither agree nor disagree*
3.	*Slightly disagree*
2.	*Disagree*
1.	*Strongly disagree*

ITEMS
In most ways my life is close to my ideal.
The conditions of my life are excellent.
I am satisfied with my life.
So far I have gotten the important things in life.
If I would live my life over, I would change almost nothing.

Table 8.2: The General Health Questionnaire (GHQ) (12 item version)

Have you recently:

*1	Been able to concentrate on whatever you're doing?
2	Lost much sleep over worry?
*3	Felt that you are playing a useful part in things?
*4	Felt capable of making decisions about things?
5	Felt constantly under strain?
6	Felt you couldn't overcome your difficulties?
*7	Been able to enjoy your normal day-to-day activities?
*8	Been able to face up to your problems?
9	Been feeling unhappy and depressed?
10	Been losing confidence in yourself?
11	Been thinking of yourself as a worthless person?
*12	Been feeling reasonably happy all things considered?

Source Goldberg (1972)
Note: *These items are scored in reverse; 1 means agree strongly.

To score your responses, add up your ratings across all five items.

The following interpretations were suggested by Diener (2002):

(i) Scores below 20 indicate a degree of dissatisfaction with one's life, which can range from extremely dissatisfied (scores of 5 through 9), to very dissatisfied (10 through 14), to slightly dissatisfied (15 through 19).

(ii) A score of 20 is the natural point (i.e., not particularly satisfied or dissatisfied).

(iii) Levels of satisfaction can very from somewhat satisfied (21 through 25), through very satisfied (26 through 30), to extremely satisfied (31 through 35).

(iv) Data from large scale surveys show that most Americans are somewhat satisfied with their lives (scoring between 21 and 25) (Diener, 1985).

"Quality of life" researchers take a different route to assess the levels of satisfaction in different domains. They ask about everything from satisfaction with physical health and the environment one lives in, to satisfaction with body appearance and sex life (Power, 2003). People are asked how satisfied they are with their jobs, families, health, leisure activities and social relationships. Overall life satisfaction would be expressed in terms of the average or sum of satisfaction ratings for these different aspects of life.

However, to obtain a more detailed picture of the basis for people's overall life satisfaction, one model of SWB suggests that domain satisfaction be included as a fourth component of SWB (Diener, 2004). Assessment of domain satisfaction provides information on what specific aspects of a person's life make the largest contribution to his or her overall satisfaction. This measure is particularly important if a researcher is interested in how different life domains (e.g., work, family, health) affect life satisfaction as a whole.

Positive Affect, Negative Affect and Happiness

Different scales are used to measure people's emotional experiences (Argyle, 2001, Larsen, 2003). Some scales ask only about positive emotions, like happiness and joy, while others assess both positive and negative feelings. The most common method of assessing feelings is to ask people to rate the frequency and intensity of different emotions they experience during a given time period.

A different scale which is widely used to measure positive or negative affect is the Positive Affectivity and Negative Affectivity schedule (PANAS) (Watson & Clark, 1988). Using this scale, researchers can ask people to rate the intensity and/or the frequency of their emotional experiences. To measure longer-term emotions, a researcher might ask people how frequently they experience positive and negative emotions during the past week, the past month or past few months. Positive and negative affect can also be measured by facial and physiological expression of emotions as the human face is highly expressive of emotion.

Studies of happiness are also concerned with the intensity and frequency of emotional experiences contribute to SWB. Researchers have found that frequency of emotions is more important then their intensity (Diener, 1997). Happiness is not built so much on intense feelings of happiness or joy, but rather on milder positive emotions that are experienced most of the time. In other words, happy people are those who experience positive emotions relatively frequently and negative emotions relatively infrequently. This is true even if the positive emotions are mild rather than intense. Researchers have found that intense positive emotions are very rare, even for the happiest people (Diener and his colleagues, 1991). People with high SWB report frequent experiences of mild to moderate positive emotions and infrequent negative emotions.

Many psychologists use more global "life as a whole" measures that assess a person's overall happiness-unhappiness instead of separate measures for positive or negative affect. A person's judgement about whether he or she is a happy or unhappy person would seem to be a good summary and a useful, brief measure of positive and negative affect.

Coming to reliability and validity of SWB measures, researches found that measures of SWB are internally reliable and coherent, stable over time and validated by behavioural measures and the reports of others. The internal reliabilities of life satisfaction scales and measures of positive and negative affect are quite high ($r = 0.80$ or so) (Angle, 2001). Measures of SWB also show reasonably high stability over time. Measures of positive and negative affect also show moderate stability. Research has shown that positive or negative changes in our lives can affect our level of happiness.

A question arises here: If people say they are happy on measures of SWB, do they also behave in ways that confirm their self-reported happiness and do other see them as happy?

This question is related to the validity of the test. Is it measuring what it claims to be measuring? A number of studies support the validity of SWB measures. Individual self-reported happiness has been confirmed via assessment by peers (Watson & Clark, 1991), family members, friends and spouses (Costa, 1988). When asked to recall positive and negative life events, happy people recall more positive events than unhappy people (Wyer & Diener, 1997). Persons with high SWB are more likely to perceive life in positive ways, expect a positive future and express confidence in their skills as well as abilities. Individuals with lower SWB are more focused on negative life events and show more self-absorbed rumination about themselves and their problems.

Measurements of SWB are not free from potential biases despite evidence supporting their reliability and validity. A significant source of bias which may be introduced is by distortions in memory and the effects of temporary mood.

Suppose there is a question for you: "Taking all things together, how happy are you these days?"

What is the basis for your answer? You may recall and reflect on the many significant events in your life (both positive and negative) and then make a reasoned judgement about what they all add up to in terms of your overall level of happiness. But what if you recall only good experiences or only bad experiences or only your most recent experiences? What if your recent mood affected your judgement of overall happiness? Only experiences from memory or current mood might bias and distort your rated level of happiness.

Research findings indicate that this sort of bias can occur. Finding a small amount of money, hearing your country's cricket team won the championship or being interviewed on a sunny day can increase people's self-reports of general life satisfaction (Schwarz & Strack, 1999). On the contrary, hearing that your cricket team has lost, spending time in a noisy and overheated atmosphere or being interviewed on a rainy day can decrease reports of satisfaction.

Studies also suggest that people may summarise and remember emotional experiences in complex and counterintuitive ways (Kohneman, 1999). Common sense would say that the larger an emotional episode lasts, the more effect it should have on how we evaluate it. For example, people who go through a long and uncomfortable remedial surgical procedure, should rate it as more negative than people who endure the same procedure, but for a shorter time span. But this may not always be so.

Studies also show that people's moods tend to fluctuate predictably over days of the week (Larsen, 1990). Moods are generally more positive on the weekends than during week days. This is perhaps because on weekends, people have greater freedom in choosing what they want to do and they participate in more enjoyable activities and pleasant social interactions than on weekdays (Gable & Ryan, 2000).

Self-Realisation: The Eudaimonic Basis of Happiness

The three-component view of SWB has been expanded by some researchers and psychologists to include personal qualities and life activities believed to be the psychological underpinnings of happiness. Seligman and Diener (2002) expanded concepts to express the eudaimonic view of defining happiness in terms of striving for self-realisation. As we have discussed earlier, happiness, from the eudaimonic perspective, results from the development and expression of our inner potentials (daimon) which include our talents, personalities and values.

Following the hedonic view, measures of SWB ask people if they are happy and satisfied with their lives. Eudaimonic measures of happiness also ask, "Why are people are happy?"

Psychological Well-Being and Positive Functioning

Carl Ryff (1989) said that the three-component model of SWB fails to describe the features in a person's life which provide the basis and meaning of well-being. She discussed this in an article titled, "Happiness is everything or is it? Explorations on the meaning of psychological well-being."

According to Ryff's view, well-being is more than happiness with life. Well-being should be a source of resilience in the face of adversity and should reflect positive functioning, personal strengths and mental health. Ryff argues that well-being and happiness are based on human strengths, personal striving and growth. Drawing on theories of positive mental health in personality and clinical psychology, Ryff and her colleagues have developed a model called "Psychological well-being" (PWB).

PWB is based on description of positive psychological and social functioning (Keyes,

1998). Originally used to describe positive functioning across the life-span, this conceptualisation has been extended to describe positive mental health (Moe, 2003). As expanded by Keyes and his colleagues, this model incorporates both hedonic and eudaimonic views of happiness.

Well-being is conceived as involving the two broad dimensions of "emotional well-being" and "positive functioning". Emotional well-being is defined by the three-component view of SWB. It includes life satisfaction and positive and negative affect. A psychological dimension and a social dimension define positive functioning. All together, well-being is described as a global combination of emotional well-being, psychological well-being and social well-being. This comprehensive model is meant to serve as a more complete description of SWB.

Need Fulfilment and Self-Determination Theory

Another concept of well-being which embraces a eudaimonic view of happiness was proposed by the self-determination theory (SDT). SDT states that well-being and happiness result from the fulfilment of three basic psychological needs: autonomy, competence and relatedness.

Autonomy needs are fulfilled when activities are freely chosen rather than imposed by others and are consistent with the individual's self-concept. Competence needs are satisfied when our efforts bring about designed outcomes that make us more confident in our abilities. Needs for relatedness are fulfilled by close and positive connections to others. Social interactions which produce feelings of closeness and support contribute to satisfaction of this need. Researches by Ryan, Deci and their colleagues have confirmed the relationship between need satisfaction and well-being (Ryans & Deci, 2001).

What Makes a "Good" Day?

What makes a good day? What makes for a bad day?

Reis and his colleagues (2000) said that the ingredients of a bad day are fairly well established. Negative life events (both big and small) which produce stress and conflict have consistently been shown to diminish our feelings of well-being, happiness and enjoyment. These negative events include failure at work, arguments and conflicts with others, financial problems, illness, frustration and these are causes of anger, sadness and disappointment.

But what about a "good day"? Is a good day just the absence of negative events, that is, no failure, conflict or disappointment? As we have discussed earlier, positive and negative emotions are somewhat independent, with each emotion making a separate contribution to happiness and well-being. A good day may involve different activities and experiences than those that make for a bad day.

According to SDT, the needs for autonomy, competence and relatedness are shared by all humans. These needs are described as the "essential nutrients" from which people grow (Ryan & Deci, 2000). These three needs together form the foundation of well-being and happiness. Each need can be thought of both as a "trait" and "state". A trait refers to an enduring personal disposition, whereas a state refers to the particular situation we are in at the moment. The fulfilment of the three needs can vary from day-to-day and from situation-to-situation.

Sheldon, Reis and their colleagues (2000) measured autonomy, competence and relatedness in a study of 76 college students. Both traits and states were taken into account. The results were consistent with SDT. Reis and colleagues found that a "good day" was related to the fulfilment of the needs for autonomy, competence and relatedness. Trait measures of need fulfilment were positively correlated with well-being and positive mood during the day. Students who scored higher in autonomy, competence and relatedness also showed higher levels of well-being and happiness across the 14 days of the study. On the whole, people who have personal qualities that contribute to need fulfilment tend to enjoy more well-being and more positive moods on a day-to-day basis. The more these three needs were positively engaged by activities during the day, the higher their ratings of well-being and positive mood. However, of the three needs, relatedness had the most significant impact on daily well-being.

From this study interesting results were found. The degree to which needs were fulfilled was also significantly related to the days of the week.

Monday produced the lowest ratings of positive emotion. Negative emotion and feelings of competence were fairly stable across the seven days of the week.

Bad moods and feelings of confidence were dependent on activities that did not vary systematically with day of the week.

Friday, Saturday and Sunday were rated highest with regard to positive emotion, relatedness and autonomy. Our moods tend to be more positive during weekends because we can enjoy desirable activities more readily.

Research findings suggest that a good day, even on the weekend, involves more than just having fun. Needs for autonomy and relatedness are more likely to be satisfied on the week-ends. Monday through Friday, we often have to follow the expectations, assignments and demands of others. On the weekends, we are more free to choose what we want to do, resulting a greater sense of self-direction and expression that satisfies our need for autonomy. Weekends often involve getting together with friends and family members. These interactions are enjoyable and they also fulfil our desire for intimacy and meaningful connections with others.

In conclusion, we can say that more "good days" occur during weekends because we are more likely to fulfil needs that increase our sense of well-being and happiness.

Comparing Hedonic and Eudaimonic Views of Happiness

We have already discussed a number of measures and two major models of happiness. It is too early to tell which measures and models are the most useful and accurate factors that underlie happiness. Most of the experts agree that refinement of measures and the formulation of more comprehensive theories are essential to the growth and development of positive psychology. In the following section, we will discuss the similarities and differences between the hedonic and eudaimonic view of happiness. Recent research centres around one or more combination of these two conceptions of well-being and happiness.

Definition and Causes of Happiness and Well-Being

(a) As we know, the hedonic view was expressed in the model and measures of SWB which defined happiness as an individual's global assessment of positive/negative emotion and satisfaction with life. Individuals who experience maximum positive emotions and few negative emotions and who also feel satisfied with their lives are defined as happy or high in SWB. SWB does not specify or measure why a person is happy or unhappy. Proponents of hedonic view regard the basis for happiness as an empirical question to be answered by research. Researchers in this area hold that, by comparing the traits and behaviours of people high in SWB to those low in SWB, the psychological meaning and foundations of happiness will emerge through continued investigation.

(b) Subjective well-being investigators have adopted a research-driven approach to happiness and well-being. Their motto is "get the research facts first", then theory can be created later.

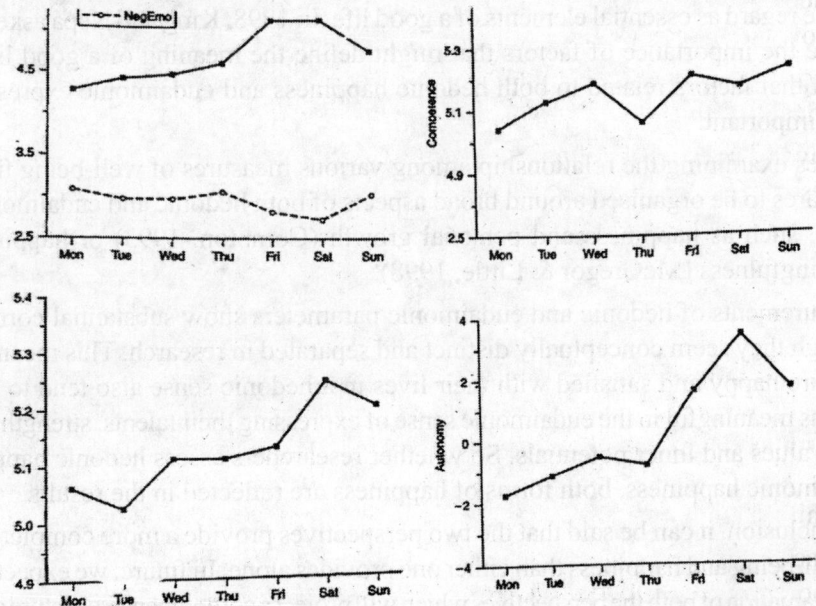

Fig. 8.2: Positive and Negative Emotions, Competence, Relatedness and Autonomy Ratings across days of the week

(c) SWB allows people to judge for themselves whether they are happy and satisfied, on the basis of their own criteria. The nature of these criteria is the focus of many SWB studies and will hopefully lead to a theory that explains the psychological underpinnings of happiness and well-being.

(d) The eudaimonic view was expressed in models and measures of self-realisation and positive mental health. It defines well-being as positive or optimal functioning and the fulfilment of basic needs and inner potentials.

(e) A happy individual is one who has actualised or is striving to actualise his or her human potential to be a fully functioning, competent and psychologically healthy person. In contrast to the hedonic concept, eudaimonic models describe the psychological and social traits, behaviours and needs that are the basis of happiness and psychological health.

(f) Proponents of the eudaimonic view believe well-being and happiness involve more than emotional happiness and life satisfaction. Models of well-being and happiness should tell us about psychological health and effective functioning. Psychologists as well as researchers taking the eudaimonic view are particularly interested in developing models of well-being that will describe positive mental health.

Complementarity and Interrelationship

It is wise to emphasise a complementary rather than a conflicting relationship between the hedonic and eudaimonic views. Both perspectives seem to be reflected in what people regard as essential elements of a good life. In 1998, King and Nepa asked people to rate the importance of factors that might define the meaning of a good life. They found that factors related to both hedonic happiness and eudaimonic expressiveness were important.

Studies examining the relationship among various measures of well-being find these measures to be organised around broad aspects of both hedonic and eudaimonic well-being, such as happiness and personal growth (Compton, 1993) or happiness and meaningfulness (McGregor & Little, 1998).

Measurements of hedonic and eudaimonic parameters show substantial correlations, through they seem conceptually distinct and separated in research. This means people who are happy and satisfied with their lives in a hedonic sense also tend to see their lives as meaningful in the eudaimonic sense of expressing their talents, strengths, deeply held values and inner potentials. So whether researchers assess hedonic happiness or eudaimonic happiness, both forms of happiness are reflected in the results.

In conclusion, it can be said that the two perspectives provide a more complete picture of well-being and happiness than either one provides alone. In future, we expect a happy amalgamation of both the perspectives which will project a comprehensive picture of human happiness. However, hedonic and eudaimonic views of well-being express two broad themes within positive psychology: one focused on personal happiness and life satisfaction and the other focused on personal meaning, personal growth and positive functioning.

Subjective Well-Being, Age and Personal Growth

A prominent contemporary psychologist, Ed Diener (2000) studied happiness defined as Subjective well-being (SWB). Measures of SWB assesses a person's level of life satisfaction and the frequency of positive and negative emotional experiences. In psychology, the view of well-being is expressed in the study of SWB (Diner, 1999). SWB takes a broad view of happiness, beyond the pursuit of short-term or physical pleasures defining a narrow hedonism. SWB is defined as life satisfaction, the presence of positive affect and a relative absence of negative affect. Together, the three components are often referred to as happiness.

> *Self-Determination Theory*
> - *Self-determination theory (SDT)* states that well-being and happiness result from the fulfilment of three basis psychological needs: (i) autonomy (ii) competence and (iii) relatedness.
> - *Autonomy needs* are fulfilled when activities are freely chosen rather than imposed by others and are consistent with the individuals self-concept.
> - *Competence needs* are satisfied when our efforts bring about designed outcomes that make us mere confident in our abilities.
> - *Needs for relatedness* are fulfilled by close and positive connections with others. Social interactions that produce feelings of closeness and support contribute to satisfaction of this need. This need involves feelings of intimacy and connection with other people. People who are skilled in the development and maintenance of close relationships are most likely to have this need fulfilled.

Many studies use global and summary measures of SWB. Psychologists have wondered whether a more complex theory of aging and happiness might be revealed in the specific components of SWB. That means global measures of SWB (i.e., life satisfaction and balance of positive and negative affect) might not be sensitive to subtle, age-related changes. Psychologists have examined the emotional aspects of SWB separately to get a clear picture of what may or may not change with age. Studies have compared the frequency, intensity and balance of positive and negative emotions among people of widely differing ages. One way that overall SWB could stay the same despite differences in emotional experiences has to do with the frequency of intense emotions.

Several studies suggest that intense emotions are fairly typical among teens and young adults, but decline with age. Some researchers found that mood among teens can go down from extreme highs and up from extreme lows in less than an hour. Both elation and despair can go and come within a short period of time. The emotional lives of older adults tend to be more even-keeled and stable (Larsen, 1985). As people age, they show a dramatic decline in high arousal emotions. Many studies suggested that the effects of everyday life events soften with age. Happiness of young adults reflects an averaging-out of more extreme emotions, while for older adults happiness reflect a steady and less fluctuating emotional life with a lower frequency of extreme emotions.

It is not true that older adults do not enjoy life. Their accumulated life experience teaches them not to get too excited or too upset about the many daily events, the effects of which are often temporary. Elders and senior citizens learn to focus on longer-term satisfactions such as developing supportive, high quality relationships or personally meaningful activities.

So, despite changes in the frequency of intense emotions, overall happiness remains stable across the life-span. Our overall emotional experiences appear to shift from an averaging out of strong reactions to life events, to less extreme and more steady emotional experiences.

Another way that differences in emotional experience might result in similar overall SWB has to do with the balance between positive and negative emotions. The emotional component of well-being is typically assessed by subtracting rating totals on the negative affect scale from the totals on the positive affect scale. This combined scoring method may mask important and independent changes in positive and negative affects. If positive and negative affects are examined separately, rather than combined into a single score, researchers can determine whether the overall score obscures important changes. For example, if both positive affect and negative affect each increased to the same degree, the results would show stable overall affect balance across the life-span. Studies examining the age-related changes in positive and negative affect have found independent changes in the two types of emotions.

Personal growth refers to an individual's feelings of continued development and effectiveness and an openness to new experiences and challenges. Personal growth is exhibited by a person who is still excited about life and learning new things. Research has shown that this factor is predictive of resilient responses in the face of adversity and in successful aging and the maintenance of good mental health (Singer, 2003). It describes aspects of an individual's personality, self-concept, competence and social relationships that represent resources for effective living.

> *Gender and Happiness: Who Is Happier – Men or Women?*
> - *Who is happier – men or women? The overall answer seems to be neither. Large-scale surveys find that women and men report approximately the same levels of happiness (Inglehart, 1990). Other national surveys affirm the general conclusion that there are few (if any) significant gender differences in overall happiness (Diener & Smith, 1992). Men and women are, on an average, equally likely to report feeling happy and satisfied with their lives as a whole. In their meta analytic review of research, Haring and Okun (1984) suggested that men showed a slight tendency to report higher levels of well-being than women. Knowing a person's gender won't tell you much about his or her happiness. Yet there are significant differences in the emotional lives of men and women, as affirmed by everyday experience.*

The Psychology of Happiness

❑ Key Terms

1. Anxiety
2. Authentic happiness
3. Autonomy needs
4. Competence needs
5. Complementarity
6. Daimon (Happiness)
7. Depression
8. Emotional well-being
9. Essential nutrients
10. Eudaimonic
11. Eudaimonic happiness
12. Good life and bad life
13. Happiness
14. Hedonic happiness
15. Hedonic psychology
16. Interrelationship
17. Need fulfilment
18. Needs for relatedness
19. Negative affect
20. Negative emotion
21. Personal Growth
22. Positive affect
23. Positive Affectivity and Negative Affectivity Schedule (PANAS)
24. Positive emotion
25. Positive functioning
26. Positive psychology
27. Quality of life
28. Satisfaction
29. Satisfaction-with-Life Scale
30. Self-actualisation
31. Self-determination
32. Self-determination theory (SDT)
33. Self-realisation
34. Subjective well-being (SWB)
35. Well-being

❑ Chapter Summary and Review

1. Happiness is found to be a single factor of experience, but it consists of at least three partly independent factors – satisfaction with life, positive affect and negative affect. Larger scales are used to measure all these concepts.
2. The measurements are affected by certain biases, such as immediate mood. An alternate means of assessing well-being is by social indicators, but it is hard to decide which ones to use. There are some inconsistencies between objective and subjective measures.
3. Social surveys have been widely used, together with longitudinal designs such as "high risk" studies, experiments and correlations with personality traits. Experiments are done usually to study the effects of positive moods.
4. Now many studies are conducted on "Subjective Well-being" (SWB). SWB means exactly the same thing, an alternative to "happiness". "Well-being" is different, since it usually includes objective variables such as income and health.
5. Defining a good life in terms of personal happiness is the general thrust of the hedonic view of well-being. Hedonic psychology parallels aspects of the philosophy of hedonism. A general version of hedonism holds that chief goal of life is the pursuit of happiness and pleasure. Within psychology, this view of well-being is expressed in the study of SWB.
6. SWB is defined as life-satisfaction, the presence of positive affect and relative absence of negative affect. Together, these three components are often referred to as "happiness".
7. Eudaimonic conception (happiness) borrowed ideas from Aristotle. It defines happiness as self-realisation, meaning the expression and fulfilment of inner potentials. From this perspective, good life results from living in accordance with our "true selves". Happiness results from striving towards self-actualisation. Self-actualisation is a process in which our talents, needs and deeply held values direct the way we conduct our lives.
8. Eudaimonic happiness has much in common with humanistic psychology's emphasis on the concepts of self-actualisation and the fully-functioning person as the criteria for optimal functioning and healthy development.
9. Positive affect is a summary term for pleasurable emotions such as joy, contentment, laughter and love. Meaningfulness refers to more personally expansive and engaging activities that may connect us to a broader and even transcendent view of life.
10. The final judge of happiness is "whoever lives inside the person's skin". An individual with high SWB has a pervasive sense that life is "good". SWB refers to people's evaluations of their lives.
11. "Life satisfaction" is a cognitive judgement concerning how satisfied an individual is with his or her life. The emotional components – positive and negative affect – refer to people's feelings about their lives. Positive affect refers to the frequency and intensity of pleasant emotions such as happiness and joy. Negative affect refers to the frequency and intensity of unpleasant emotions such as sadness and worry.

12. Life-satisfaction is the "satisfaction-with-life scale". Quality-of-life researchers took a different turn to assess the levels of satisfaction in different domains. To obtain a more detailed picture of the basis for people's overall life satisfaction, a model of SWB suggests that domain satisfaction be included as the fourth component of SWB. Assessment of domain satisfaction provides information on what specific aspects of a person's life make the largest contribution to his or her overall satisfaction.
13. Studies of happiness are concern with how much the intensity and how much the frequency of emotional experiences contribute to SWB. Happiness is not built so much on intense feelings of happiness or joy, but rather on milder positive emotions which are experienced most of the time. Happy people are those who experience positive emotions relatively frequently and negative emotions relatively infrequently.
14. Measures of SWB are internally reliable and coherent, stable over time and validated by behavioural measures and the reports of others. Measures of SWB also show reasonably high stability. These measures are not free from potential biases despite evidence supporting their reliability and validity.
15. Well-being should be a source of resilience in the face of adversity and should reflect positive functioning, personal strengths and mental health. Self-determination theory (SDT) states that well-being and happiness result from the fulfilment of three basic psychological needs: autonomy, competence and relatedness.
16. Autonomy needs are fulfilled when activities are freely chosen rather than imposed by others and are consistent with the individual's self-concept. Competence needs are satisfied when our efforts bring about desired outcomes that make us more confident in our abilities. Needs for relatedness are fulfilled by close and positive connections with others.
17. The self-determination theory (SDT) states that the needs for autonomy, competence and relatedness are shared by all humans. These needs are described as the "essential nutrients" from which people grow. These three needs together form the foundation of well-being and happiness. Each need can be thought of both as a "trait" and "state".
18. A trait refers to an enduring personal disposition, whereas a state refers to the particular situation we are in at the moment. The fulfilment of these three needs can vary from day-to-day and from situation-to-situation.
19. Researchers interested in investigating subjective well-being (SWB) adopted a research-driven approach to happiness and well-being. Their motto was "get the research facts first", then theory can be created later.
20. A person's feelings of continued development and effectiveness and an openness to new experiences and challenges are known as "personal growth". These are exhibited by an individual who is still excited about the life and learning new things.

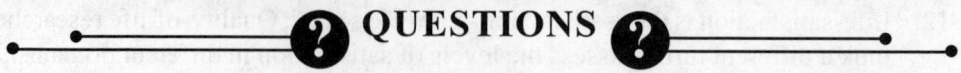

QUESTIONS

1. What is happiness? Distinguish between Hedonic and Eudaimonic happiness, with examples.
2. What three components define subjective well-being (SWB)?
3. Briefly describe the three major components of the eudaimonic model of well-being.
4. What do you mean by eudaimonic happiness? How it is different from hedonic happiness?
5. How do the hedonic and eudaimonic views of happiness differ in their definitions and causes of happiness?
6. How are the hedonic and eudaimonic conceptions complementary and interrelated?
7. How can happiness or SWB be measured?
8. Point out the relationship between psychological well-being and positive functioning.
9. What makes a good day?
10. Write short notes on:
    (a) Personal growth
    (b) Subjective well-being (SWB)
    (c) Gender and happiness
    (d) Self-realisation
    (e) Self-actualisation
    (f) Positive affect

KEY TERMS IN PSYCHOLOGY

Ability	– Present level of performance on some task. It is a general term referring to the potential for the acquisition of a skill. The term covers intelligence and specific aptitudes.
Abnormal	– "Ab" means "away from". Hence this means diverging from normal. It also refers to psychological deficit.
Abnormal psychology	– The branch of psychology that is concerned with behaviour disorders, their diagnosis, classification, treatment and theories that explain them.
Absolute threshold	– Minimal level of stimulation that the organism can detect.
Abstract thinking	– It is the capacity to generalise, to utilise one's experiences in thinking and planning, logically transcending immediate experiences.
Accommodation	– (i) In vision, it refers to the adjustment of the eye for vision at various distances. (ii) As used by Jean Piaget, it is the process by which the individual, in adapting to new experiences, modifies internal cognitive structures.
Acetylcholine	– A chemical neurohormone found in synaptic transmission.
Achievement motive	– A need to achieve for its own sake rather than for the benefits derived from such achievement.
Acquisition	– It refers to a new response added through learning to the organism's repertoire of responses.
Action potential	– It is the change in electrical potential associated with the activity of nerves and muscles.
Action research	– It refers to a research whose ends are practical as opposed to theoretical.
Adrenalin	– A hormone secreted from the endocrine glands (i.e., from adrenal gland).
Affrent neuron	– A neuron that conducts impulses towards the central nervous system (CNS).
Afterimage	– The image or sensory impression immediately after the cessation of the stimulus.
Agnosia	– Inability to recognise objects.
Agoraphobia	– Fear of being alone.
All-or-none law	– The property of a neuron or gland cell either to respond to its fullest extent or not to respond at all.
Alpha rhythm	– A rhythm of EEG typically obtained from the occipital region of the cortex during relaxed wakefulness.
Ambivalence	– The existence of conflicting feelings or attitudes, e.g., love and hate towards the same object or person.
Ambivert	– A person who is both extrovert and introvert.
Analgesia	– Insensitivity to pain without loss of consciousness.

Anal stage	– A stage from Freudian theory of psychosexual development. Here behaviour is focused on anal pleasure and activities.
Anamia	– Disregard of social norms and values.
Androgen	– A hormone associated with the development and maintenance of male characteristics.
Animism	– The primitive belief that immediate objects have a spirit or soul.
Anoxia	– Insufficient supply of oxygen.
Antisocial personality	– A personality disorder characterised by a marked lack of ethical or moral development.
Anxiety state	– A transitory experience of fear and apprehensiveness, specific to the situation.
Apparent motion	– Perception of motion under conditions in which no physical movement occurs.
Approach-approach conflict	– A state of indecision produced by the necessity of choosing between two desirable objects.
Approach-avoidance conflict	– A state of indecision produced when a single object or activity is simultaneously attractive and unattractive.
Aptitude	– The capacity to profit from training in some particular skill.
Aqueous humor	– A fluid transparent to light filling the space between the lens and the cornea of the eye.
Assimilation	– In Piaget's theory, it is a process whereby a child, by taking a new information, modifies it or even distorts it to agree with the internal cognitive system. The child gives meaning to an act by assimilating it to something already known.
Attitude	– A predisposition to react in a certain way, a readiness to react, a determining tendency.
Autokinetic effect	– The apparent drifting movement of a small, fixed spot of light in a darkroom.
Autonomic nervous system	– An independent system which controls the body's internal environment. It consists of both parasympathetic and sympathetic system.
Avoidance learning	– A type of instrumental conditioning where the organism avoids punishment by making an appropriate anticipatory response.
Behaviourism	– A school which originated with J.B. Watson and believes in environmentalism and external behaviour.
Behaviour therapy	– A therapeutic procedure based on learning principles.
Bilateral transfer	– The effect of practice with one hand on learning the same skill with the other.
Bimodal distribution	– A frequency distribution having two modes.
Biofeedback-information	– Provided to a person about biological events in his or her own body. The perception of this information may allow individuals to gain control over biological events in their bodies.
Blind spot	– The region of the retina where the optic nerve passes to the brain. It contains no rods or cones. Therefore what is focused on it is not seen.
Broca's area	– An area advocated by Broca in the frontal lobe which is responsible for speech.

Case history	–	The investigation of psychological problems through the assembling and examination of people's biographies.
Castration anxiety	–	A concept in Freudian theory of psychosexual development. It is a fear on the part of the boy that his father will castrate him because of his sexual attraction towards his mother.
Central nervous system (CNS)	–	The brain and the spinal cord.
Chromosome	–	A long, threadlike strand which is located in the nucleus of the cell and plays a central role in heredity. The genes are found in chromosomes. The human cell contains 23 pairs of chromosomes. One of each pair has been derived from the sperm cell (father) and the other from egg cell (mother).
Chromosomes X and Y	–	Sex chromosomes. An XX pair produces a female offspring, an XY combination a male.
Chronological age	–	Age in years and months. It is generally used in the computation of I.Q.
Client-centred therapy	–	Nondirective therapy advocated by Carl Rogers. Here the emphasis is placed on the client's awareness of feelings and potentialities.
Conditioned response (CR)	–	A response resembling the UR that is evoked by the CS as a result of repeated pairing of CS and US.
Conditioned stimulus (CS)	–	A neutral stimulus which does not have the neural capacity to elicit a response.
Conflict	–	The situation in which there is simultaneous instigation by two incompatible responses.
Continuous reinforcement	–	A schedule of reinforcement in which the subject is rewarded for every correct response.
Control group	–	A reference group in an experiment which does not receive any treatment.
Controlled variable	–	A variable whose value is held constant for all groups in an experiment.
Counterbalanced design	–	A design (ABBA) in which practice and fatigue effects are balanced in all treatments.
Convergent thinking	–	Thinking which moves towards the selection of a single solution to a problem.
Coping	–	Facing and finding necessary expedients to overcome problems and difficulties.
Cornea	–	The outermost, transparent coating in front of the eye.
Creativity	–	The ability to generate many new and useful ideas.
Cretinism	–	An abnormality of structure and behaviour which results from insufficient thyroid secretion during early period of childhood.
Dark adaptation	–	Increasing visual sensitivity which is a function of time spent in darkness or in low illumination.
Defence mechanism	–	Unconscious strategies used to avoid anxiety, resolve conflict and enhance self esteem.
Delusion	–	A false belief. For example, people suffering from mental illness may believe that some persons are putting ground glass in their food. This is a common symptom found in Paranoid Schizophrenia. There may be delusion of grandeur and delusion of persecution.

Dementia praecox	– It is a name formerly given to schizophrenia. It means youthful insanity.
Dendrite	– It is a part of the neuron which carries the nerve impulse toward the cell body.
Dependent variable	– The variable in an experiment which changes with the change in independent variable.
Depth perception	– Perceiving depth (tridimensionality) or distance.
Depth psychology	– A branch of psychology which probes into the motivational or dynamic aspects of personality.
Displacement	– A defence mechanism in which a person copes with an anxiety provoking motive by substituting another goal for the original one.
Distributed learning	– A practice in learning which includes substantial rest pauses between trials.
DNA (deoxyribonucleic acid)	– Molecules found in the cell nucleus that are the fundamental determiners of heredity of the organism.
Effector	– An organ capable of producing a response, for example, a muscle or gland.
Efferent neuron	– A neuron which conducts impulses away from the central nervous system.
Ego	– A concept in psychoanalytic theory by Freud. It is the portion of the personality that behaves realistically.
Egocentricism	– It is a characteristic behaviour of children in which there is little differentiation of self from others in the external world.
Electra complex	– The little girl's erotic attachment to her father in the psychoanalytic theory of Freud.
Empathy	– The capacity to recognise and share vicariously the emotions of others.
Endocrine system	– The glands which excrete their products directly into the bloodstream.
Endomorphy	– A personality type advocated by Sheldon. These people are round and oval faced.
Episodic memory	– It is the opposite of semantic memory. It is the memory related to personally experienced events.
Experimental group	– The group in an experiment that receives the independent variable, but is otherwise equivalent to the control group.
Extirpation	– The removal of brain tissue for experimental purposes.
Extrasensory Perception (ESP)	– Awareness of thought or object without direct participation of senses.
Extraversion	– Sociable, adventurous, talkative, frank and open behaviour in dealing with others.
Fantasy	– Daydreaming, imagining another private and pleasant world.
Figure and ground	– Perception of objects or events as standing out clearly from a background.
Foetus	– In the human species, the conceptus from the eighth week following conception to birth.

Forgetting	– Apparent loss of information that has been stored in the long term memory (LTM).
Frustration	– Blocking of goal-directed behaviour.
Genes	– The essential elements in the transmission of hereditary characteristics.
Gradient of generalisation	– It is a graphical representation of the strength of response in the presence of stimuli similar to discriminative stimuli, varying along a continuum. Gradients vary in the degree of their steepness.
Hallucination	– False perception. Sensory experience in the absence of stimulation of receptors.
Hippocampus	– A part of cerebrum, limbic system which is responsible for memory formation.
Homeostasis	– The tendency of the body to maintain a stable internal condition through interacting physiological processes.
Hormone	– A secretion of endocrine gland, often called a chemical messenger.
Hypnosis	– A trance-like state in which the person is very susceptible to suggestions.
Hypothalamus	– A group of nuclei in the forebrain that controls many emotional and motivational processes.
Iconic image	– A faint copy of the visual input which persists in the visual sensory register for a few seconds before it gradually decays.
Id	– In Freudian psychoanalytic theory, the aspect of personality concerned with primitive reactions. The id contains the biological instincts and seeks immediate gratification of motives with little regard for the consequences or the realities of life.
Identification	– The process by which the children assimilate the values of the parents and see themselves in some sense as the same as parents.
Illusion	– Wrong perception. A misinterpretation of real external stimulus.
Imprinting	– The development of young in many species of a filial attachment to the first large moving object they see.
Incentive	– Any goal or external condition which impels an organism to action.
Independent variable	– Any variable which serves as a basis for making a prediction. A condition manipulated by the experimenter to see whether it would have any effect on behaviour.
Inferiority complex	– A concept developed by Alfred Alder, a feeling developed out of frustration in striving for superiority.
Interneuron	– A neuron which connects a sensory and motor neuron within the CNS.
Introspection	– The process of examining and reporting the content of one's own consciousness.
Introvert	– A type of personality. An introvert person is one who is not sociable. He or she is a lover of seclusion.

I.Q.	– Intelligence Quotient. A measure of intelligence found by dividing a person's mental age (MA) by his or her chronological age (CA) and multiplying by 100. $I.Q = MA/CA \times 100$.
Latent learning	– Learning that becomes evident only when the occasion for using it arises.
Level of aspiration	– The level at which a person sets certain goals.
Libido	– In Freudian psychoanalytic theory, general sexuality which provides the energy for all behaviour.
Lie detector	– An apparatus which measures blood pressure, pulse, respiration and skin resistance changes during the course of questioning an individual. The assumption is that lying is accompanied by changes in these emotional indices.
Life instinct	– In psychoanalytic theory, the basic instinct or drive under the control of the pleasure principle.
Life space	– A term used by Kurt Lewin to denote all phenomena making up the world of actuality for a person, thus determining behaviour.
Linear perspective	– The convergence of parallel lines as they become more distant; a secondary cue to distance.
Long term memory (LTM)	– A memory system of long duration, following after short term memory (STM).
LSD (lysergic acid diethylamide)	– A hallucinogenic drug which can induce vivid perceptual experiences, hallucinations and disorganised thinking.
Macrocephaly	– An abnormally large head; a condition which causes mental retardation.
Massed practice	– Practice in which the trials are crowded closely together. Contrast with distributed practice.
Mental retardation	– A condition of significantly sub-average intellectual functioning and of deficits in adaptive behaviour which are first manifested during childhood.
Mental set	– A readiness to respond in a certain way. Sometimes called "mindset" or just "set".
Mesomporphy	– A Sheldon's typology of personality. These persons are vigorous and powerfully boned.
Microcephaly	– A condition in mental retardation. These people have abnormally small heads.
Mitosis	– The process of cell division in which the chromosomes duplicate, then line up in pairs within the cell nucleus.
Moon illusion	– A visual illusion in which the moon appears closer than it is to the horizon.
Narcissism	– In psychoanalysis, erotic feelings associated with the individual's own body or self. More generally, self-love, egocentrism.
Negative transfer	– Process in which learning one task interferes with the learning of another task. Contrast with positive transfer.
Neonate	– A newborn infant.
Neurons	– Nerve cells. A typical neuron has a cell body, dendrites and an axon.

Neurotransmitter	— A chemical substance stored in vesicles and released into synaptic clefts.
Nondirective therapy	— A psychotherapeutic procedure in which the client is dominant and is given the greatest possible opportunity for self-expression.
Normal probability curve (NPC)	— A bell-shaped frequency distribution also called the normal curve. It is an ideal approximated by many distributions obtained in psychology and the biological sciences.
Nucleus	— (i) The area within a cell that contains the genetic material (ii) A relatively compact collection of the cell bodies of neurons.
Null hypothesis	— The hypothesis that there is no true difference between experimental and control groups after they have been treated differently in an experiment.
Obesity	— Excessive fatness, 20 per cent overweight by arbitrary definition.
Obsessions	— Recurring, intrusive and uncontrollable thoughts.
Oedipus complex	— In Freudian psychoanalytic theory, the erotic attachment of the boy in the phallic stage for his mother and his desire to eliminate his father as a rival. These id impulses are usually repressed in some way through fear of punishment.
Omission training	— In operant conditioning, a procedure in which reward fails to follow a designated response but is given if that response is not made.
Operation	— In Piaget's theory, the basic and logical mental manipulation and transformation of information.
Oral stage	— In Freud's psychoanalytic theory, the first stage of psychosexual development where the infant acquires its most important pleasures from activities of the mouth – chewing, sucking, biting, etc.
Overlearning	— Practice beyond the point of mastery in learning a set of materials.
Perception	— The interpretation of sensory experience.
Perceptual constancy	— The tendency to perceive objects in their correct sizes, shapes and colours in spite of great variations in the pattern of proximal stimulation.
Perceptual defence	— A hypothetical, not fully validated, tendency for a person to fail to perceive psychologically threatening stimuli.
Personal unconscious	— According to Carl Jung, the portion of the unconscious that contains specific experiences of the individual.
Person perception	— Inferences made about the disposition, motives and intentions of a person.
Phallic stage	— According to psychoanalytic theory, the stage of psychosexual development during which the child, of 3 to 5 years age, becomes interested in the sexual organs and forms a romantic attachment to the parent of the opposite sex.
Phobia	— Intense, irrational fears of specific things.
Place learning	— Learning the place where some event occurs without making a specific response and without reinforcement.

Plasticity of perception	– Modifiability of perceptual processes by learning or other special experiences.
Positive reinforcer	– A reward or an event which increases the probability that the response it follows will be made again in similar circumstances.
Positive transfer	– A process in which learning of one skill aids in the learning of a second.
Primacy effect	– In memory, a tendency to remember the first learned things best.
Primary circular reactions	– In Piaget's theory, the movements repeated for pleasure by 1 to 4 months olds.
Primary drive	– An unlearned biological motive.
Primary reinforcement	– Reinforcement which depends little or nothing on previous learning.
Proactive inhibition	– A process whereby earlier learning interferes with the learning and later recall of new material.
Progestin	– A female sex hormone, secreted by ovaries. It prepares uterine lining for pregnancy and the breasts for lactation.
Programmed instruction	– The presentation of materials to be learned in carefully planned sequences, often with the aid of a computer.
Projection	– A defence mechanism in which the individuals attribute unwittingly their own usually undesirable traits to others.
Prototype	– The standard or ideal exemplar of a concept.
Psycholinguistics	– The study of the psychological aspects of language and its acquisition.
Psychometrics	– The study of the techniques and theories of mental measurement.
Psychophysics	– The study of the relationships between physical stimulation and psychological judgement. The study of relationship between variations in physical energy and reported experience and behaviour.
Psychosexual development	– In psychoanalytic theory, the idea that the instinctual drives are expressed in different ways as children grow older.
Psychotherapy	– The treatment of psychological disorders and mild adjustment problems by means of psychological techniques.
Puberty	– The period during which the capability for sexual reproduction is attained. It is marked by changes in both primary and secondary sexual characteristics.
Punishment	– The application of an unpleasant or noxious stimulus for the purpose of suppressing behaviour.
Questionnaire	– A test which asks a set of questions about typical performance that can be answered "yes" or "no". A survey of opinions and experiences.
Range	– It is a measure of variability. It is the interval between the highest and lowest scores.
Rationalisation	– A defence mechanism, providing oneself with good reasons for one's undesirable behaviour or position in life.
Reaction formation	– A type of defence mechanism in which a person acts (often unconsciously and in an exaggerated manner) in exactly the

opposite manner to his or her own disturbing or socially unacceptable thoughts or emotions.

Reaction time	– The interval between the onset of a stimulus and the beginning of the organism's response.
Realism	– In Piaget's theory of intellectual development, the tendency of children in the preoperational stage to think of symbols and concepts as real things.
Reality principle	– In Freudian psychoanalytic theory, the principle that the ego becomes aware of and adapts to the realities of life situations thereby inhibiting or delaying the expression of the id's impulses or drives.
Reality testing	– In Freudian psychoanalytic theory, the exploratory probing by which the young person learns about the environment.
Recall method	– A standard way of measuring memory in which people, after being exposed to the to-be-remembered items, are asked to call back the items from memory.
Receptor	– A cell or group of cells specialised to respond to relatively small changes in a particular kind of physical energy.
Receptor potential	– The electrical activity generated in a receptor cell during transduction.
Recognition method	– A way of measuring memory in which a person is asked to recognise the to-be-remembered items when they are presented along with incorrect items.
Reflex	– A simple adaptive bodily movement produced when motorneurons are excited by some sensory input.
Regression	– A defence mechanism in which a person copes with anxiety by retreating to childish or earlier forms of behaviour. Often encountered in children and adults faced with frustration and motivational conflict.
Reinforcement	– Any process which increases the probability of occurrence of a response that is being learned.
Relative refractory period	– A brief period following stimulation of a nerve or muscle during which it is unresponsive to all but a very strong stimulus.
Reliability	– The extent to which a measuring instrument yields consistent results at each time the same individual is tested.
Rapid eye movement (REM)	– Eye movements which occur during sleep and usually denote dreaming.
Replication	– The repetition of an experiment under identical conditions.
Representative sample	– A sample whose characteristics match those of the population.
Repression	– A defence mechanism and process in which certain memories and motives are not permitted to enter awareness but are operative at an unconscious level. This results in a failure of retrieval of anxiety-provoking material from long-term memory.
Retinal disparity	– The slight difference in images of the same object received by the two eyes. It provides a very sensitive primary cue to depth.

Retrieval	– The process of calling up an item from memory.
Retroactive inhibition	– The interference with retention by learning interpolated between the original learning and its attempted recall.
Retrograde amnesia	– Forgetting of events immediately preceding some injury or other traumatic experience.
Reversibility	– In Piaget's theory of cognitive development, the ability of children to understand that a changed object or state of affairs can be returned to its original state if the changes are reversed.
Reward training	– A form of operant conditioning employing a positive reinforcer.
Rhodopsin	– A light-sensitive substance found in the rods of the retina.
Ribonucleic acid (RNA)	– Complex molecules which are believed to be the "enforcers" of the genetic code by directing the formation of enzymes out of amino acids found in the cell.
Rote learning	– Learning of verbal sequences with little attention to meaning.
Scapegoating	– Aggression displaced towards a person or group that is the object of prejudice.
Schema	– A mental representation of objects, events and their relationships.
Sensory register	– The storage of information for a brief time in a sensory channel.
Set	– In problem solving, a readiness to react in a certain way when confronted with a problem or stimulus situation.
Short term memory (STM)	– The temporary store of information held in memory for a few seconds while it is being processed for long-term storage or use; holds information for about 30 seconds and has a very limited storage capacity.
Social conditioning	– Learning in a social context.
Social intelligence	– The ability to get along well in social situations.
Social interaction	– The interplay between individuals or groups.
Standard deviation	– A statistical index of the variability within a frequency distribution, represented by the Greek symbol sigma.
Standardisation	– The establishment of uniform conditions for administering a test and interpreting test results.
Status	– The position an individual holds within a group.
Storage processes	– The means by which information is actually put into memory.
Stress	– An internal condition which can be caused by physical demands on the body or by environmental or social situations which are evaluated as potentially harmful, uncontrollable or exceeding the individual's resources for coping.
Stressors	– The situation or events which cause stress.
Stroboscopic motion	– Apparent motion due to successive presentations of visual stimuli.
Sublimation	– A defence mechanism which converts one's unacceptable impulses into socially acceptable outlets.

Sympathetic nervous system	– A division of the autonomic nervous system concerned with emotional excitement. It prepares the organism for emergency and acts as the opposite of parasympathetic nervous system.
Synapse	– The functional connection between two neurons.
Synaptic cleft	– The narrow gap separating neurons at a synapse.
Systematic desensitisation	– A form of behaviour therapy or behaviour modification using the principles of counterconditioning and reciprocal inhibition.
Tachistoscope	– An apparatus for presenting perceptual materials for a very brief time.
Temperament	– The aspect of personality that includes mood, activity level and emotion.
Temporal summation	– A form of summation in which two threshold stimuli occurring in rapid succession succeed in firing a neuron.
Token economy	– A therapeutic technique used in institutions or by the family in which rewards (tokens) are given for socially constructive behaviour and can later be exchanged for material goods, services and privileges.
TOT phenomenon	– A state that may occur during an attempt at retrieval of information from long-term memory during which a person may retrieve incorrect information that is related in some way to the correct item, indicates that information in long-term memory is organised incorrectly.
Trait	– An enduring attribute of a person that is manifested in a variety of situations.
Trait theory	– A theory of personality that emphasises traits as enduring and persistent aspects of personality.
Transfer of training	– The process whereby learning one skill has an effect, beneficial or interfering, on learning another somewhat similar skill.
Unconditioned Response (UR)	– A response elicited by the US without special training.
Unconditioned Stimulus (US)	– A stimulus which produces a consistent response (UR) at the onset of training.
Validity	– The extent to which test scores measure what they are intended to measure.
Variance	– A measure of dispersion; the square of standard deviation.
Vitreous humor	– The transparent, jelly-like substance filling the eyeball between the retina and the lens.
Wechsler tests	– A family of tests of intelligence developed by the psychologist David Wechsler.
Zeigarnik effect	– The tendency to remember interrupted or unfinished tasks better than completed tasks.

❖❖❖

ABBREVIATIONS

ABBA Design	–	Counter balancing Design in Experiments
ACE Test	–	The American Council of Education Test of Intelligence
ACH	–	Acetylcholine
ACHE	–	Acetylcholine sterose
ACTH	–	Andronocorticotrophic Hormone
AD	–	Average Deviation
ADH	–	Antidiuretic Hormone
ANS	–	Autonomic Nervous System
BMR	–	Basal Metabolism Rate
B-type	–	A Personality Pattern
C	–	Constant
CA	–	Chronological Age
CAL	–	Computer-Assisted Learning
CCC Trigram	–	Consonant-Consonant-Consonant, for example, SKV, PNZ, etc.
CNS	–	Central Nervous System
CR	–	Conditioned Response
CRT	–	Cathode Ray Tube
CS	–	Conditioned Stimulus
CV	–	Controlled Variable
CVC	–	Consonant-Vowel-Consonant trigram, e.g., XOY, KIZ, etc.
D	–	Drive
DAT	–	Differential Aptitude Test
DL	–	Differential Limen
DNA	–	Deoxyribonucleic Acid
DQ	–	Developmental Quotient
DV	–	Dependent Variable
E	–	Experimenter, Experimental Group
ECG	–	Electrocardiogram
ECS	–	Electro-convulsive shock
EDR	–	Electrodermal Response
EEG	–	Electroencephalogram
E-F Scale	–	A scale from Minnesota Multiphasic Personality Inventory
EMG	–	Electromyogram
EOG	–	Electro-oculogram
EQ	–	Educational Quotient, Emotional Quotient
ERG	–	Electroretinogram

ESP	–	Extrasensory Perception
EST	–	Electroshock Therapy
EV	–	Extraneous Variable
FI	–	Fixed Interval
F scale	–	Fascism Scale
F score	–	A score in MMPI
FSH	–	Follicle-stimulating Hormone
GIGO	–	Garbage In Garbage Out
GPS	–	General Problem Solver
GSR	–	Galvanic Skin Response
ICD	–	International Classification of Diseases
ICS	–	Intracranial Stimulation
ICSH	–	Interstitial Cell-Stimulating Hormone
I/E ratio	–	Ratio of the rate of inspiration to the rate of expiration
I.E. scale	–	A scale of introversion-extraversion
IPA	–	Interpretative Phenomenological Analysis
I.Q.	–	Intelligence Quotient
IRT	–	Interresponse Time
ITI	–	Intertrial Interval
ITPA	–	Illinois Test of Psycholinguistic Ability
IU	–	Interval of Uncertainty
IUD	–	Intrauterine Device
J-curve	–	A curve describing the frequency of compliance with a rule or standard
JND	–	Just Noticeable Difference
LAS (or LAD)	–	Language-acquisition Device
LD	–	Learning Disability or Language Disability
LH	–	Luterinizing Hormone
LSD	–	Lysergic Acid Diethylamide
LTM	–	Long Term Memory
MA	–	Mental Age
MAT	–	Miller Analogies Test
MBD	–	Minimal Brain Dysfunction or Damage
N	–	Abbreviation for "Number"
O	–	Organism
P	–	Person
PGR	–	Psychogalvanic Response
PI	–	Proactive Inhibition
PNS	–	Peripheral Nervous System
Q	–	Quartile Deviation
R	–	Response
RAS	–	Reticular Activating System
REM	–	Rapid Eye Movement (Sleep)
RGB	–	Red-Green-Blue: a system for specifying colours

RI	–	Retroactive Inhibition
RIBT	–	Rorschach Inkblot Test (personality)
RL	–	Reiz Limen
RNA	–	Ribo Nucleic Acid (Messenger)
S	–	Subject, Stimulus
SD	–	Standard Deviation
SES	–	Socioeconomic Status
St.	–	Standard
STM	–	Short Term Memory
T	–	Temperature or Time
TAT	–	Thematic Apperception Test
THC	–	Tetrahydrocannabinol
TM	–	Transcendental Meditation
TOT	–	Tip of the Tongue phenomenon (memory)
T-test	–	A statistical test for significance of differences between means
UCR	–	Unconditioned Response
UCS	–	Unconditioned Stimulus
U Test	–	A nonparametric test for significance of differences between means and unmatched groups
V	–	Variable
VI	–	Variable Interval
VIB	–	Vocational Interest Blank
VOT	–	Voice Onset Time
VTE	–	Vicarious Trial and Error
WAT	–	Word Association Test
WHO	–	World Health Organisation
X	–	Mean (statistics)
X	–	Score, Chromosome
X-O test	–	A test of attitude and interest
XX	–	Sex chromosome (female)
XY	–	Sex chromosome (male)
Y	–	Variable, Chromosome
Y-Maze	–	A maze shaped like "Y"
ZPG	–	Zero Population Growth
Z-score	–	A statistical score